Designing Services and Programs for High-Ability Learners

Second Edition

Designing Services and Programs for High-Ability Learners

A Guidebook for Gifted Education

Second Edition

Rebecca D. Eckert

Jennifer H. Robins

Editors

A Joint Publication

FOR INFORMATION:

Corwin

A SAGE Company

2455 Teller Road

Thousand Oaks, California 91320

(800) 233-9936

www.corwin.com

SAGE Publications Ltd.

1 Oliver's Yard

55 City Road

London EC1Y 1SP

United Kingdom

SAGE Publications India Pvt. Ltd.

B 1/I 1 Mohan Cooperative Industrial Area

Mathura Road, New Delhi 110 044

India

SAGE Publications Asia-Pacific Pte. Ltd.

3 Church Street

#10-04 Samsung Hub

Singapore 049483

Program Director: Jessica Allan

Senior Associate Editor: Kimberly Greenberg

Editorial Assistant: Katie Crilley

Production Editor: Melanie Birdsall

Copy Editor: Deanna Noga

Typesetter: C&M Digitals (P) Ltd.

Proofreader: Ellen Howard

Indexer: Amy Murphy

Cover Designer: Glenn Vogel

Marketing Manager: Jill Margulies

Printed in the United States of America

Library of Congress Cataloging-in-Publication Data

Names: Eckert, Rebecca D., author. | Robins, Jennifer H., author. | National Association for Gifted Children (U.S.)

Title: Designing services and programs for high-ability learners : a guidebook for gifted education / Rebecca D. Eckert, Jennifer H. Robins.

Description: Second Edition. | Thousand Oaks, California : Corwin, a SAGE Company, [2017] | "A Joint Publication with the National Association for Gifted Children." | Previous edition authored by Jeanne H. Purcell and Rebecca D. Eckert. | Includes bibliographical references and index.

Identifiers: LCCN 2016016030 | ISBN 9781483387024 (Paperback : acid-free paper)

Subjects: LCSH: Gifted children—Education—United States. | Educational planning—United States.

Classification: LCC LC3993.9 .P87 2017 | DDC 371.95—dc23 LC record available at https://lccn.loc.gov/2016016030

This book is printed on acid-free paper.

16 17 18 19 20 10 9 8 7 6 5 4 3 2 1

Contents

Acknowledgments

We have been fortunate in this endeavor to begin with a meaningful task and a solid foundation: Jeanne Purcell's original vision of a guidebook for practitioners seeking advice about how to best serve gifted students in a variety of educational settings. Her tireless efforts to move this research-based conversation forward and to bring the first edition to light have provided us with inspiration as well as a responsibility to connect with practitioners in the field working with gifted students. As we updated this text, we had the privilege of working collaboratively with a number of talented individuals.

First, we would like to thank the chapter authors whose scholarly ideas, experiences, and research interests have shaped this publication. Their generous contributions of time and effort are a clear demonstration of their commitment to high-quality education for gifted students.

We owe a debt of gratitude to Amelia Wildman for her careful attention to detail and scholarly questions raised about each chapter. She brought both a fresh perspective and enthusiasm to the review of each chapter in this book. Her help and insight has been invaluable throughout this process.

Other colleagues reviewed new chapters added to this edition. In this review process, we asked for the help of state directors, leaders within the National Association for Gifted Children (NAGC), and other experts within the field of gifted education. We asked these colleagues to help us ensure that the content of each chapter was up to date, comprehensive, and that it transcended the idiosyncratic policies and legislation of each state. Each of these reviewers, listed below, provided authors with a carefully crafted set of recommendations and thoughts. We want to thank each of them:

Wendy Behrens, Laura Beltchenko, Elissa Brown, Ginny Burney, Meredith Green Burton, Carolyn Callahan, Jane Clarenbach, Jeff Danielian, Tamara Fisher, Keri Guilbault, Angela Housand, Claire Hughes, Joan Jacobs, Jennifer Jolly, Lauri Kirsch, Tracy Missett, Kristie Speirs Neumeister, Kathy Nilles, and Mary Cay Ricci.

Jane Clarenbach has been a constant ally and advocate for this book—and for the field of gifted education. Her regular inquiries about the need for updating the guidebook along with her successful efforts as an editorial matchmaker finally got this project rolling. She has been a willing, energetic, thoughtful, and steady companion. Jane cheered us on when all seemed impossible; she rallied and organized reviewers; she reminded us of deadlines; she read every word of the manuscript and offered her insights. We are indebted to her as a critical friend.

We also extend our appreciation to the members of the NAGC Publications Committee for their continued commitment to providing high-quality resources for practitioners in the field of gifted education and willingness to support this book as a service publication.

Finally, we would like to thank family and friends (and the many caring medical professionals) who have offered support and encouragement to bring this project to completion. In all honesty, there were difficult moments when the path forward was far from clear, and the effort needed seemed immense. Fortunately, we were not alone on this journey, and that has made all the difference.

About the Editors

 **Rebecca D. Eckert**, PhD, is an associate clinical professor in Teacher Education at the Neag School of Education at the University of Connecticut, where she works with preservice teachers as they navigate the joys and challenges of their first classroom experiences. In her former role as the Gifted Resource Specialist for the National Association for Gifted Children (NAGC), Rebecca helped redesign the NAGC website and develop practical resources for educators and advocates of gifted students. Her previous work at The National Research Center on the Gifted and Talented included participation in Javits research at both the elementary and secondary levels. Her research interests include talented readers, recruitment and preparation of new teachers, arts in the schools, and public policy and gifted education. She is a former middle school teacher with experience in geography, history, and theater arts.

 **Jennifer H. Robins**, PhD, is the Director of Publications and Professional Development at the Center for Gifted Education at William & Mary and a clinical assistant professor. She teaches graduate courses in gifted education, working with teachers who are pursuing their gifted endorsement. She is a former teacher of elementary gifted and talented students and was senior editor at Prufrock Press, focusing on the development of scholarly materials, including gifted education textbooks and professional development books, as well as classroom materials for teachers of gifted and advanced students. She is managing editor of the *Journal for the Education of the Gifted* and a board member of The Association for the Gifted, Council for Exceptional Children. Her areas of interest include the history of gifted education and underrepresented populations.

About the Contributors

Brittany Nicole Anderson is a doctoral student in the Department of Educational Psychology at the University of Georgia (UGA) and is enrolled in the Gifted and Creative Education Program (GCE). She is a member of the GCE University-School Partnerships for Achievement, Rigor, and Creativity (Project U-SPARC) initiative. Her research interests focus on university-school partnerships that promote talent development among low-income, ethnic minority youth, as well as the training and development of preservice educators. Brittany is a former elementary educator, who received her bachelor's in early childhood education from Baylor University and master's in curriculum and instruction at the University of North Texas. Brittany has served as the Mary Frasier STEM Conference Graduate Coordinator, UGA's Torrance Center Summer Institute graduate student coordinator, and on the African-American Female Faculty Workshop committee at UGA. She is a proud member of Phi Kappa Phi Honor Society.

Mallory M. Bagwell, PhD, received his doctorate in gifted education from the University of Connecticut and teaches creativity and the arts at Eastern Connecticut State University. A teaching movement artist who works throughout New England keeping the "A" in the STE(A)M curriculum, his work involves translating curricular concepts into various kinesthetic experiences and creating supporting visual aids and tactile models. *Motion is Life* is his modus operandi. He has designed and taught online and site-based courses in Canada, Korea, Kuwait, and the United States. Experience with, and interest in, early childhood parenting practices led to the development of the ASPIRE Survey, a web-based app for parent-community engagement used around the country. His is currently interested in examining the relationship between sustainable house/building design/practices and education/personal growth outcomes.

Jennifer G. Beasley, EdD, is currently an assistant professor in curriculum and instruction at the University of Arkansas where she teaches courses in the Masters of Arts in Teaching program. Her professional contributions include serving as a regular columnist for the National Association for Gifted Children's publication *Teaching for High Potential* as well as Chair of the Curriculum Studies Network. Her research interests include student engagement, teacher efficacy, curriculum design, and differentiated instruction.

Carolyn M. Callahan, PhD, developed the master's and doctoral programs in gifted education, teaches classes in gifted education, and developed the Summer and Saturday Enrichment Programs at the University of Virginia. She was principal investigator on projects of the National Research Center on the Gifted and Talented (NRC/GT), serves as a co-PI on the National Center for Research in Gifted Education, and has been principal investigator on six Javits grants. Her research has focused on evaluation, curriculum development, and implementation. She has conducted evaluations of Javits grants and state- and local-level gifted programs large and small. She has been recognized as Outstanding Professor of the Commonwealth of Virginia and Distinguished Scholar of the National Association for Gifted Children (NAGC). She served as president of NAGC and The Association for the Gifted, a division of the Council for Exceptional Children (CEC-TAG) and as editor of *Gifted Child Quarterly*. Dr. Callahan has published more than 200 articles and 50 book chapters on topics in gifted education.

Carolyn R. Cooper, PhD, is a seasoned district-level administrator who has coordinated programs for gifted and talented students in Baltimore County, MD, as well as in Wichita and suburban St. Louis. As an assistant superintendent for four small school districts in Massachusetts, and earlier, as an assistant to the superintendent of a Connecticut school district, she was responsible for budget oversight and streamlining the annual school budget development process. She has been an active volunteer leader at the National Association for Gifted Children and has served on the Board of Directors and the Finance Committee. Dr. Cooper earned her doctorate from the University of Connecticut.

Alicia Cotabish, EdD, is an associate professor of education at the University of Central Arkansas. She is the immediate past-president of the Arkansas Association of Gifted Education Administrators and is president-elect of The Association for the Gifted, a division of the Council for Exceptional Children (CEC-TAG). She has authored and coauthored four books and more than 50 journal articles, book chapters, and products focused on K–20 STEM and gifted education. Her recent research has focused on STEM and gifted education and examining the effects of virtual coaching on the quality of gifted and teacher candidates using Skype and Bluetooth Bug-in-the-Ear (BIE) technology.

Debbie Dailey, EdD, is an assistant professor and the gifted education program coordinator at the University of Central Arkansas. She is the secretary of The Association for the Gifted, a division of the Council for Exceptional Children (CEC-TAG) and serves on the board of Arkansans for Gifted and Talented Education. Additionally, she is the director of a

xii   DESIGNING SERVICES AND PROGRAMS FOR HIGH-ABILITY LEARNERS

summer camp for talented youth, STEMulate Engineering Academy, and she will be investigating the effects of the program on students' engineering knowledge, skills, and perceptions.

Alissa Doobay, PhD, is a licensed psychologist and Supervisor of Psychological Services at the Belin-Blank Center for Gifted Education and Talent Development at the University of Iowa; she is also an adjunct assistant professor in psychological and quantitative foundations at the University of Iowa. Dr. Doobay's clinical and research interests include assessment and intervention of twice-exceptional students, including students with attention and learning disorders, autism spectrum disorders, and mood and anxiety disorders. Awards include the AERA Path Breaker Award and Mensa Education and Research Foundation Award.

Michele Femc-Bagwell, PhD, holds a doctorate in educational administration and is a faculty member in the Educational Leadership Department at the University of Connecticut Neag School of Education where she teaches graduate courses to preservice teachers and aspiring school leaders. She is also the Director of the CommPACT Community Schools Collaborative designed to support community and family involvement in Connecticut urban school districts. During her career as an educator, she has been a high school teacher, gifted and talented coordinator, middle school assistant principal, and principal. She is the coauthor of the ASPIRE Survey, a web-based asset mapping inventory designed to identify the interests and skills of parent and community members in an effort to connect them as enrichment resources to schools in more meaningful and purposeful ways. She shares her passion locally and nationally as she works with teachers and school administrators to embrace these important stakeholders as integral partners in supporting students' success.

Megan Foley-Nicpon, PhD, is a licensed psychologist, associate professor of counseling psychology, and Associate Director for Research and Clinic at the Belin-Blank Center for Gifted Education and Talent Development, both at the University of Iowa. Dr. Foley-Nicpon's research and clinical interests include assessment and intervention with high-ability students with ASD, ADHD, and emotional/learning difficulties, and the social and emotional development of talented and diverse students. Awards include the NAGC Early Scholar Award; AERA Research on Giftedness, Creativity, and Talent Path Breaker Award; AERA Division E Outstanding Research Award in Human Development; and, twice, the Mensa Research Award, Mensa Education & Research Foundation.

Tarek Cy Grantham, PhD, is professor of educational psychology at the University of Georgia (UGA). He has served as coordinator in the Gifted and Creative Education (GCE) graduate program, where he teaches primarily in the diversity and equity strand. He codirects the GCE University-School Partnerships for Achievement, Rigor, and Creativity

(Project U-SPARC) initiative. Dr. Grantham's research addresses equity for underrepresented ethnic minority students in advanced programs, gifted Black males, motivation, and creativity policy. He has coedited two books: *Gifted and Advanced Black Students in School: An Anthology of Critical Works* and *Young, Triumphant, and Black: Overcoming the Tyranny of Segregated Minds in Desegregated Schools.* Dr. Grantham serves as the Chair for the Special Populations network of the National Association for Gifted Children. He is a recipient of the Mary M. Frasier Excellence and Equity Award by the Georgia Association for Gifted Children for outstanding achievement in gifted education.

E. Jean Gubbins, PhD, is professor of educational psychology at the University of Connecticut. She teaches graduate courses in gifted education and talent development related to identification, programming, curriculum development, and program evaluation. She has published articles in *Roeper Review*, *Journal of Advanced Academics*, *Gifted Child Quarterly*, and *Journal for the Education of the Gifted* and contributed book chapters for major textbooks. Through grant funding from the United States Department of Education for The National Research Center on the Gifted and Talented, Dr. Gubbins implemented research studies on curricular strategies and practices in science, technology, engineering, and mathematics (STEM) high schools, reading and mathematics education, professional development, and gifted education pedagogy for all students. Currently, she is the Associate Director for the National Center for Research on Gifted Education. In addition, she has conducted more than 45 program evaluations for school districts around the country and implemented literacy and arts-integrated evaluations for nonprofit organizations.

Meg Easom Hines, PhD, is a lecturer and the coordinator of Gifted and Creative Education (GCE) Online Programs in the Department of Educational Psychology at the University of Georgia. She codirects the GCE University-School Partnerships for Achievement, Rigor, and Creativity (Project U-SPARC) initiative. Before her position at UGA, Dr. Hines was an elementary educator and an adjunct professor at the College of Charleston in Charleston, South Carolina. She consults with teachers, administrators, and policy makers in local schools and districts on creativity, differentiated instruction, curriculum design, and innovative programming. Her research interests include programming that uses creativity and how creative problem solving and critical thinking meet the needs of special populations. Dr. Hines is a recipient of the National Association for Gifted Children's (NAGC) Doctoral Student Award. Currently, she serves as a member of NAGC's Special Populations network and as a member of the editorial review panel for *Teaching for High Potential.*

Marcia B. Imbeau, PhD, is currently a professor at the University of Arkansas in the department of curriculum and instruction where she teaches in the Master of Arts in Teaching and gifted education programs. Her professional contributions include serving as a former At-Large Board Member and Divisions Secretary of the National Association for Gifted Children, At-Large Member of The Association for the Gifted, a division of the Council for Exceptional Children (CEC-TAG), editorial advisory board member for *Teaching for High Potential* as well as Chair for the Curriculum Studies Network. Her research interests include differentiated instruction, curriculum development, gifted education services, preservice teacher education, students' engagement, and action research.

Nykela Jackson, PhD, is an assistant professor of education at the University of Central Arkansas where she is an instructor in the Masters of Arts in Teaching and Gifted Education programs. Her current research has focused on building cultural competence in the gifted classroom, preparing culturally responsive educators, and modeling differentiated instruction in teacher preparation courses.

Joan K. Jacobs, PhD, has earned a bachelor's degree in English, a master's degree in English, a master's degree in educational management, and a doctoral degree in educational psychology with a focus on gifted education and assessment at the University of Connecticut. She has spent 30 years in education, most of which focused on the needs of gifted students. She has taught English and business in high school and colleges and currently works as the gifted supervisor for Lincoln Public Schools.

Susan K. Johnsen, PhD, is a professor in the Department of Educational Psychology at Baylor University where she directs the PhD program and programs related to gifted and talented education. She is editor-in-chief of *Gifted Child Today* and coauthor of *The Practitioner's Guide for Using the Common Core State Standards for Mathematics*, *Using the Common Core State Standards for Mathematics With Gifted and Advanced Learners*, *Using the NAGC Pre-K–Grade 12 Gifted Programming Standards*, *Math Education for Gifted Students*, and more than 250 articles, monographs, technical reports, chapters, and other books related to gifted education. She has written three tests used in identifying gifted students: *Test of Mathematical Abilities for Gifted Students* (TOMAGS), *Test of Nonverbal Intelligence* (TONI-4), and *Screening Assessment for Gifted Elementary and Middle School Students* (SAGES-2). She is past president of The Association for the Gifted, a division of the Council for Exceptional Children (CEC-TAG) and past president of the Texas Association for the Gifted and Talented (TAGT). She has received awards for her work in the field of education, including NAGC's President's Award, CEC's Leadership Award, TAG's Leadership Award, TAGT's President's Award, TAGT's Advocacy Award and Baylor University's Investigator Award, Teaching Award, and Contributions to the Academic Community.

Jann H. Leppien, PhD, is an associate professor and the Margo Long Chair in Gifted Education at Whitworth University in Spokane, WA. She teaches courses in gifted education for teachers obtaining their gifted education specialty endorsement or a master's degree in gifted education. She also teaches curriculum and thinking skills courses online and in the Three Summers Program at the University of Connecticut. She has been a classroom teacher, enrichment specialist, and coordinator of a gifted education program in Montana. She is the coauthor of *The Multiple Menu Model: A Practical Guide for Developing Differentiated Curriculum*, *The Parallel Curriculum: A Design to Develop High Potential and Challenge High-Ability Students*, and seven other texts that complement *The Parallel Curriculum Model*. She is active in the National Association for Gifted Children, where she has served as a board member and treasurer, and a member on the Diversity and Equity Committee. Currently, she is the secretary of the Association for the Education of Gifted Underachieving Students (AEGUS), an executive board member of the 2E Center for Research and Professional Development at Bridge's Academy in Studio City, CA, and a member for Washington State's Gifted and Talented Advisory Board.

Julie Lenner McDonald, EdD, currently serves as the Chief Academic Officer for Sandusky City Schools, a small urban district in Ohio. Dr. McDonald holds an EdD in leadership studies from Bowling Green State University and has taught gifted K–8 students in various service settings. Her administrative experience includes coordinating gifted services; Title programs; and local, state, and national grants involving curriculum, instructional design, assessment, and gifted identification. Dr. McDonald and her team successfully opened a fully funded public school for regional gifted students in 2013.

Jay McIntire has been a school superintendent in Maine and New Hampshire for the last decade. Prior, he was very involved with students with specialized learning needs, including serving as a staff member of the Council for Exceptional Children (CEC) and as executive director of the Texas Association for the Gifted and Talented (TAGT). He served on NAGC's Legislative and Advocacy Committee for a number of years. His teaching experience was as a special education teacher and teacher of students with gifts and talents. Mr. McIntire's master's degree is from Lesley University, and he did advanced coursework at the University of Virginia.

Sidney M. Moon, PhD, is Professor Emerita of Gifted, Creative, and Talented Studies in the Department of Educational Studies at Purdue University. She has been involved in the field of gifted, creative, and talented studies for 33 years. In that time, she has contributed more than 75 books, articles, and chapters to the field. Dr. Moon has been active in the National Association for Gifted Children, where she has served as Chair of the Research and Evaluation Division, a member of the Board of Directors, and Association Editor. In the American Educational Research Association Special Interest Group (SIG), Research on Giftedness, Creativity, and Talent, she has served as treasurer. Her research interests include gifted education programs, the social and emotional development of talented persons, and talent development in the STEM (science, technology, engineering, and mathematics) disciplines.

Tonya R. Moon, PhD, is a professor in the Curry School of Education at the University of Virginia where she teaches courses in research design, statistics, and assessment. Her scholarship focuses on understanding teachers' personal practice assessment theories and the ways in which contextual factors facilitate or constrain teachers' use of data. She is also the Chair of the University's Institutional Review Board for the Behavioral and Social Sciences.

Maureen Neihart, PsyD, is a licensed clinical child psychologist and associate professor at the National Institute of Education in Singapore. She is a former member of the board of directors of the National Association for Gifted Children. Her research interests include the social and emotional development of gifted children, mobile behavioral health, psychological interventions for children with special needs, and the psychology of high performance.

Soeun Park is a doctoral student in counseling psychology at the University of Iowa. Soeun is interested in ethnic, racial, and cultural issues in psychology, parenting children with special needs, and social and emotional development of high-ability students.

Kristina Ayers Paul, PhD, is a special assistant for program evaluation with the Lower Merion School District. Dr. Paul is a graduate of the University of Connecticut and has worked with more than 10 school districts to evaluate or develop their gifted programs and nearly 20 state- and federal-funded grant programs focused on professional development programs for teachers. Her research and teaching focuses on policy and program development in gifted education, with specific interests in program evaluation, professional development, talent development in rural contexts, and how technology can be used to enhance and transform those practices.

Sally M. Reis, PhD, is the Vice Provost for Academic Affairs, a Board of Trustees Distinguished Professor, and the Letitia Neag Morgan Chair in Educational Psychology at the University of Connecticut. She has authored or coauthored more than 250 publications. Her research interests are related to special populations of gifted and talented students, including students with learning disabilities, gifted females, and diverse groups of talented students. She has been a consultant to numerous schools and ministries of education throughout the United States and abroad, and her work has been translated into several languages and is widely used around the world. She has been honored with the highest award in her field as the Distinguished Scholar of the National Association for Gifted Children and named a fellow of the American Psychological Association.

Julia Link Roberts, EdD, Mahurin Professor of Gifted Studies at Western Kentucky University (WKU), is Executive Director of the Carol Martin Gatton Academy of Mathematics and Science in Kentucky and The Center for Gifted Studies at WKU. Dr. Roberts is on the Executive Committee of the World Council for Gifted and Talented Children and is past president of The Association for the Gifted. Dr. Roberts enjoys working with children and young people, directing Saturday and summer programming, and traveling abroad with high school students. She has focused her writing on differentiation, gifted education, STEM education, and advocacy and is coauthor of six books, several chapters, and numerous articles and columns. She received the 2011 Acorn Award as the outstanding professor at a Kentucky 4-year university, the first NAGC David Belin Advocacy Award, the 2012 NAGC Distinguished Service Award, and the 2011 William T. Nallia Award for innovative leadership from the Kentucky Association for School Administrators.

Karen L. Westberg, PhD, is a professor at the University of St. Thomas (UST) where she teaches coursework in gifted education and research methodology. Before joining the faculty at UST, she was a principal investigator at The National Research Center on the Gifted and Talented and a faculty member in gifted education at the University of Connecticut. She has been actively involved with the National Association for Gifted Children by serving as member of the Board of Directors, finance secretary, and member of the Editorial Board for the *Gifted Child Quarterly*. She has published articles in several journals including *Parenting for High Potential*, *Journal for the Education of the Gifted*, *Gifted Education International*, *Gifted Child Today*, and *Gifted Child Quarterly*. Earlier in her career, she was a teacher and gifted education specialist in the Burnsville/Eagan/Savage school district in Minnesota.

Introduction

HOW WE GOT HERE

When *Designing Services and Programs for High-Ability Learners: A Guidebook for Gifted Education* was released as a service publication of the National Association for Gifted Children (NAGC) in 2006, it was the first text in more than 30 years to provide practical, comprehensive advice for developing and supporting high-quality programs and services for gifted students. A decade later, this handbook for educators, administrators, and university personnel continues to fill the need for research-based, practical guidance about how to best utilize resources to meet the needs of gifted students.

Believe it or not, much of the correspondence with first-edition authors and reviewers was through the U.S. Postal Service and the trusty NAGC fax machine. This reminds us that although the publication of the original guidebook seems like it occurred just yesterday, the world in which we—and our students—live moves at an increasingly rapid pace. Therefore, the goal for this text is to update and continue the comprehensive discussion of practical issues related to the provision of educational opportunities for gifted and talented students begun with the publication of the first edition a decade ago. Each of the chapters is focused on a key feature or aspect of gifted education and provides detailed guidelines to help new or experienced practitioners create and sustain these programs and services.

HOW THIS BOOK IS DIFFERENT

Much has been written about gifted education, and what we know is contained in countless monographs, journal articles, dissertations, position papers, videos, and books; however, the options are still limited for practitioners seeking a consolidated and comprehensive discussion of the numerous practical issues related to services and programs for high-achieving students. Although robust standards have been articulated for the field, there continue to be few publications that provide detailed guidelines to help new or experienced practitioners create and sustain gifted programs and services. This guidebook does both. We hope it provides a comprehensive discussion of the key features that characterize programs and services for the gifted. In addition, we provide guidelines, practical tips, templates, and suggestions to help practitioners determine where they are now, where they are going, and how they are doing along the way.

FOR WHOM IS THIS BOOK WRITTEN?

This book contains practical, research-based information about the key features of successful programs and services for high-ability learners, so a wide variety of audiences will find this guidebook helpful. Teachers of the gifted and talented and specialists who have major responsibilities for program or service delivery will be able to use this book as a reference. District administrators, charged with monitoring the development of services for high-achieving students, will be able to use this book as a roadmap to help identify the services that currently exist and as a compass to identify how services can be enhanced. Advocates for enhanced opportunities for gifted students can use this book as a reference for defining exemplar programs and services. State directors for the gifted and talented, who play leadership roles in their respective states, can use this publication as a manual to support their work with school districts. This guidebook can be readily understood by those who are new to the field as well as those who have years of experience in gifted education. In these times of turnover in district positions, the guidebook can provide continuity when leadership changes. Finally, university personnel who teach introductory courses in gifted education can use this publication.

THE BOOK'S STRUCTURE

The book contains 17 chapters that address key features of gifted education programs and services. Readers will recognize many of the updated topics that are included such as construction of identification procedures, advocacy, and program evaluation, for example. Other key features, reflecting current trends in education, have been added to this new edition: collaborating with families, aligning programs and services with national standards, and developing local policies to support gifted education. In addition, the NAGC Pre-K–Grade 12 Gifted Programming Standards, which were updated in 2010, can be found in Appendix B, page 261.

In an effort to provide consistency and structure for those who select to read the book from beginning to end or as isolated chapters, chapters in the book share parallel components to elucidate key features of services and programs for high-ability learners:

- **Definition:** A definition is provided to ensure a common understanding of the key feature under consideration.
- **Rationale:** This section explains the critical importance of the key feature and outlines current research to guide decisions about the development or redesign of programs and services for gifted students.

- **Guiding Principles and Attributes That Define High Quality:** Chapter authors provide a parsimonious list of assumptions and high-quality markers that form the foundation of each key feature and determine the effective implementation of an aspect of programming. This ensures that those charged with creating or supporting programs and services can assess the overall effectiveness of each key feature.
- **Example in Need of Revision:** We asked authors to reflect on their experiences in the field and to generate a carefully crafted example of the key feature gone awry. Examples, as well as exemplars, help us clearly understand what we are seeking.
- **Makeover Example:** The revised example in each chapter serves as a contrast to the lackluster example and makes explicit the differences between a less-than-satisfactory implementation of gifted services and programs and one that is of high quality. This section includes a brief description of what is wrong with the lackluster example, as well as strategies used to improve it, and the improved result from these efforts. The lackluster example and the exemplar provide readers with bookends, so to speak, to help them better understand the continuum of quality in the field and to keep us aiming for excellence.
- **Advice for Getting Started:** Too often we underestimate the amount of time and effort that will be required to create or redesign a key feature of gifted education programs or services. Therefore, this section provides a strategic plan to uncover the complex process that is required to develop high-quality features of programs and services. Many chapters also include a graphic organizer or configuration map to guide reflection and planning with regard to the key feature under consideration. The goal with this section is to help readers jump-start the creation or remodeling process.
- **Advice for the Sole Practitioner:** In many instances, educators or advocates may be working on their own to conceptualize, plan, or implement services and programs for gifted students. Because the enormity of this task can be quite daunting, targeted advice and guidance is provided to improve the likelihood of success for practitioners working alone.
- **Suggested Resources:** Authors for each chapter were selected for their expertise related to the key feature, and they have a working knowledge of resources that deal with that aspect of gifted programming. We asked them to select a few suggested resources that would be most beneficial to practitioners seeking additional information on the topic.

NEXT STEPS

Although the isolation of key features of gifted education within individual chapters is somewhat artificial, the hope is that this structure will allow readers to better appreciate the function and subtleties of these program components and use this knowledge in their own contexts to navigate the complex and multifaceted process of designing services and programs for gifted and talented students. Although grounded in research and guided by the NAGC Pre-K–Grade 12 Gifted Programming Standards, the practical insights and advice found in this text are only the beginning of the journey toward the development and/or expansion of high-quality educational services for gifted students. We encourage you to seek out opportunities to discuss and share the ideas in this guidebook (either in person or online). We also urge you to take this base and expand on it, providing up-to-date information for your schools and classrooms for years to come. These continued efforts and further collaboration will provide the gateway to the future of gifted education.

Rebecca D. Eckert, PhD

Jennifer H. Robins, PhD

Editors

Chapter 1

Aligning Gifted Programming and Services With National and State Standards

Alicia Cotabish, EdD, Debbie Dailey, EdD, and Nykela Jackson, PhD

OVERVIEW OF THE PRE-K–GRADE 12 GIFTED PROGRAMMING STANDARDS

The NAGC Pre-K–Grade 12 Gifted Programming Standards serve as an important benchmark for student outcomes and for describing effective educational practices for gifted students. Grounded in theory, cognitive and social science research, and practice, the design of the standards focuses on student outcomes, reflects an emphasis on diversity, and emphasizes a relationship between gifted education, general education, and special education (National Association for Gifted Children [NAGC], 2010). The most recent version of the standards is supported by the following principles: (a) giftedness is evolving and never static, (b) giftedness is found among students from diverse backgrounds, (c) standards should focus on student outcomes rather than practices, (d) educators are responsible for the education of the gifted, and (e) services for gifted and talented students should reflect student abilities, needs, and interests (NAGC, 2010). As such, the

NAGC Pre-K–Grade 12 Gifted Programming Standards serve as an important foundation for programs and services for all gifted learners and provide a basis for designing and developing educational and experiential options for gifted students. Specifically, the six gifted education programming standards focus on: (a) learning and development, (b) assessment, (c) curriculum and instruction, (d) learning environments, (e) programming, and (f) professional development. Furthermore, the standards should be used in the early stages of program planning, for internal analysis, and for defensibility of plans and programs (NAGC, 2010). They help document the program necessity, justify the approach to programming, and "identify program strengths and weaknesses, determine new directions or components, and provide support to maintain current programs and services" (NAGC, 2010, p. 6).

In addition to the aforementioned uses, the standards often serve as indicators of progress in program development and delivery. The organization of the programming standards into six broad categories allows them to serve as a mechanism to document gaps in program services, which can lead to the creation of program action plans (Cotabish & Krisel, 2012). Utilizing the standards as a framework for Pre-K–12 gifted programs can assist gifted education personnel in evaluating current programming services, setting program goals, constructing a plan for strategically meeting those goals, and aligning curriculum, instruction, and programmatic components to multiple state and national standards (e.g., Achieve, Inc., 2014; National Governors Association Center for Best Practices & Council of Chief State School Officers, 2010).

The standards also send an important message to policy makers and the general public about the specialized needs of gifted learners. In recent years, a major objective of federal and state education policy has been to narrow K–12 achievement gaps. Unfortunately, the principal focus of legislation has been focused on minimum competency; therefore, it is of critical importance that policy makers and the general public are made aware of the specialized needs of gifted learners. The NAGC Pre-K–Grade 12 Gifted Programming Standards address this need.

RATIONALE

The NAGC Pre-K–Grade 12 Gifted Programming Standards represent collaboration between two advocacy organizations: the National Association for Gifted Children and The Association for the Gifted, a division of the Council for Exceptional Children (CEC-TAG). Johnsen (2012) eloquently provided the following rationale for the development of standards:

> Growing out of the need for more rigorous and measurable standards and higher expectations for academic performance, standards have been developed for teacher preparation, programming, and specific content or discipline areas. These standards have

been used for the design of assessment-based accountability systems and the accreditation of both teacher preparation and K–12 programs. (p. ix)

Programming standards help define the comprehensiveness necessary in designing and developing options for gifted learners at the local level. Students who are performing at advanced levels require accommodations such as differentiated curriculum and instruction and specialized programming services. Although the implementation of the standards varies from district to district and state to state, the standards provide an important direction and focus for program development.

According to Cotabish and Krisel (2012), "accountability of districts has increasingly placed gifted educators in the position of having to prove their worth and demonstrate their impact on student achievement" (p. 231). With this in mind, the NAGC Pre-K–Grade 12 Gifted Programming Standards can serve as a guide to document the effects of gifted programming on student performance, particularly as it relates to higher levels of student engagement, critical and divergent thinking, and creativity.

It is not uncommon for the standards to be used to guide state department personnel in the development and evaluation of state standards for gifted programming. Furthermore, program coordinators typically use the standards to improve local plans, assist with curriculum planning and program development, and guide professional development activities. Notably, "the programming standards may also provide language, rationale, and direction for effective advocacy for high-quality services for students with gifts and talents" (Cotabish & Krisel, 2012, p. 232). For example, the standards can serve as a guide for educators, parents, and policy makers who advocate for improved services for gifted and talented students.

Figure 1.1 depicts six common categories in which the NAGC Pre-K–Grade 12 Gifted Programming Standards are often used, specifically among state department personnel, gifted program coordinators, and classroom teachers. One can see that the utilization overlap primarily occurs in efforts focused on advocacy and professional development planning.

GUIDING PRINCIPLES AND ATTRIBUTES THAT DEFINE HIGH-QUALITY PROGRAMS

Program planning, design, development, implementation, and evaluation all work in concert and become the basis for high-quality gifted programs and services. Using the NAGC Pre-K–Grade 12 Gifted Programming Standards, gifted education personnel can develop a process for assessing their gifted programs according to attributes that define high-quality programs. The key features of each (as outlined in the standards) can provide direction to continuous improvement in gifted programming and can redirect poor programming and instructional practices. When done skillfully, the

Figure 1.1 Six Categories of Use

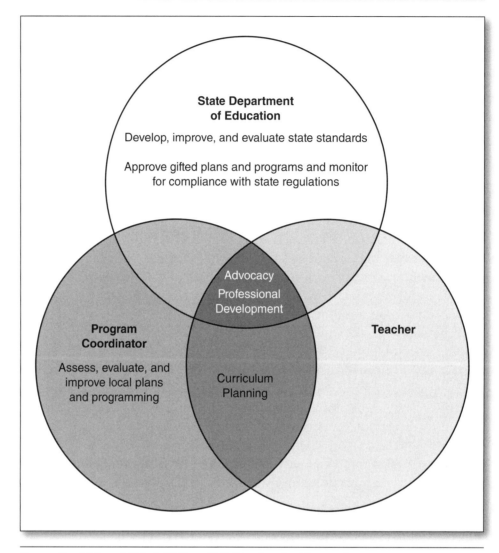

Source: Cotabish and Krisel (2012, p. 232). Reprinted with permission.

overall result is that programs should experience change in ways that improve the design, development, and delivery of gifted programming.

Developing Program Goals

To begin the process of program development and/or refinement, you must start with the end in mind. Typically, program goals are aligned with a larger school mission; therefore, it is important for goals to be feasible, which may require coordinated efforts between gifted education personnel and other school personnel. When considering program goals, less is more—regardless of whether the goal's focus is on alignment to national standards, curriculum planning and development, or the identification of traditionally underrepresented groups. We recommend focusing more efforts on short-term, feasible goals that can be accomplished in an academic year. Longer-term overarching goals could possibly be accomplished over time by meeting a number of articulated shorter-term goals. It is also important to seek input from all involved with teaching and providing services to gifted children. For example, general classroom teachers can be of great assistance to gifted education personnel, particularly in the coordination phase of standard alignment—and ultimately, the delivery of aligned curriculum and instruction in the general education classroom.

Aligning the NAGC Pre-K–Grade 12 Gifted Programming Standards With National and State Standards

Given the current focus on education policy and resources, it is important for gifted educators to consider aligning curriculum and instructional practice to existing state and national standards. For example, as the Common Core State Standards (CCSS) (National Governors Association Center for Best Practices & Council of Chief State School Officers, 2010) and the Next Generation Science Standards (NGSS) (Achieve, Inc., 2014) have become more widely adopted, interest in how the NAGC Pre-K–Grade 12 Gifted Programming Standards connect to these standards has increased. Although there are a number of standards that lend themselves to alignment with the NAGC programming standards, Figure 1.2 on the next page depicts the student-centered expectations and relationships among the NGSS, CCSS, and the NAGC Pre-K–Grade 12 Gifted Programming Standards.

According to Adams, Cotabish, and Ricci (2014), overlap among the four sets of standards is found in the middle of the graphic with specific student expectations associated with each set of standards highlighted in separate boxes. The broad similarities among the standards can serve as the basis for curriculum planning and development. Be mindful that aligning multiple standards does not provide a rationale to replace gifted education programming; rather, it provides a framework for strategic gifted education program planning. Regardless of aligned components, advanced learners require substantially differentiated curriculum and instructional services to meet their unique learning needs.

USING A PROGRAM ASSESSMENT TOOL ALIGNED TO THE PRE-K–GRADE 12 GIFTED PROGRAMMING STANDARDS TO GUIDE GIFTED PROGRAMMING AND SERVICES

Several programming standards tools have been developed by NAGC to assist gifted program coordinators, school administrators, and teachers of the gifted in assessing programmatic and professional development needs in relation to implementing the six national gifted programming standards. The latest tool, featured in *Self-Assess Your P–12 Practice or Program Using the NAGC Gifted Programming Standards* (Cotabish, Shaunessy-Dedrick, Dailey, Keilty, & Pratt, 2015), provides an easy-to-use, self-study

Figure 1.2 Relationships and Convergences Found in the Next Generation Science Standards (NGSS), the Common Core State Standards for Mathematics, the Common Core State Standards for English Language Arts, and the National Association for Gifted Children (NAGC) Pre-K–Grade 12 Gifted Programming Standards

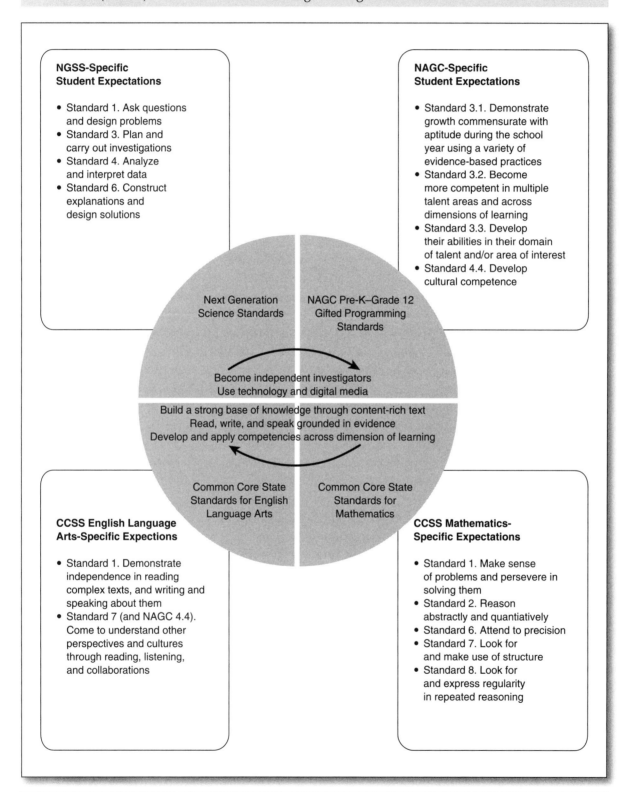

NGSS-Specific Student Expectations

- Standard 1. Ask questions and design problems
- Standard 3. Plan and carry out investigations
- Standard 4. Analyze and interpret data
- Standard 6. Construct explanations and design solutions

NAGC-Specific Student Expectations

- Standard 3.1. Demonstrate growth commensurate with aptitude during the school year using a variety of evidence-based practices
- Standard 3.2. Become more competent in multiple talent areas and across dimensions of learning
- Standard 3.3. Develop their abilities in their domain of talent and/or area of interest
- Standard 4.4. Develop cultural competence

Next Generation Science Standards

NAGC Pre-K–Grade 12 Gifted Programming Standards

Become independent investigators
Use technology and digital media

Build a strong base of knowledge through content-rich text
Read, write, and speak grounded in evidence
Develop and apply competencies across dimension of learning

Common Core State Standards for English Language Arts

Common Core State Standards for Mathematics

CCSS English Language Arts-Specific Expections

- Standard 1. Demonstrate independence in reading complex texts, and writing and speaking about them
- Standard 7 (and NAGC 4.4). Come to understand other perspectives and cultures through reading, listening, and collaborations

CCSS Mathematics-Specific Expectations

- Standard 1. Make sense of problems and persevere in solving them
- Standard 2. Reason abstractly and quantiatively
- Standard 6. Attend to precision
- Standard 7. Look for and make use of structure
- Standard 8. Look for and express regularity in repeated reasoning

Source: Adapted with permission from Cheuk (2012).

checklist for each of the six standards that can give the user a quick visual indication of priorities and needs when implementing the standards. The checklist is oriented around student outcomes and is relevant to those who serve as a teacher of the gifted, program coordinator, and/or in dual capacities, regardless of service delivery model. Completing a checklist entails a rating response to a set of four questions that directly relate to the programming standards. After rating each component, the user will add up the total number of points across each row. Once a Standards section is completed and the points have been added up, the user can use the total number of points to put program priorities in rank order (lower points indicate a higher priority). A snapshot of the self-study checklist for Standard 3 is provided in Figure 1.3 on the next page.

After using the self-study checklist to identify program priorities and alignment with standards-based practices, the next step is to explore gaps between current practices and those that have been shown to improve outcomes for gifted learners (Cotabish et al., 2015). A gap analysis chart is a strategic tool that can help an individual determine the steps needed to move from a current state of implementation or development to a future desired state. Typically, a gap analysis chart consists of a simple matrix in which data relevant to current practice and future goals are recorded and organized. (See Table 1.1 on page 9 for an example.)

The following example scenario and gap analysis chart (Table 1.1) reference the specific evidence-based practices that are linked to the NAGC Pre-K–Grade 12 Gifted Programming Standards. A full description of the NAGC evidence-based practices can be found in Appendix B, page 261.

EXAMPLE SCENARIO

The Trellis School District is a small urban school system with enrollment of approximately 30,000 students. A large percentage of students come from economically challenged families, whose economic statuses fall in the low-income to working-class range. Classrooms are comprised of more than 50% of children from immigrant families. The population is very diverse (30% White, 40% Black, 25% Hispanic, 3% Asian, 2% other), with a variety of ethnicities and racial groups. In contrast, most of the teachers' backgrounds are quite different when compared to those of their students. The majority of the teachers are White, middle-class females who reside outside the community (suburban areas) in which they teach. Most of the teachers' experiences have been in affluent suburban districts. Teacher evaluations and standardized test scores prove that the school has effective teachers who understand the mission of the school district and are making an impact on students' lives.

Recently, the Office of Gifted Services conducted a trend analysis across the district to evaluate their programs and services. Data revealed extreme disparities between percentages of students from underrepresented minority groups (URM) enrolled in the gifted program and Advanced Placement (AP) courses compared to White students. Even though there is a large

Figure 1.3 Self-Study Checklist for Standard 3

NAGC Standard 3: Curriculum Planning and Instruction	Question 1 To what degree do I address the student outcome?				Question 2 To what degree have current practices improved this student outcome?				Question 3 How high of a priority do I place on meeting this standard element?				Question 4a Is support readily available in my district? (Check 4b to indicate need to address with coordinator or other administrator.)				4b ☑	Total Points	Rank Order of Priorities to Address
	Not at all			To a great extent	Not at all			To a great extent	Low			High	Not at all			To a great extent			
Student Outcomes	1	2	3	4	1	2	3	4	1	2	3	4	1	2	3	4			
3.1. *Curriculum Planning.* Students with gifts and talents demonstrate growth commensurate with aptitude during the school year.																			
3.2. *Talent Development.* Students with gifts and talents become more competent in multiple talent areas and across dimensions of learning.																			
3.3. *Talent Development.* Students with gifts and talents develop their abilities in their domain of talent and/or area of interest.																			
3.4. *Instructional Strategies.* Students with gifts and talents become independent investigators.																			
3.5. *Culturally Relevant Curriculum.* Students with gifts and talents develop knowledge and skills for living and being productive in a multicultural, diverse, and global society.																			
3.6. *Resources.* Students with gifts and talents benefit from gifted education programming that provides a variety of high-quality resources and materials.																			

Source: Cotabish, Shaunessy-Dedrick, Dailey, Keilty, and Pratt (2015, p. 15). Reprinted with permission.

Table 1.1 Gap Analysis Chart

Standard	Evidence-Based Practice	What We Do to Support This Practice	Desired Student Outcomes	What Evidence Do We Have That Current Practices Are Leading to Desired Student Outcomes?	What Additional Evidence/Information Do We Need? (Gaps)
1	1.2.1	Teachers differentiate instruction to match students' developmental levels.	Students with gifts and talents possess a developmentally appropriate understanding of how they learn and grow; they recognize the influences of their beliefs, traditions, and values on learning and behavior.	According to student feedback (e.g., exit slips, reflections, discussion) and assessments, instruction is being differentiated based on students' developmental levels.	Additional evidence is needed that ensures instructional strategies in gifted and AP classes value student diversity and differences in learning.
1	1.4.1 1.4.2	Currently, we neither adequately involve community members nor utilize community resources.	Students with gifts and talents access resources from the community to support cognitive and affective needs, including same-age peers and mentors or experts.	There is no evidence supporting the use of role models or out-of-school learning opportunities that match students' abilities or interests.	Additional information is needed on how the community can provide resources to support cognitive and affective needs of students.
1	1.5	Parents are invited to the parent-teacher conferences held each fall and spring.	Students' families and communities understand similarities and differences with respect to the development and characteristics of advanced and typical learners, and they support the needs of students with gifts and talents.	Particular students' learning differences and needs are discussed at parent-teacher conferences as documented by a sign-in sheet.	Additional information is needed on efforts to better communicate and collaborate with parents and community members.
2	2.3	Parents and teachers are able to nominate students for the gifted program.	Students with identified needs represent diverse backgrounds and reflect the total student population of the district.	There is a lack of evidence supporting student diversity in the gifted program. According to gifted program and AP student data, the total student population is not represented in the gifted program or AP courses.	Additional information is needed to ensure use of nonbiased and equitable approaches for identifying students with gifts and talents. Evidence is also needed that parents and students are informed of the benefits of AP courses.

(Continued)

9

Table 1.1 (Continued)

Standard	Evidence-Based Practice	What We Do to Support This Practice	Desired Student Outcomes	What Evidence Do We Have That Current Practices Are Leading to Desired Student Outcomes?	What Additional Evidence/ Information Do We Need? (Gaps)
3	3.3.1	Teachers integrate instructional strategies and activities that differentiate for content, process, and product.	Students with gifts and talents participate in multiple learning experiences and activities that allow them to develop and apply knowledge in ways that are meaningful and relevant.	According to student feedback (e.g., exit slips, reflections, discussion) and assessments, differentiated instruction is effective.	Additional evidence is needed to ensure that the instructional strategies used are culturally relevant and appropriately responsive.
3	3.5.1	Minimal cultural aspects have been integrated other than contributions related to holidays and celebrations.	Students with gifts and talents actively engage in rigorous, culturally significant learning experiences.	Multicultural education is integrated at a basic level, which yields very little evidence.	Additional evidence is not required because there is a recognized gap.
3	3.5.2	Few opportunities are provided for students to construct their own knowledge through the curriculum.	Students with gifts and talents participate in exploratory learning opportunities that are responsive and related to their interests.	Very little evidence since student-centered opportunities are limited.	Additional evidence is not required because there is a recognized gap.
3	3.5.3	Nothing has been implemented to support this practice.	Students with gifts and talents use personal and multiple perspectives to analyze and reflect on cultural issues, interests, and challenges.	No evidence.	Additional evidence is not required because there is a recognized gap.

Standard	Evidence-Based Practice	What We Do to Support This Practice	Desired Student Outcomes	What Evidence Do We Have That Current Practices Are Leading to Desired Student Outcomes?	What Additional Evidence/Information Do We Need? (Gaps)
5	5.2.1	Minimal collaborative opportunities have been initiated to discuss how best to help gifted students.	Students with gifts and talents demonstrate achievement as result of collaborative efforts and shared vision among all school divisions and personnel.	Very little evidence other than the results presented from the needs assessment at the school site meetings.	Additional evidence is not required because there is a recognized gap.
5	5.3.1	The school occasionally invites parents and community members to help with fundraisers, serve on hiring committees, and come to school events.	Students with gifts and talents experience enriched learning opportunities through team-based planning and communication among community, parents, and the school.	Data from needs assessment revealed that parents/community felt more of an observer relationship with the school and did not fully understand how the gifted courses affected post-high-school plans.	More evidence is needed on how to employ school and community resources directly in the classroom and collaborate with community members (e.g., university, healthcare facilities, parents, field-based opportunities, local resources, mentors) to enhance learning.
6	6.1.1 6.1.2 6.1.3	Gifted education and AP teachers are required by the state to have 60 hours of continuing education each year.	Students develop their talents and gifts as a result of interacting with educators who meet the national teacher preparation standards in gifted education.	Evidence from standardized test scores suggests teachers are effective. Additional evidence indicates that learning may not be culturally relevant to all students.	Evidence is needed that encourages classroom, gifted education, and AP teachers to seek professional development opportunities that model how to develop environments and instructional strategies that support gifted learners, including those from underrepresented minority (URM) groups.

population of URM students in the school district, this number is not reflected in the gifted program or AP courses. Currently, the percentage of URM students identified and served in the gifted program is less than 10%, well below their represented population in the district. Additionally, over the past 3 years, the percentage of URM students enrolled in high school AP courses decreased by 20%, although school enrollments remained stable. To further investigate the lack of identification of URM gifted students and the retention and persistence of URM students in AP courses, a needs analysis survey was administered to teachers, community/parents, and URM students currently enrolled in gifted services as well as students who had withdrawn. This was followed by focus group interviews with all stakeholders. The surveys revealed that many teachers and parents were unaware of gifted program identification procedures. Parents did not realize they could request that their child be tested for identification into the gifted program. Furthermore, teacher responses indicated a limited knowledge of the diverse characteristics of URM gifted students. In the gifted and AP classrooms, data revealed that teachers planned effective differentiated lessons focused on content, process, and products that occasionally required students to use technology; however, the students were less than enthusiastic about the activities and readings. Former and current students felt that there was a divide because the teachers did not understand or value their cultural differences. Community members and parents divulged that there was not a reciprocal relationship with the school. Parents rarely received information from the school except through occasional newsletters, teacher calls and e-mails, and the twice-a-year parent-teacher conferences. As an example, parents were unaware of how an AP course would prepare their children any differently than a regular content course in the same area. Because state tests are based on the traditional content areas and are used as the standard for college and career readiness, many parents did not understand why their child should take a course with higher expectations, increased homework, and more challenging assignments.

The Office of Gifted Services is convinced that to identify URM students for gifted services and increase enrollment in advanced classes, teachers and parents must be educated on the characteristics of URM gifted students, teachers must integrate more culturally relevant practices and utilize community resources to support learning, and the district office must do a better job at communicating the importance of gifted education and AP courses to parents and the community while at the same time advocating for their help. The district coordinator refers to the NAGC Pre-K–Grade 12 Gifted Programming Standards as a resource to help meet the students' individual learning needs. To address areas of needed improvement in instruction and programming, the coordinator and teachers complete a self-evaluation using Cotabish and colleagues' (2015) *Self-Assess Your P–12 Practice or Program Using the NAGC Gifted Programming Standards*. After completing the self-study checklist, school site meetings—followed by a district-wide meeting—are held to collaborate and complete a gap analysis chart (see Table 1.1) and finally create an action plan (see Table 1.2).

Table 1.2 Action Plan Chart

Standard	Evidence-Based Practice	Desired Student Outcomes	Identified Gaps	Information to Be Collected/ Action to Be Carried Out	Person(s) Responsible	Timeline
1	1.2.1	Students with gifts and talents possess a developmentally appropriate understanding of how they learn and grow; they recognize the influences of their beliefs, traditions, and values on learning and behavior.	Student diversity and differences in learning are not addressed in gifted or AP classrooms.	The district will seek professional development and community assistance in efforts to educate teachers on culturally responsive instructional practices.	District administrators	Yearly
1	1.4.1 1.4.2	Students with gifts and talents access resources from the community to support cognitive and affective needs, including same-age peers and mentors or experts.	There is no evidence supporting the use of role models or out-of-school learning opportunities that match students' abilities or interests.	Gifted and AP teachers will seek community and industry members to serve as mentors or role models for students.	Gifted and AP teachers	Ongoing
1	1.5	Students' families and communities understand similarities and differences with respect to the development and characteristics of advanced and typical learners and support the needs of students with gifts and talents.	There is minimal communication with parents regarding student learning and programming options.	The district will establish a parental involvement committee to seek additional avenues for communicating with parents. The parental involvement committee will survey parents on their preferred mode of communication. The communication efforts will be implemented in the following year.	Parental Involvement Committee	Year 1 and then ongoing

(Continued)

Table 1.2 (Continued)

Standard	Evidence-Based Practice	Desired Student Outcomes	Identified Gaps	Information to Be Collected/ Action to Be Carried Out	Person(s) Responsible	Timeline
2	2.3	Students with identified needs represent diverse backgrounds and reflect the total student population of the district.	According to gifted program and AP student data, the total student population is not represented in the gifted program or AP courses.	District administrators, classroom teachers, gifted education teachers, and AP teachers will be provided professional development targeting nonbiased approaches for identifying students with gifts and talents. Parents will receive communication regarding the benefits of AP courses.	District gifted and AP administrators	Yearly
5	5.2.1	Students with gifts and talents demonstrate achievement as result of collaborative efforts and shared vision among all school divisions and personnel.	More evidence is needed to ensure that all educators and professional staff are trained to implement culturally responsive teaching practices, how cultural factors influence positive and negative behaviors in school and gifted/advanced classes, and how to address the social and emotional and psychological needs of culturally diverse gifted students.	Conduct an internal and external evaluation of the gifted services offered in the district. Examine data and make informed instructional decisions to establish deeper awareness of best practices for culturally diverse gifted students.	Administrators and coordinators from specific divisions, counselors, instructional facilitators, and teachers	Ongoing

Standard	Evidence-Based Practice	Desired Student Outcomes	Identified Gaps	Information to Be Collected/ Action to Be Carried Out	Person(s) Responsible	Timeline
5	5.3.1	Students with gifts and talents experience enriched learning opportunities through team-based planning and communication from community, parents, and the school.	A reciprocal relationship between school and stakeholders should be established.	Seek out parents and community members to volunteer or get involved with curriculum planning and to help relate content to real-world practice. Create a living document resource guide with a compilation of resource people, educational experiences, and/or places to visit in the local and surrounding community.	Classroom teacher with assistance from the counselor, PTO, students, parents, and community members	Once every two months
6	6.1.1 6.1.2 6.1.3	Students develop their talents and gifts as a result of interacting with educators who meet the national teacher preparation standards in gifted education.	There is student dissatisfaction with activities and readings in gifted and AP classes.	Gifted education and AP teachers should seek professional development opportunities that model how to develop environments and instructional strategies that support gifted learners, including those from URM groups.	District gifted and AP administrators	Ongoing

NEXT STEPS

As indicated by the gap analysis chart (Table 1.1) and action plan (Table 1.2), Trellis School District has a strategy to make needed improvements to the gifted program across several standards. As outlined by the action plan, individuals are responsible for specific tasks to help improve the program and provide a better, more equitable education for all students. The scenario was fictional and many of the situations were not probabilistic; however, many school districts face similar problems, especially with implementing culturally relevant and responsive teaching and the lack of diversity representation in gifted classrooms. By using the self-study checklist, school districts, gifted and AP programs, and teachers of the gifted can better recognize areas for improvement. After the Action Plan is implemented, school personnel should revisit the self-study checklist for continuous evaluation and program improvement.

BRINGING IT ALL TOGETHER

In conclusion, meeting the needs of students with gifts and talents takes a community effort. When addressing gifted programming, it is important for educators to consider the state and national standards, including the NAGC Pre-K–Grade 12 Gifted Programming Standards and content standards such as the CCSS and the NGSS. Additionally, educators must be cognizant of students' cultural differences. To make learning interesting and relevant for students, there needs to be a connection with their real world. To increase the relevancy of student learning, community resources need to be identified and utilized. Using guest speakers, providing field trips, and arranging professional mentoring opportunities allow students opportunities to view learning in the context of the real world. No longer should students ask, "How will I use this when I grow up?" Instead, we should show them how they will use the content when they grow up.

SUGGESTED RESOURCES

Johnsen, S. K. (Ed.). (2012). *NAGC Pre-K–Grade 12 Gifted Education Programming Standards: A guide to planning and implementing high-quality services*. Waco, TX: Prufrock Press.

This book offers a guide to planning and implementing high-quality services across the six standards addressing areas critical to effective teaching and learning. Example assessments of student products and performances are provided.

Cotabish, A., Shaunessy-Dedrick, E., Dailey, D., Kielty, W., & Pratt, D. (2015). *Self-assess your P–12 practice or program using the NAGC gifted programming standards*. Washington, DC: National Association for Gifted Children.

This NAGC publication is designed for teachers and gifted education coordinators to reflect on and improve their teaching practices and gifted education programs to support the student outcomes. Through this process, teachers and coordinators can identify areas of needed improvement and develop an action plan.

Johnsen, S. K., & Clarenbach, J. (Eds.). (2017). *Using the national gifted education standards for prek–12 professional development.* Waco, TX: Prufrock Press.

This book summarizes how to use the NAGC-CEC national teacher preparation standards in gifted education to guide teachers in professional development opportunities and to design and assess in-service training programs.

REFERENCES

Achieve, Inc. (2014). *Next Generation Science Standards.* Washington, DC: Author.

Adams, C. M., Cotabish, A., & Ricci, M. K. (2014). *Using the Next Generation Science Standards with gifted and advanced learners.* Waco, TX: Prufrock Press.

Cheuk, T. (2012). *Relationships and convergences found in Common Core State Standards for Mathematics, Common Core State Standards for ELA/Literacy, and a Framework for K–12 Science Education.* Arlington, VA: National Science Teachers Association.

Cotabish, A., & Krisel, S. (2012). Action plans: Bringing the program standards to life. In S. K. Johnsen (Ed.), *NAGC Pre-K–Grade 12 Gifted Education Programming Standards: A guide to planning and implementing high-quality services* (pp. 231–253). Waco, TX: Prufrock Press.

Cotabish, A., Shaunessy-Dedrick, E., Dailey, D., Kielty, W., & Pratt, D. (2015). *Self-assess your P–12 practice or program using the NAGC Gifted Programming Standards.* Washington, DC: National Association for Gifted Children.

Johnsen, S. K. (2012). Preface: Overview of the NAGC Pre-K–Grade 12 Gifted Programming Standards. In S. K. Johnsen (Ed.), *NAGC Pre-K–Grade 12 Gifted Education Programming Standards: A guide to planning and implementing high-quality services* (pp. ix–xiii). Waco, TX: Prufrock Press.

National Association for Gifted Children. (2010). *NAGC Pre-K–Grade 12 Gifted Programming Standards: A blueprint for quality gifted education programs.* Washington, DC: Author.

National Governors Association Center for Best Practices, & Council of Chief State School Officers. (2010). *Common Core State Standards.* Washington, DC: Authors.

Chapter 2

Developing a Mission Statement on the Educational Needs of Gifted and Talented Students

Rebecca D. Eckert, PhD

DEFINITION

A mission statement is a short, written passage that communicates the beliefs and purpose of an organization. School districts often develop a mission statement as a tool for strategic management and leadership with the hope of generating a shared focus on positive results for an entire learning community (Slate, Jones, Wiesman, Alexander, & Saenz, 2008; Stemler & Bebell, 2012). Within a school system, a mission statement on the educational needs of gifted and talented students serves a twofold purpose: (a) to foster a collective understanding of those needs, and (b) to guide subsequent actions with regard to programming and service delivery.

Therefore, an effective mission statement clarifies the beliefs of a school district about the nature of giftedness and the need for educational services to meet the learning needs of gifted and talented students. It should illuminate who gifted and talented children are, explain why educational services for them are necessary, provide one or two overarching program goals, and offer a clear message about the district's commitment to meeting the learning needs of these students. Mission statements may be presented in paragraph or bulleted form, or a combination of both formats.

RATIONALE

Like successful businesses, successful schools invest resources in crafting a vision and fostering values because they recognize that community culture determines how and why people work together toward excellence. According to Knowling (2002), "[m]ost leaders love to make strategy, but it is vision and values that spawn strategic action. The absence of a vision will doom any strategy—especially a strategy for change" (p. 129). Essentially, a mission statement helps community members understand what is crucial to the success of any organization or program, including gifted education.

There are several important reasons for developing a clear and cogent mission statement.[1] Thoughtfully crafted mission statements inform and shape the educational programming available for gifted students within a school district and community. With a coherent set of statements that put forth beliefs about gifted students and their educational needs, educators, parents, and other community members also will gain an understanding of how gifted education is viewed by policy makers (Berg, Csikszentmihalyi, & Nakamura, 2003). Moreover, a gifted program mission statement aligned with the purpose and values of a broader learning community is powerful because meeting the educational needs of gifted and talented students becomes an essential part of the overall school mission (Keeling, 2013).

Equally important, a clear mission statement provides constituents with a solid reference point to understand the reasons for decisions and actions related to gifted and talented education (Knowling, 2002). It frees educators and administrators from the trap of "this is how we've always done it" to map out a new path and dedicate resources to pursuing positive results for students with specialized—and recognized—needs in their community (Carver, 2000; Slate et al., 2008). Finally, the mission statement is the foundation for all other tasks described in subsequent chapters in this text; it supports and is the rationale for designing and implementing programs and services for gifted students (Lawrence, 2002).

GUIDING PRINCIPLES AND ATTRIBUTES OF A HIGH-QUALITY MISSION STATEMENT

Researchers who reviewed documents from more than 300 elementary schools in Texas noted that "a properly worded mission statement can contribute to the success of a school" (Slate et al., 2008, p. 26). This conclusion

---

[1]Interestingly, research suggests that schools with mission statements that focus on academic success and providing challenges for students are more likely to be described as academically successful (Slate et al., 2008).

emphasizes the need for attention to detail and clear communication when developing a mission statement. Specifically, a high-quality mission statement will encompass four key attributes:

1. comprehensiveness,

2. rationale,

3. consistency, and

4. clarity.

Comprehensiveness

Mission statements should express beliefs about how giftedness and talents develop and define the word *gifted* for the school district. A high-quality mission statement balances brevity with the recognition that there is no simple, one-size-fits-all definition. Therefore, it addresses broadly the intellectual, social, and emotional needs of students identified as gifted and talented in the school district, as well as the way in which these talents are developed.

Comprehensive mission statements also provide a focus for moving forward—or adapting to change—in a coordinated, thoughtful way. The mission statement should specify one or two overarching, long-term outcomes that will result from programs and services. Additionally, the mission statement may address the issue of responsibility (i.e., identifying who is responsible for meeting the needs of high-achieving students).

Rationale

Mission statements should explain why educational services for students are necessary. To foster a shared purpose, a high-quality statement includes solid justification for providing educational programs and services for gifted and talented students. Moreover, the credibility of the mission (and subsequent programming and services) is enhanced when it is grounded in tested theories and supported by research.

Consistency

Mission statements should align philosophically with the broad educational goals of the school system and reflect an understanding of state laws and policies. Architects of a high-quality mission statement recognize that programs and services for gifted and talented students represent parts of a whole educational system rather than an isolated entity. Therefore, to serve as an effective guide for action and decision making, the mission statement must be reflective of the school community and character. The educational vision for gifted and talented students should align with the district's general goals for education as stated in strategic plans and district statements of vision and mission.

Clarity

Mission statements should be clear and easily understood. A high-quality mission statement will serve as a starting point for conversations with a variety of stakeholders (e.g., teachers, administrators, parents, students, community members) about how best to meet the needs of gifted and talented students within a school system. Therefore, it should avoid educational jargon and specialized terms so that all users will understand its intent and purpose.

EXAMPLE IN NEED OF REVISION

Jonesville School District's Mission Statement: Academically talented children in Jonesville may possess characteristics that necessitate qualitatively different instruction. Our program is designed to provide the atmosphere for stimulating above-average-ability students.

Often, statements of goals and beliefs are most meaningful when developed in collaboration with a team of individuals with an interest in the project (Keeling, 2013). Therefore, the first recommended step in the revision process it to assemble a task force to critically examine the four defined traits of a high-quality mission statement.

Comprehensiveness

Although the Jonesville School District's mission statement explicitly states that academically talented students may need qualitatively different instruction, the statement shows little evidence of comprehensiveness. In their revision, the task force plans to address or elaborate on the following:

- what giftedness looks like in Jonesville and areas of potential gifts and talents that the current mission statement overlooks (e.g., creativity),
- how children develop giftedness and what the school district can do to uncover hidden talents,
- one or two broad goals for the services to gifted and talented students, and
- the responsibility of the school and larger community to meet the learning needs of this population.

Rationale

The original mission statement does not explain why it is necessary to provide an atmosphere that will stimulate students of above-average abilities. The task force needs to justify why educational services are necessary to meet the learning needs of this population and communicate this shared purpose effectively. Even though it may not become a specific part of the final polished mission statement, the task force members also plan to collect research-based evidence to inform their work and support their statements.

Consistency

As originally written, the Jonesville mission statement shows no evidence of consistency with other goals and programs within the school district or a broader school mission. To successfully shape future programming and positively influence district decisions, the mission statement must reflect the linkages between the character and mission of the larger learning community and the broad goals for the services provided to gifted and talented children. Moreover, the task force members intend to review state laws and policies to ensure that their revised mission statement is aligned.

Clarity

Finally, the brevity and use of educational terms (e.g., qualitatively different) in the original mission statement limit the clarity of the document. After all other concerns have been addressed, the task force members plan to ask a broad sample of individuals to review the document. Based on their feedback, they will simplify and/or modify the language and detail to ensure that all constituents can understand its intent.

MAKEOVER EXAMPLE

After several productive conversations and the inclusion of feedback from a wide range of community members, the final, revised mission statement developed by the Jonesville strategic task force reads as follows:

> The mission of the Jonesville School District is to ensure that each child has equal opportunity to reach his or her academic potential. The school board recognizes that some students possess, or are capable of possessing, extraordinary learning ability and/or outstanding talent. These students come from all socioeconomic, cultural, and ethnic backgrounds. The school board affirms the following:
>
> - Curricular modifications as described in our comprehensive program design will occur in the regular classroom to provide continuous levels of challenge for all students, including those with unique gifts and talents.
> - In addition to the regular classroom, a range of instructional settings, both within the school as well as the community, will be available for specialized instruction that is integrated with the regular curriculum and the intellectual and social and emotional needs of gifted and talented children.

- It is the responsibility of the school district and the larger community to ensure the following:
  - ○ ongoing identification of gifted and talented children, and
  - ○ provision of appropriate and systematic educational services to meet the unique learning needs of gifted and talented children.

The Jonesville strategic task force designed the mission statement above as a mixture of narrative and bulleted items. They could have also conveyed the same information in one or two paragraphs, as in the following example:

> The Jonesville Board of Education believes that there are gifted students whose intellectual capacity, rate of learning, and potential for creative contributions demand experiences apart from, but connected to, the regular classroom. These students exhibit high performance, or the potential to achieve, in intellectual, creative, or artistic areas; possess strong leadership capacity; or excel in specific academic fields. It is essential to provide diverse, appropriate, and ongoing learning experiences and environments that incorporate the academic, psychological, and social needs of students. It is our responsibility to provide students with educational alternatives that teach, challenge, and expand their knowledge, while simultaneously stressing the development of independent and self-directed learners who continuously generate questions, analyze, synthesize, and evaluate information and ideas.
>
> We are committed to the belief that gifted students are individuals with potential who require guidance in discovering, developing, and realizing their potentials as individuals and as members of society. Under this philosophy, it becomes the responsibility of the entire staff to meet the needs of gifted students by identifying their gifts and talents and developing those areas. This philosophy also requires a strong partnership between the school system and community.

When comparing the two different formats, note that both mission statements begin with a clear definition of giftedness connected to the broader school district purpose. In addition, both statements describe program services that address the cognitive and affective needs of students as well as services that can be made available in the larger community. Finally, the mission statements address the responsibility of the school district to provide ongoing levels of challenge for all students, including those who are gifted and talented.

ADVICE FOR GETTING STARTED

Admittedly, the final goal in the development of a mission statement is an articulate, polished document that communicates clearly the needs of gifted and talented students in your school and the purpose and goals of educational programs or services. However, there are numerous benefits to be gained from the collaborative work involved when developing or revising a mission statement with a task force or team.

> The process requires participants to negotiate the meaning of words, phrases, and concepts, an activity that invests generic-sounding language with deep meaning for members of the community. Through these discussions, members of a group come to understand how all members contribute to the enterprise. (Keeling, 2013, p. 31)

The strategic plan provided in Table 2.1 can be used to jump-start your own process of assembling a team to uncover and communicate the mission for your gifted program.

Table 2.1 Strategic Plan

Objective: To create or revise a mission statement on the education of gifted and talented students	
Evidence: A completed mission statement on the education of gifted and talented students	
Tasks: Create a mission statement or revise an existing mission statement	
Timeline	
February 15	Send invitations to all task force members for a working meeting.
	Ask each member to come prepared to discuss: "Who are the gifted and talented students in our school system, and what do they need to reach their full potential?"
March 1	Convene a meeting of the task force on gifted education to discuss the mission and purpose of gifted education in the school district.
	Provide school district documents (e.g., demographics, district mission statement, state definition of gifted) and attributes template to inform the conversation.
March 2	Send out meeting notes and a brief article about creating a mission statement to all task force members; include a reminder for the next meeting.
March 14	Convene a meeting of the task force to develop a working draft of the mission statement and assemble research evidence to support it. (If the task force is large, a subcommittee may make the writing process more manageable.)
March 15–29	Post the working draft online and invite comments and refinements from all task force members; use the four attributes to prompt feedback (i.e., consistency, comprehensiveness, rationale, and clarity).
April 1–15	Distribute an updated draft to a broad sample of individuals for review and feedback.
April 24	Present completed mission statement to the school board and superintendent for final approval.

As you work to craft your own mission statement, remember that

> a vision is usually formed by looking both inward and outward—
> looking inside the school at the people there and looking outside
> the school at the challenges society and individuals are facing, the
> challenges schools are supposed to prepare youngsters to deal
> with. (Starratt, 1995, p. 16)

The template in Table 2.2 was designed to aid in this introspective process and guide conversations, as you work to design or revise a mission statement.

Although this chapter is about how to create a mission statement, it is important to consider what will happen once you have completed this foundational task. How will your finely crafted statement of purpose and values be used to guide program and service development for gifted

Table 2.2   Template to Design or Revise a Mission Statement

Trait	Focusing Question	Our Thinking
Comprehensiveness	What is giftedness?	
	How are students' gifts and talents developed in an educational setting?	
	Broadly speaking, how do the intellectual and social and emotional needs of gifted students differ from those of their chronological peers?	
	What are the broad, long-term outcomes (1–2) that will result from programs and services focused on the needs of gifted and talented students?	
Rationale	What is the justification for providing educational services to gifted and talented students?	
	Why is it important that students' unique learning needs are met?	
	What is the research base that supports our conclusions?	

(Continued)

Table 2.2 (Continued)

Trait	Focusing Question	Our Thinking
Consistency	What are the policies and regulations regarding gifted education in our state and district?	
	What is the linkage between the broad learning goals for gifted and talented students and the academic goals for all students in the district or school?	
Clarity	Is the language clear, succinct, and free of educational jargon?	
	Is it written so that all readers (including students) will understand the intent of the document?	

students? What actions will be sparked by a clear communication of the academic and social needs of high-ability learners in your community? Ultimately, it will be the responsibility of the gifted education coordinator, task force members, and administrators to ensure that the mission statement comes to life.

ADVICE FOR THE SOLE PRACTITIONER

Although consensus building is one of the most important side benefits of crafting a mission statement, the sole practitioner can still reap positive rewards from clarifying and sharing an ideal vision of education for the gifted and talented students within his or her district. Begin by assembling district and school goals and mission statements as well as policies and decisions that relate to the gifted education program. Then, seek out examples of mission statements online or from neighboring school districts to help guide your thinking. If you are unable to assemble a task force to assist you in crafting a mission statement, try to elicit feedback from a few stakeholders and colleagues familiar with your students and your school system. Once you are satisfied with your polished and thoughtful mission statement, you are prepared to share your vision with your school community and get down to work.

SUGGESTED RESOURCES

Keeling, M. (2013). Mission statements: Rhetoric, reality, or road map to success? *Knowledge Quest, 42*(1), 30–36.

This article provides thoughtful advice and background for practitioners about developing a mission statement for an educational program within the context of a larger school district mission. Although focused on communicating a shared purpose for school libraries, the author's description of the collaborative process and insights gained from crafting a meaningful mission statement for the community translates well to the experience of those seeking to develop a statement of purpose for gifted programming and/or services. (For additional advice on establishing a gifted educational advisory committee and building consensus, see Appendix A, page 256.)

Stemler, S. E., & Bebell, D. J. (2012). *The school mission statement: Values, goals, and identities in American education.* Larchmont, NY: Eye on Education.

For readers seeking foundational understanding, this comprehensive text explores "the purpose of school" as defined in the mission statements of 111 diverse schools from across the United States. The authors also include advice for crafting your own school mission statement, providing specific examples from the 11 most common themes found in their research. Although gifted education is not specifically discussed, examples from magnet and award-winning schools are provided, and the common themes of mission statements could be used to guide conversations among stakeholders and/or strategic planning groups.

REFERENCES

Berg, G. A., Csikszentmihalyi, M., & Nakamura, J. (2003). A mission possible? Enabling good work in higher education. *Change, 35*(5), 41–47.

Carver, J. (2000). Managing your mission: Advice on where to begin. *About Campus, 4*(6), 19–23.

Keeling, M. (2013). Mission statements: Rhetoric, reality, or road map to success? *Knowledge Quest, 42*(1), 30–36.

Knowling, R. (2002). Why vision matters. In F. Hesselbein & R. Johnston (Eds.), *On mission and leadership* (pp. 128–140). San Francisco, CA: Jossey-Bass.

Lawrence, D. M. (2002). Maintaining a mission: Lessons from the marketplace. In F. Hesselbein & R. Johnston (Eds.), *On mission and leadership* (pp. 89–101). San Francisco, CA: Jossey-Bass.

Slate, J. R., Jones, C. H., Wiesman, K., Alexander, J., & Saenz, T. (2008). School mission statements and school performance: A mixed research investigation. *New Horizons in Education, 56*(2), 17–27.

Starratt, R. J. (1995). *Leaders with vision: The quest for school renewal.* Thousand Oaks, CA: Corwin.

Stemler, S. E., & Bebell, D. J. (2012). *The school mission statement: Values, goals, and identities in American education.* Larchmont, NY: Eye on Education.

Chapter 3

Developing a Definition of Giftedness

Kristina Ayers Paul, PhD, and Sidney M. Moon, PhD

DEFINITION

There are two types of definitions of giftedness—conceptual and operational—both of which are important for schools. Conceptual definitions provide a theoretical description of giftedness and are incorporated into a school district's mission statement for gifted education programming. They define the construct of giftedness and the nature of gifted students in the abstract, thereby illustrating the general characteristics of the students for whom the gifted education programming is intended to serve. On the other hand, operational definitions provide detailed, concrete guidance on how the giftedness of students will be assessed and identified in a particular context and for a particular purpose. Operational definitions stem from more general conceptual definitions, and they provide logistical information for guiding identification procedures. Generally, a school district selects one conception of giftedness to serve as a foundation for all the gifted programming in the district and then creates related operational definitions for each programming component within a continuum of services. Thus, definitions of giftedness link broad mission statements to specific programs and services through identification procedures.

RATIONALE

Conceptions of giftedness have changed over time (Tannenbaum, 2000), moving from narrow, intellectually based conceptions of giftedness to broader, more inclusive definitions that recognize talents in specific domains (McClain & Pfeiffer, 2012). Early scholars such as Lewis Terman (1925) and Leta Hollingworth (1926, 1942) defined giftedness as the ability to achieve a very high score on an individualized intelligence test. These scholars defined giftedness primarily as an advanced ability to think and learn. Current scholars view giftedness more broadly. For example, Gardner (1983, 1999, 2011) spoke of multiple intelligences, only three of which are measured on traditional intelligence tests. Sternberg (2000) conceptualized giftedness as developing expertise, a more dynamic way of conceptualizing advanced abilities. In his WICS model of giftedness, Sternberg (2003) described giftedness as the synthesis of wisdom, intelligence, and creativity, but he ultimately emphasized the role of culture in determining how giftedness is conceptualized (Sternberg, 2007, 2012). Renzulli (1978, 1986, 2012) focused on the development of gifted behaviors. He believed that gifted performance, what he called creative productivity, requires above-average ability in combination with creativity and task commitment. Gagné (1985, 1999, 2000, 2004, 2009) combined many of these more current conceptions into a complex theory of giftedness that suggests that natural abilities (gifts) of many kinds are developed into demonstrated competencies (talents) through a long-term process that involves intrapersonal catalysts, environmental catalysts, and chance factors. Gagné (1998) also has presented a proposal for considering subcategories, or levels of giftedness, within any particular talent domain.

The various types of conceptual definitions can be summarized in six categories:

1. Psychometric definitions are based on test scores. For example, Lewis Terman (1925) defined giftedness as a score over 140 on the Stanford-Binet IQ test, and Julian Stanley and his colleagues (Benbow & Stanley, 1983; Stanley, 1996) defined giftedness as a high score on an off-grade-level test of mathematical or verbal reasoning ability. These definitions are very easy to operationalize; in fact, they are examples of situations where conceptual and operational definitions merge. Although some states adopted psychometric definitions of giftedness in the past, the trend has been to move away from psychometric definitions toward composite definitions (see below).

2. Neurobiological/cognitive definitions are based on findings from neuroscience and/or cognitive science. Gardner's (1999) multiple intelligences and Sternberg's (1985; Sternberg & Clinkenbeard, 1995) analytical, creative, and practical intelligences are examples. These definitions are somewhat harder to operationalize through standardized tests than are psychometric tests and generally are operationalized with multiple measures, including both tests, when available, and performance-based assessments.

3. Creative-productive definitions are based on examining the life histories of creative-productive adults. Renzulli's (1978) three-ring conception of giftedness is an example. These definitions are usually operationalized with multiple measures, including standardized

tests of intellectual ability and academic achievement in combination with authentic assessments; portfolios; interviews; teacher, peer, and self-nominations; and other subjective measures of talent potential.

4. Psychosocial definitions emphasize the role of both the individual and his or her environment in the development of giftedness. Tannenbaum (1986) and Gagné (2000) are examples of scholars who have developed psychosocial conceptions of giftedness. Operationalization of these definitions is complex because the definitions are so broad. These definitions provide the broadest possible framework for giftedness and, as a result, provide the least guidance for creating operational definitions for specific programming options.

5. Composite definitions borrow from multiple theoretical perspectives. The Marland Report (Marland, 1972), the *National Excellence* Report (U.S. Department of Education, 1993), and the National Association for Gifted Children's (NAGC, 2010) position statement defining giftedness promoted composite definitions of giftedness for school settings. John Feldhusen (1995) developed a composite definition called TIDE that focused on talent identification and development in four domains in school settings. Legal definitions are often composite definitions modeled after the original Marland Report definition. The federal Jacob K. Javits Gifted and Talented Students Education Act includes a composite definition of giftedness, as do many state definitions. Composite definitions are generally operationalized with separate multiple assessment identification procedures for each of the talent areas addressed (e.g., intellectual, academic, creative, visual and performing arts, leadership).

6. The advanced academics approach (Peters, Matthews, McBee, & McCoach, 2014) focuses on developing specific advanced academic options that are needed within a school program, based on the needs of students, and then systematically identifying the students who are suited for each advanced academic option. In other words, this approach favors contextualized, composite definitions that focus on academic talent development. The approach aligns with the idea of using operational definitions of giftedness for each advanced academic option without combining qualified students into one broad category of "gifted."

Notions of giftedness are influenced by culture, politics, and research findings (Moon & Rosselli, 2000). Because giftedness is a somewhat controversial construct in school settings, it is important for school districts to examine different theories of giftedness and select a conceptual definition that is consistent with current theory and research, existing state policies that define giftedness, and the values of most of the stakeholders in the district. These contexts are constantly evolving, so it is also important that school districts regularly review their definition of giftedness for relevance within the changing context. For example, McClain and Pfeiffer (2012) found that 48% of the state definitions had changed during the period of 2000 to 2012, which highlights the need for school districts to continually monitor changes in state policy to maintain alignment.

State policies have tremendous influence over the implementation of gifted education services within local school districts (VanTassel-Baska, 2006). Definitions of giftedness adopted by local school districts should be aligned with the state within which they reside. Local definitions may be broader than that of the state—but never more restrictive—and similar terms should be maintained (i.e., gifted and talented, gifted, and high ability). For example, in a 2012 review of the 48 states that have adopted an official definition of giftedness, 27 states use the term *gifted and talented*, 18 states use only *gifted*, and 3 states use the term *high ability* (McClain & Pfeiffer, 2012). The definitions that accompany these terms vary considerably regarding the combination of traits and categories included; intelligence, high achievement, creativity, domain-specific giftedness (e.g., artistic), leadership, and motivation are represented among the definitions. It is important that schools align their conceptual definition of giftedness with their state's definition, even if the school's definition takes a broader, more inclusive approach.

GUIDING PRINCIPLES AND TRAITS THAT DEFINE HIGH QUALITY

When developing or revising conceptual and operational definitions of giftedness, keep the following principles in mind:

- Giftedness is a social construction that is influenced by culture, values, and politics.
- Definitions of giftedness should reflect current theory and research.
- Definitions of giftedness must reflect state or legal definitions.
- Definitions of giftedness must reflect the context in which they are implemented.
- Effective definitions of giftedness provide a foundation for identification and programming.

High-quality definitions of giftedness will embody a set of traits that are logical extensions of the principles listed above. They are legality, soundness, cultural relevance, feasibility, equity, clarity, and utility. Table 3.1 includes guiding questions that can be used to assess the presence of these traits in definitions of giftedness and suggestions for addressing needed improvements.

EXAMPLE IN NEED OF REVISION

Imagine a school district in a state that defines giftedness as having outstanding intellectual ability, the development of which requires that students

Table 3.1   Traits of High Quality in Conceptual Definitions of Giftedness

Traits	Guiding Questions	Strategies for Improvement
Legality	To what extent does the definition reflect current legal definitions of giftedness?	Review the legal definitions that apply to your district to ensure the definition reflects current existing legal definitions and the needs of your students.
Soundness	To what extent is the definition aligned with the research and/or theory?	Review current theories of giftedness and reports on gifted education, and select one or more that is consistent with your district's values and context to serve as a theoretical framework for your definition.
Cultural Relevance	To what extent does the definition reflect the cultural values of the community?	Ask a variety of stakeholders to share their impressions of what is valued most by the community.
Feasibility	What features of the definition are particularly appropriate for our students and our particular educational context (e.g., age of students, grade levels served)?	Review the definition in light of available resources and, if necessary, clarify language and/or priorities so that operationalizing the definition is more manageable and affordable.
Equity	To what extent is the definition free of cultural, ethnic, and gender bias?	Eliminate any biased language and include a specific statement indicating that your program will serve students from all cultural and economic groups.
Clarity	To what extent will the definition be clear and understandable to all constituents?	Ask a variety of stakeholders to read the draft and provide suggestions for improvement. Tell them you want to know if there are parts that are hard to understand. Revise and repeat based on their feedback.
Utility	To what extent does the definition provide guidance for the development of gifted education services?	Ask a sample of school leaders (e.g., principals, superintendents, school board members) if they think the definition will provide guidance for the development of gifted programming and future decisions.

participate in specially designed programs or services. The state also requires students to score 130 or better on an individualized intelligence test to be classified as a gifted student. The district defines giftedness as follows: Giftedness is exceptional ability to learn.

MAKEOVER EXAMPLE

At first glance this might seem like a fine way to characterize giftedness in general, yet the feasibility, clarity, and utility of this definition for the purpose of guiding identification and programming is questionable. Elaboration of what it means to have exceptional ability to learn is needed, as well as more information about the local context within which this definition will be used.

Scenario 1: Urban Setting

Malcolmville School District is a large, urban school district serving a diverse student population. Two members of Malcolmville's broad-based planning committee recently completed online coursework with a leading university in gifted education. Consequently, they realized that their current state and local definitions of giftedness were limited in scope and not serving their population well. They shared their concerns with their fellow committee members and provided literature to support their arguments. As a result, the Malcolmville planning committee recommended that the board of education consider broadening the local definition of giftedness to serve more students. The Malcolmville Board of Education agreed that intellectually gifted students are an important population to serve, but noted that the district served many students talented within particular domains. The board members also acknowledged that over the past 15 years a thriving arts scene had emerged within their city. The board of education agreed that the school district should broaden its definition so that intellectually, academically, creatively, and artistically gifted students could be identified and served with specialized programming. Therefore, the board members approved the recommendation of the planning committee to create a new, composite definition, which they adapted from the *National Excellence* Report as follows:

> Children and youth with outstanding talent perform or show the potential for performing at remarkably high levels of accomplishment when compared with others of their age, experience, or environment. These children and youth exhibit high performance capability in intellectual, creative, and/or artistic areas, or within specific academic fields. These outstanding talents are present in children and youth from all cultural groups across all economic strata. They require services or activities not ordinarily provided within the standard curriculum by the schools. (U.S. Department of Education, 1993, p. 26)

The Malcolmville Board of Education's members stated that they believed this broadened definition was consistent with their state definition in that it still encompassed students with an IQ of 130 or greater, but was more appropriate for their urban, multicultural context within an artistic, creative community. This conceptual definition of giftedness was adopted, and the planning committee began working on developing operational definitions for giftedness in the areas of intellectual ability, creativity, the arts, and specific academic fields.

Scenario 2: Rural Setting

Blooming Valley School District is a rural district with one elementary school and one junior and senior high school. It is among the smallest school districts in the state, with approximately 50 students in each grade level. It is primarily a working-class community with the majority of jobs concentrated around three companies located within an hour's drive: a tile factory, a natural gas company, and a regional hospital located 40 miles away. A new superintendent of schools moved into town, and she became puzzled when she realized that the school district was serving only six gifted students across all grade levels. She realized that the state's use of a psychometric definition of giftedness requiring an IQ score of at least 130 was preventing many of her district's top students from qualifying for gifted services, and she felt strongly that advanced learning opportunities should be available to the top students in each grade level, whether or not their IQ met the threshold of 130. She decided to hire a consultant with expertise in gifted education who could work with her gifted advisory committee to address this issue. They learned about the concept of using local norms to create a talent pool of the top students in each class according to aptitude and achievement, an idea that stemmed from the work of Renzulli and Reis (2014). Students in the talent pool, including, but not limited to, those with high IQs, would have access to a menu of advanced learning opportunities that could be personalized according to the strengths and interests of the individual students. The advisory committee prepared a proposal for the school board that included a short summary of background information, key points from theory and research, links to related information on NAGC's website, and a draft of a new definition of giftedness—an adaption of NAGC's (2010) definition of giftedness—as follows:

> Gifted and talented students are those who demonstrate outstanding levels of aptitude (defined as an exceptional ability to reason and learn when compared with age-mates) or competence in one or more domains (as documented by performance or achievement in the top 10% or rarer). It can be evident as exceptional performance on tests and/or other measures of ability or achievement compared to other students of the same age or in actual achievement in a domain. Students who demonstrate these characteristics require advanced learning opportunities not ordinarily provided within the general school curriculum.

Members of the Blooming Valley Board of Education reviewed the background materials provided by the gifted advisory committee and prepared questions to ask of the advisory committee and consultant at the board meeting. The consultant presented the characteristics of high-quality definitions, as described in this chapter, and provided a short narrative related to each of the guiding questions listed in Table 3.1. The school board members ultimately agreed that a talent pool approach would be suitable for the school district and that the conceptual definition of giftedness proposed by the advisory committee was a high-quality definition. They charged the advisory committee with preparing an operational definition to guide identification of students for the talent pool and a proposal for expanding the scope of services currently provided to gifted students identified through state criteria.

ADVICE FOR GETTING STARTED

Whether you are updating an existing definition, or starting from scratch, consider the following action steps:

1. Select a writing team (preferably the same group that will be working on a mission statement).

2. Read and discuss current theories of giftedness and summarize each briefly.

3. Read and discuss statewide legislation and/or local policy on giftedness.

4. Review existing data and discuss the needs, values, and culture of the local school district community.

5. Reach consensus on a sound, feasible, conceptual definition.

6. Examine the definition using the information in Table 3.1 and revise as needed.

7. Circulate the draft for feedback from key stakeholders.

8. Revise the definition based on feedback.

9. Test the definition by translating it into one or two sample operational definitions (identification procedures) for projected program components at different developmental levels; revise again, as needed.

10. Seek adoption of the definition through all appropriate channels (e.g., administrators, central office staff, board of education).

11. Incorporate the definition into your mission statement and other program documents.

ADVICE FOR THE SOLE PRACTITIONER

The most important thing for sole practitioners to do in developing a definition of giftedness is to develop their own knowledge about both definitions of giftedness and the contexts in which they are working. This knowledge will help the sole practitioner to promote and adopt a definition that is consistent with current research on giftedness, existing laws or policies that govern the district, the student population of the district, and the values of the community. The second most important thing for the sole practitioner to do is to make sure that he or she seeks broad input into the definition adoption process to build support for and understanding of the definition that is promoted. A good way to do this is to chair a task force, committee, or planning group charged by the superintendent or board of education to work on the task of adopting a definition that is consistent with current research and effective in the local context. (See Appendix A, page 256, for procedures to establish an advisory committee.)

SUGGESTED RESOURCES

Dai, D. Y., & Chen, F. (2013). Three paradigms of gifted education: In search of conceptual clarity in research and practice. *Gifted Child Quarterly, 57,* 151–168.

This journal article describes three ways of thinking about gifted education: the gifted child paradigm, the talent development paradigm, and the differentiation paradigm. Considering these three paradigms may help individuals develop a definition of giftedness that bridges theory and practice to reflect local culture and values.

Moon, S. M., & Rosselli, H. (2000). Developing gifted programs. In K. A. Heller, F. J. Mönks, R. J. Sternberg, & R. F. Subotnik (Eds.), *International handbook of giftedness and talent* (pp. 499–522). Amsterdam, The Netherlands: Elsevier.

This chapter provides an overview of contextual issues that affect definitions of giftedness from an international perspective.

Sternberg, R. J., & Davis, J. E. (Eds.). (2005). *Conceptions of giftedness* (2nd ed.). New York, NY: Cambridge University Press.

This edited volume contains a collection of theoretical definitions of giftedness from leaders in the field. Each chapter describes implications for schools.

U.S. Department of Education. (1993). *National excellence: A case for developing America's talent.* Washington, DC: Author.

Although it is somewhat dated at the time of printing, this foundational document remains the best current national policy document on gifted education.

REFERENCES

Benbow, C. P., & Stanley, J. C. (Eds.). (1983). *Academic precocity: Aspects of its development.* Baltimore, MD: Johns Hopkins University Press.

Feldhusen, J. F. (1995). *TIDE: Talent identification and development in education.* Sarasota, FL: Center for Creative Learning.

Gagné, F. (1985). Giftedness and talent: Reexamining a reexamination of the definitions. *Gifted Child Quarterly, 29,* 103–119.

Gagné, F. (1998). A proposal for subcategories within gifted or talented populations. *Gifted Child Quarterly, 42,* 87–95.

Gagné, F. (1999). My convictions about the nature of abilities, gifts, and talents. *Journal for the Education of the Gifted, 22,* 109–136.

Gagné, F. (2000). Understanding the complex choreography of talent development. In K. A. Heller, F. J. Mönks, R. J. Sternberg, & R. F. Subotnik (Eds.), *International handbook of giftedness and talent* (pp. 67–79). Amsterdam, The Netherlands: Elsevier.

Gagné, F. (2004). Transforming gifts into talents: The DMGT as a developmental theory. *High Ability Studies, 15,* 119–147.

Gagné, F. (2009). Building gifts into talents: Detailed overview of the DMGT 2.0. In B. MacFarlane & T. Stambaugh (Eds.), *Leading change in gifted education: The festschrift of Dr. Joyce VanTassel-Baska* (pp. 61–80). Waco, TX: Prufrock Press.

Gardner, H. (1983). *Frames of mind: The theory of multiple intelligences.* New York, NY: Basic Books.

Gardner, H. (1999). *Intelligence reframed: Multiple intelligences for the 21st century.* New York, NY: Basic Books.

Gardner, H. (2011). *Frames of mind: The theory of multiple intelligences* (3rd ed.). New York, NY: Basic Books.

Hollingworth, L. S. (1926). *Gifted children.* New York, NY: World Press.

Hollingworth, L. S. (1942). *Children above 180 IQ.* New York, NY: World Book.

Marland, S. P., Jr. (1972). *Education of the gifted and talented: Report to the Congress of the United States by the U.S. Commissioner of Education.* Washington, DC: U.S. Government Printing Office.

McClain, M.-C., & Pfeiffer, S. (2012). Identification of gifted students in the United States today: A look at state definitions, policies, and practices. *Journal of Applied School Psychology, 28,* 59–88.

Moon, S. M., & Rosselli, H. C. (2000). Developing gifted programs. In K. A. Heller, F. J. Mönks, R. J. Sternberg, & R. F. Subotnik (Eds.), *International handbook of research and development of giftedness and talent* (2nd ed., pp. 499–521). Amsterdam, The Netherlands: Elsevier.

National Association for Gifted Children. (2010). *Redefining giftedness for a new century: Shifting the paradigm* (Position statement). Retrieved from http://www.nagc.org/sites/default/files/Position%20Statement/Redefining%20Giftedness%20for%20a%20New%20Century.pdf

Peters, S. J., Matthews, M. S., McBee, M. T., & McCoach, D. B. (2014). *Beyond gifted education: Designing and implementing advanced academic programs.* Waco, TX: Prufrock Press.

Renzulli, J. S. (1978). What makes giftedness? Re-examining a definition. *Phi Delta Kappan, 60,* 180–184, 261.

Renzulli, J. S. (1986). The three-ring conception of giftedness: A developmental model for creative productivity. In R. J. Sternberg & J. E. Davidson (Eds.), *Conceptions of giftedness* (pp. 53–92). Cambridge, England: Cambridge University Press.

Renzulli, J. S. (2012). Reexamining the role of gifted education and talent development for the 21st century: A four-part theoretical approach. *Gifted Child Quarterly, 56,* 150–159. Retrieved from http://doi.org/10.1177/0016986212444901

Renzulli, J. S., & Reis, S. M. (2014). *The Schoolwide Enrichment Model: A how-to guide for talent development* (3rd ed.). Waco, TX: Prufrock Press.

Stanley, J. C. (1996). In the beginning: The study of mathematically precocious youth. In C. P. Benbow & D. Lubinski (Eds.), *Intellectual talent: Psychometric and social issues* (pp. 225–235). Baltimore, MD: Johns Hopkins University Press.

Sternberg, R. J. (1985). *Beyond IQ: A triarchic theory of human intelligence*. Cambridge, England: Cambridge University Press.

Sternberg, R. J. (2000). Giftedness as developing expertise. In K. A. Heller, F. J. Mönks, R. J. Sternberg, & R. F. Subotnik (Eds.), *International handbook of giftedness and talent* (pp. 55–66). Amsterdam, The Netherlands: Elsevier.

Sternberg, R. J. (2003). WICS as a model of giftedness. *High Ability Studies, 14*, 109–137.

Sternberg, R. (2007). Cultural concepts of giftedness. *Roeper Review, 29*, 160–165.

Sternberg, R. J. (2012). Intelligence. *Wiley Interdisciplinary Reviews: Cognitive Science, 3*, 501–511.

Sternberg, R. J., & Clinkenbeard, P. R. (1995). The Triarchic Model applied to identifying, teaching, and assessing gifted children. *Roeper Review, 17*, 255–260.

Tannenbaum, A. J. (1986). Giftedness: A psychosocial approach. In R. J. Sternberg & J. E. Davidson (Eds.), *Conceptions of giftedness* (pp. 21–52). Cambridge, England: Cambridge University Press.

Tannenbaum, A. J. (2000). A history of giftedness in school and society. In K. A. Heller, F. J. Mönks, R. J. Sternberg, & R. F. Subotnik (Eds.), *International handbook of giftedness and talent* (2nd ed., pp. 23–53). Amsterdam, The Netherlands: Elsevier.

Terman, L. M. (1925). *Genetic studies of genius: Vol. 1. Mental and physical traits of a thousand gifted children*. Stanford, CA: Stanford University Press.

U.S. Department of Education. (1993). *National excellence: A case for developing America's talent*. Washington, DC: Author.

VanTassel-Baska, J. (2006). State policies in gifted education. In J. H. Purcell & R. D. Eckert (Eds.), *Designing services and programs for high-ability learners: A guidebook for gifted education* (pp. 249–261). Thousand Oaks, CA: Corwin.

Chapter 4

Constructing Identification Procedures

Susan K. Johnsen, PhD

B eginning with the development of Binet's (1905) Individual Test of Intelligence and Terman and Oden's (1959) subsequent work related to gifted individuals, educators have been interested in identifying gifted students. Through the first half of the 20th century, a unitary conception of intelligence guided the identification process. Beginning with Guilford's (1950) address at the American Psychological Association, however, the conception of giftedness changed to include creativity. This expansion of the definition influenced subsequent federal definitions that initially incorporated creativity (U.S. Congress, 1970) and later other areas of giftedness such as academic, leadership, and artistic areas (Marland, 1972; No Child Left Behind Act, 2002; U.S. Congress, 1988; U.S. Department of Education, 1994). These more inclusive definitions, in turn, influenced theories of intelligence (Gagné, 1985; Gardner, 1993; National Association for Gifted Children [NAGC], 2010a; Renzulli, 1978; Sternberg, 1988; Tannenbaum, 1983) and educators' views of how to identify a more diverse population of gifted students.

Although most educators would agree today that there are similarities and differences between and within the gifted population as compared to the general population, identification procedures are quite varied, with some embracing more inclusive practices and others not. These differences result from the lack of a clear federal mandate in gifted education, which give states freedom to develop their own policies, rules, and regulations resulting in variations from state to state, from school district to school district, and even between schools within the same district. This chapter describes the key components of an effective identification process, which are built on current standards in the field of gifted education, and provide examples of best practices.

DEFINITION

In this chapter, identification is defined as a formalized process for recognizing students who might benefit from specialized services in gifted education. This definition is aligned to state requirements and the current federal definition of giftedness. The No Child Left Behind Act (2002) emphasized the importance of finding students who need services or activities not ordinarily provided by the school to develop their capabilities. In addition, the majority of states require schools to develop specific criteria or methods to be used in the identification process (Council of State Directors of Programs for the Gifted [CSDPG] & NAGC, 2013). Indeed, without a formal process, many students with gifts and talents might go unrecognized and underserved in general education settings.

RATIONALE

Why identify gifted and talented students? The major reason for identification is to find students who might benefit from specialized services they wouldn't normally receive in a general education classroom. For the most part, teachers do not have the training to meet the needs of gifted students in the general education classroom and focus more on struggling learners (Moon, Tomlinson, & Callahan, 1995; Reis et al., 2004). Without identification, gifted and talented students would not have access to opportunities for an outstanding education aligned to their talents and interests and would therefore not perform at a level commensurate with their abilities, which might result in domain-specific deficits that are not easily overcome (Subotnik, Olszewski-Kubilius, & Worrell, 2011; Worrell, 2010; Zuckerman, 1977).

Recognition is particularly important for fields where talents emerge and need to be developed beginning in preschool or the primary years (e.g., mathematics, music, gymnastics) and for students who have limited opportunities such as those from low-income backgrounds or minority students (Subotnik et al., 2011). The underrepresentation of students from poverty and minority students in gifted education has been well documented (Daniels, 1998; Ford & Harris, 1999; Morris, 2002) and may result from low teacher expectations and attitudes (Harris, Plucker, Rapp, & Martinez, 2009; Soto, 1997), selective referrals (Frasier, Garcia, & Passow, 1995; Peterson & Margolin, 1997), exclusive definitions (Ryser, 2011a), and unfair tests (Ford & Harmon, 2001).

For these reasons, educators need to formalize the identification process to ensure that it is not biased toward any particular group and finds all of the students who would benefit from specialized services. In this way, school districts can identify the types of resources needed to serve each gifted and talented student's strengths and needs. A common program is not sufficient when providing services to such a diverse population. A formalized identification procedure is therefore necessary to find students early, create a fair process, and tailor services to each gifted and talented student.

GUIDING PRINCIPLES: IDENTIFICATION STANDARDS IN GIFTED EDUCATION

In the NAGC Pre-K–Grade 12 Gifted Programming Standards, three student outcomes within the assessment strand address specifically the identification of gifted students. They focus on equal access, variation and interpretation of assessments, and representation of diversity in the gifted education program.

Equal Access

The first student outcome (Student Outcome 2.1, NAGC, 2010a) targets each student's ability to access a comprehensive assessment system. To address this outcome, evidence-based practices make these recommendations:

- **Differentiated classroom.** Create a classroom environment that allows all students opportunities to demonstrate diverse talents and gifts. Teachers in a differentiated environment allow students to pursue their own interests, provide more challenging content, use assessments so that students learn new information, provide options for learning activities, and enhance student interactions and independent learning. The placement of students in classrooms where teachers do not believe in gifted education or in special education resource programs should not preclude the student's nomination or need for special programming in gifted education (Johnsen, 2012b).
- **Professional development in differentiation.** Schools need to ensure that professional development in gifted education is provided to teachers, parents/guardians, and other educators who are involved with students (e.g., counselors, psychologists, administrators, content specialists) so that they learn how to support differentiation in the classroom setting and understand individual differences.
- **Individualized for roles.** Professional development needs to be individualized for each group and based on their role in the identification process. Teachers, for example, may not know how to differentiate and may nominate only those children who reflect their conceptions of giftedness—academically able, well mannered, and/or verbal (Plata & Masten, 1998; Speirs Neumeister, Adams, Pierce, Cassady, & Dixon, 2007). Parents, particularly those from minority or lower-income

backgrounds, may not understand that giftedness needs to be developed and may be reticent to nominate their children for gifted education programming (Scott, Perou, Urbano, Hogan, & Gold, 1992). Moreover, other educators in the school may not believe in gifted education because of some of the pervasive myths (e.g., gifted students will make it on their own, gifted programs are elitist). For these reasons, providing professional development that affords equal access is critical to meeting the other standards.

Variation and Interpretation of Instruments

The second student outcome stresses the importance of each student's being able to reveal his or her potential (Student Outcome 2.2, NAGC, 2010a). To address this standard, professionals in gifted education need to establish comprehensive, cohesive, and ongoing procedures; use multiple assessments (e.g., qualitative and quantitative, dynamic); interpret results; and involve parents/guardians throughout the process (see NAGC, 2010a, Evidence-Based Practices 2.2.1–2.2.6).

- **Procedures.** To be comprehensive and cohesive, identification procedures need to be aligned across grade levels (Pre-K–12) and address all areas of giftedness (e.g., academic areas, creativity, the arts, leadership). For example, if a child is recognized for her gifts in mathematics in kindergarten, then she should be able to advance according to her rate of learning across grade levels and into college-level courses when she's ready. Identification should also be available to students as the need for specialized services becomes evident to the teacher. Some students may need more time and more access to challenging activities in their areas of talent before they are able to show their potential, particularly those who may not have had early opportunities for enrichment or been taught by a special teacher who has preparation in gifted education.
- **Multiple assessments.** Multiple assessments are used because of the diversity of the population and the variation in student performance within and across assessments and environments. No one source of information can provide a comprehensive view of a student's behaviors across settings. For this reason, assessments need to be used that provide information from a variety of sources (e.g., teachers, parents/guardians, counselors, psychologists, administrators). These assessments should provide both quantitative information (How do test scores compare to others of the same age, experience, and background?) and qualitative information (What specific characteristics are present that might identify this particular student as needing services that are different from the general education setting?). Observing how students interact with tasks before and during instruction (i.e., dynamic assessment) is helpful in assessing their strengths and needs, particularly with

students who may not have been exposed to a challenging academic program. To examine abilities and discover potential, these tasks need to be novel, be problem-based, require complex strategies, and be off level so that advanced students can show their knowledge and skills (Geary & Brown, 1991; Kurtz & Weinert, 1989; NAGC, 2010a; Scruggs & Mastropieri, 1985).

In addition, assessments need to be aligned to the type of services provided and to the characteristics of the student. For example, assessments to identify students with talents in the visual arts would be different from assessments that might be used to identify students with talents in language arts. Moreover, if the student were an English language learner, then different types of assessments would need to be considered such as those that are nonverbal or linguistically reduced. Tests or assessment procedures are biased if they differentiate between members of various groups on some characteristic other than the one being measured (e.g., reading is assessed on a math test instead of mathematical problem solving; Johnsen, 2012a). To minimize bias, the assessment may include performance-based items, pantomimed instruction, practice items, untimed responses, abstract reasoning and problem solving, and nonverbal items (Jensen, 1980; Joseph & Ford, 2006; VanTassel-Baska, Feng, & Evans, 2007).

All the assessments should be technically adequate. Professional organizations have established standards to ensure that tests are reliable (i.e., consistent) and valid for their intended purposes (see American Educational Research Association, American Psychological Association, & National Council on Measurement in Education, 2014). Resources are also available to assist educators in examining the technical qualities of assessments so that they might make informed decisions (see Robins & Jolly, 2011, and Buros Institute of Mental Measurements [http://www.unl.edu/buros] for test reviews).

- **Interpretation of results.** Results from assessments need to be interpreted by a committee of professionals who are familiar with the characteristics of gifted and talented students, particularly those from special populations, and with possible options for specialized services. To interpret assessment results, the committee needs to understand basic psychometrics (e.g., reliability, validity, norming); the meaning of different types of scores (e.g., raw scores, standard scores, index scores, percentile ranks); the standard error of measurement; and the limitations of assessments (Johnsen, 2011a; NAGC, 2010a). The committee needs to determine if the assessment's stated purpose is for identifying gifted students. For example, state tests may be useful for determining if students have acquired the knowledge and skills at a particular grade level but do not have enough items at the upper end (i.e., have a ceiling) to show what gifted students might know and be able to do. Even if a test has a sufficient ceiling, extremely high cut-off scores on individual assessments should not be used because they do not consider the error in assessments. (For a more complete discussion of scores and error in assessments, see Johnsen, 2011a.) If data from assessments are presented in a format where the committee can examine students' strengths and needs, the committee has a better opportunity to identify each student's best performance and align specialized services to develop individual gifts and talents.

- **Involvement of parents/guardians.** Different sources of information such as parents or guardians may provide different perspectives of the same student because gifted students may show more of their abilities at home, with friends, or in other settings than at school. Variations in performance may also result from gifted students not having an opportunity to explore their interests in a particular setting or not wanting to exhibit behaviors associated with giftedness that others, such as friends or teachers, might not understand or approve (Coleman & Cross, 2005). For these reasons, parents/guardians need to be involved throughout the process, nominating their child for specialized services, providing information about their interests and passions, and collaborating with the school in providing appropriate services.

Representation of Diversity

The focus of the third student outcome in the assessment standard is to enhance representation from all populations in the school district (Student Outcome 2.3, NAGC, 2010a). Researchers have suggested these approaches to increase diversity in gifted education programs:

- **Inclusive definitions.** Use more inclusive definitions that include all the ways that gifts and talents might be manifested such as specific academic areas, creativity, the arts, and leadership (Passow & Frasier, 1996).
- **Nontraditional tests.** Use nonverbal, problem-solving, and performance-based types of assessments (Pierce et al., 2007; VanTassel-Baska et al., 2007; VanTassel-Baska, Johnson, & Avery, 2002).
- **Multiple sources.** Include multiple sources of information in the referral process because of educators' misconceptions about children who have disabilities, who are economically disadvantaged, or who are English learners (Johnsen & Ryser, 1994; McCoach, Kehle, Bray, & Siegle, 2001; Plata & Masten, 1998).
- **Changing attitudes.** Provide professional development to all educators who are involved in the referral process since attitudes may influence notions about who should be served in gifted programs (Johnsen & Ryser, 1994). Extensive training needs to occur to help teachers overcome negative attitudes toward special populations of gifted students and value multicultural perspectives (Kitano & Pedersen, 2002).

ASSUMPTIONS

Underlying the NAGC Pre-K–Grade 12 Gifted Programming Standards and the principles guiding the construction of identification procedures are these assumptions (Johnsen, 2008; NAGC, 2010a):

- **Gifts and talents are dynamic and constantly developing.** The development of gifts and talents is now viewed as a lifelong process (NAGC, 2010b). Theorists suggest a variety of factors that interact with one another in the developmental process (Gagné, 1985; Renzulli, 1978; Tannenbaum, 2003). A more developmental view of giftedness requires educators not only to collect information from traditional tests but also to collect information over time or in interactive learning situations to learn about students' abilities and their developmental trajectories (Lidz, 1991; McCoach et al., 2001).
- **Gifts are developed not only within a domain but also within an interest area.** For example, a student with a talent in the scientific domain may have a particular interest in astronomy, specifically black holes. He may not show his knowledge and skills on a traditional, grade-level achievement test, but might show his interest through teacher or parent/guardian observations or in products from independent research opportunities.
- **Giftedness is exhibited across all racial, ethnic, income-level, and exceptionality groups.** Because diverse groups of gifted students are underrepresented in gifted education programs (Daniels, 1998; Ford & Harris, 1999; Morris, 2002), the entire identification process needs be examined to minimize bias and explore ways of increasing diversity.
- **Early identification improves the likelihood that gifts will be developed into talents.** Early recognition is especially critical for students who have limited opportunities such as those from low-income backgrounds or minority students. When minority students are identified early and attend schools and classes for gifted and talented students, they have higher achievement than those who are placed in general education classrooms (Borland, Schnur, & Wright, 2000; Franklin, 2009).

KEY COMPONENTS OF A HIGH-QUALITY IDENTIFICATION PROCEDURE

Based on the standards and the assumptions underlying the standards, school districts should consider the following key components when developing a high-quality identification procedure.

Identification of Student Characteristics

The first key component is for educators to be aware of characteristics of students with gifts and talents in the school district, particularly those who are underrepresented, so that they can identify students needing specialized services. They need to be aware of how other factors such as cultural background, income level of the family, disability, or age might interact with these characteristics and produce different behaviors. For example, a student with a reading disability may demonstrate critical and creative thinking in oral discussions during social studies but read below grade level. Teachers need to create differentiated classroom environments, focus on children's strengths, and notice characteristics that might be indicative of high potential (Johnsen, 2011b).

Identification of Services

Another influence on identification procedures is the services that might be available to the identified students. What areas of giftedness are served? Are they related to traditional academic content areas? Are they student-interest driven? Identification procedures should focus on finding students who will benefit academically and socially from program services. In addition, programs should provide enough flexibility so that students' specific talents might be developed. In all cases, services should be differentiated for the diversity represented within the gifted population.

Identification Process

A three-phase process might be used in identifying gifted students (Johnsen, 2011a, 2014). During the first phase, *nomination or referral*, a pool of all students who exhibit one or many of the characteristics are identified. Multiple sources of information (e.g., teachers, parents/guardians, peers, students) and multiple types of assessments (e.g., checklists, portfolios, performance on problem-solving activities, group intelligence and/or achievement tests) should be used. The referral process may vary with some schools waiting for different individuals to refer a student for additional assessment, while others may incorporate the identification of gifted students within a Response to Intervention (RTI) process (Coleman & Johnsen, 2011). Every effort should be made to ensure consideration of students from special populations (e.g., students with a learning disability, English language learners, minority students). During the next phase, *screening or assessment*, a school committee selects some of the students for further screening, which may include individually administered measures or methods that allow for more clinical observations or the collection of other data needed for decision making. Depending on the state or local education agency's rules, a certain percentage of or all the students might be screened. During the final phase of the identification process, *selection or placement*, the placement committee examines all data collected on each student during the previous two phases. The placement committee then determines which students are selected for gifted services. The committee may design an individual plan for the student that identifies long- and short-term goals, classroom activities, and evaluation. All individuals who are involved in any phase of the identification process need to receive professional development training in the nature and needs of gifted and talented students. According to the NAGC Pre-K–Grade 12 Gifted Programming Standards (2010a) and the assumptions underlying the standards, this process should be comprehensive, cohesive, and ongoing.

Selection of Assessment Instruments for Each Phase in the Process

As mentioned in the programming standards, selected assessments need to provide qualitative and quantitative information from a variety of sources, be aligned to services and the characteristics of the students, and be technically adequate. Along with reliability and validity, technical adequacy includes a standardized approach for gathering information. For example, if teachers are going to be using a checklist to refer students for a specialized program in mathematics, have they received professional development in the characteristics of mathematically advanced students and how to use the checklist (e.g., under what conditions, over what period of time, how to record anecdotal information)? Other areas to consider when selecting instruments are the age of the instrument, norming sample, types of scores, qualifications of the personnel needed to administer the assessments, and practical considerations (e.g., cost, time, required training). All assessments used in the identification process, including qualitative assessments, need to meet technical standards to reduce error and ensure that the assessment is actually serving its purpose (Ryser, 2011b).

Organization of and Interpretation of Assessment Information

During the final phase of the identification process, a committee reviews all of the assessment information from all phases in the identification process to determine the best services for the student. The information may be organized in a case study format, on a profile, or on other forms that provide information regarding the student's specific strengths and needs (see Johnsen, 2011a, for specific forms). When organizing the information, the committee needs to pay special attention to weighting (e.g., placing more emphasis on information from some instruments over others); the types of scores being compared (e.g., standard scores with standard scores; not raw scores to standard scores); the standard error of measurement (e.g., the range of performance based on the consistency of the test); and the student's best performance, which shows potential.

Professional Development

As mentioned previously, all individuals who are involved in the identification process need to receive professional development. Teachers and other educators generally have no previous training in gifted education in their university programs, so they need to understand specific characteristics of gifted students to contribute to the identification process (Johnsen & Ryser, 1994). Parents/guardians also need information regarding diverse characteristics of gifted children, the identification process, and the benefits of participating in the gifted education program.

Board-Approved Policies

A final, but very important, component is to clearly describe the entire identification process for school district educators and stakeholders. The description should include policies and procedures related to the process for identifying and serving gifted and talented students, informed consent, committee review, student retention, student reassessment, student exiting, and appeals procedures for entering and exiting the program (NAGC, 2010a, Evidence-Based Practice 2.2.1). All these procedures should be aligned to the state rules and regulations and followed by everyone involved in the identification process.

EXAMPLES IN NEED OF REVISION

Example 1

The Yellow Mountain School District has an identification process that includes teacher and parent nominations as part of the referral process. Nominated students are then assessed further by the Office of Gifted Education (OGE) using norm-referenced tests. The Director of the OGE has noticed that some schools nominate a much smaller percentage of students at their campus than other schools in the district, particularly those campuses with children from poverty. In speaking with the principals of the schools with a lower number of referrals, the director discovered that the teachers didn't believe there were any gifted and talented students in their classrooms because most of their students were not passing the state assessment of knowledge and skills.

Comments: This first example illustrates the importance of professional development. Teachers and principals may not be aware of the characteristics of gifted students, particularly the ways that gifted students from poverty might manifest these characteristics. Parents also may be reticent to nominate their children for gifted classes, fearing that they may be separated from their peer group. Furthermore, the disparate referral rates between schools might be a civil rights issue and would need to be addressed by the school district (Trice & Shannon, 2002). In the revised example that follows, professional development is included along with talent development services, which will provide access to enrichment opportunities.

Example 2

The Roseview Elementary School offers specialized programming for gifted students in these core academic areas: mathematics, language arts, social studies, and science. During March, the selection committee at the school reviews assessment information collected from the identification process to determine which students need acceleration or enrichment services. Each second-grade student's assessments are organized into a case study format that includes scores and anecdotal information from teacher and parent nominations, a portfolio of work, a nonverbal intelligence test, and an above-level achievement test. During this year's meeting, the committee noted these performances for one seven-year-old boy: 128 (97th percentile) on a nonverbal intelligence test; a 118 (88th percentile) on the reading subtest of the achievement test; a 130 (98th percentile) on the mathematics subtest; and an average score on the student's portfolio. The portfolio included these planned activities: an autobiography, a creative toy created from scrap materials, and an independent research project on a famous person. Although the parent's nomination indicated that the student exhibited many of the characteristics associated with giftedness such as constructing models at home and solving problems, the teacher felt that the student was not engaged during class and wasn't responsible for turning in his homework. Although the committee noticed that this student has potential, they decided to leave him in the general education setting until he matured and became more responsible regarding his work.

Comments: This second example shows how a committee did not review all the information carefully to determine strengths and needs and was swayed by a single source of assessment information: the teacher. In this case, the youngster showed high achievement in mathematics on an above-level test, demonstrated superior performance on an intelligence test, and exhibited many of the characteristics of gifted students at home. The required products in the portfolio did not include items that related to his interests or showcased his strengths so they were not indicative of potential performance. Moreover, the lower score on the reading subtest might indicate some area of developmental delay, because he is a young second grader, or a disability, which might influence his lack of engagement in class and/or his disorganization regarding homework assignments. In the revised example, an individualized program and professional development for committee members are included.

MAKEOVER EXAMPLES

Example 1

This example showing the inconsistency in the application of the referral process across the school district calls for professional development. Professional development needs to include not only the characteristics of gifted students, particularly those from poverty, but also how to differentiate the classroom so that students can show their gifts and talents. This school district offers a wide array of services for gifted students, but the teachers and principals appear to have a limited conception of giftedness— academically able, well mannered, and verbal (Plata & Masten, 1998; Speirs Neumeister et al., 2007). The parents also need to understand the importance of developing their child's gifts and talents so the school district will want to provide ongoing workshops for parents at a convenient time for them.

In responding to the disparate referral rates, the Yellow Mountain School District developed a series of professional development opportunities for administrators and teachers, as well as workshops for parents. They provided resources and materials to teachers to assist them in differentiating the curriculum in their classrooms and providing for student interests—pre-assessments, ideas for independent learning projects, above-level activities, and forms for managing individual differences (e.g., contracts, compactors, tiered assignments). In addition, the district collaborated with a local university and identified graduate students in gifted education who provided talent development activities at the school in the general education classrooms. Talent development activities modeled ways that the teachers might add more depth and complexity to their current curriculum, incorporated independent study in students' areas of interest, and varied the pace of instruction so that students accelerated when they were ready. All these efforts resulted in improvements in referral rates and more students in these schools identified for gifted programming.

Example 2

The committee in the second example placed more emphasis on a single source rather than considering all of the assessment information. They needed to examine the strengths and weaknesses of the student to determine important areas for specialized services. In this child's case, he was young in comparison to other second graders who were mostly eight years old. He had outstanding reasoning ability as demonstrated on the intelligence test; strengths in math, scoring better than 98% of students on an above-level test; and many characteristics of giftedness that he demonstrated at home. His relative weaknesses appeared to be in reading and to manifest themselves primarily in the general education classroom— completing artifacts for the portfolio and assigned work.

After the parents appealed the committee's decision to the Department of Gifted Education (DGE), the District Oversight Council reviewed the case and decided that the student needed additional services. Specialists from the DGE went to the school to plan a program collaborative, which eventually included acceleration to third grade in math only, and differentiated activities within the general education setting, which incorporated more independent projects in his area of interest. His performance in the language arts area was reviewed by the campus RTI team, and it was determined that he needed Tier 2 services to help him with a possible delay in reading and writing. At the next general in-service for all educators in the school district, the DGE provided an overview of characteristics of gifted students who might also have delays or disabilities (e.g., twice-exceptional students) to increase awareness of this underrepresented group. The DGE also provided professional development for all individuals who were serving on selection committees at individual campuses. This professional development consisted of (a) weighting all assessments equally; (b) comparing quantitative and qualitative information; (c) interpreting scores, including the standard error of measurement; and (d) examining the best performance for indicators of potential. In evaluating the success of these professional development activities, the district noticed fewer parent appeals and more students from underrepresented groups receiving gifted education services.

A PLAN FOR CONSTRUCTING EFFECTIVE IDENTIFICATION PROCEDURES

Table 4.1 shows a synthesis of the information in this chapter and should help districts in constructing an effective identification procedure.

Table 4.1 A Framework for Constructing Effective Identification Procedures

Focusing Questions	Characteristics	Our Plan
What are the characteristics of students in our schools? How will we ensure that each group is represented in the identification process?	• Overall school district demographics (ethnicity/race, income level, gender) • Each campus's demographics	
What areas of giftedness are included in the state or local district definition? Which ones will we serve beginning at which grade levels? How will we address individual student interests?	• General intellectual • Academic • Leadership • Artistic • Creative	
What types of services will we provide at each grade level to ensure a comprehensive and cohesive system so that each identified student's talents are developed?	• Cluster groups within general education classroom(s) • Resource/support services • Separate courses/classes • Advanced classes • Magnet schools • Afterschool activities • Mentoring • Competitions	

(Continued)

Table 4.1   (Continued)

Focusing Questions	Characteristics	Our Plan
What phases will be used in the identification process so that all students have equal access?	• Referral/nomination (within RTI?) • Screening/assessment • Selection/placement	
What assessments will be used at each phase in the process so that underrepresented populations are included?	• Aligned to students • Aligned to services • Multiple sources • Qualitative and quantitative • Technically adequate • Minimize bias	
How will data be organized so that each student's strengths and needs are readily identified?	• Case study • Profile • Other format	
Who will be involved in interpreting the data? How will the data be interpreted to minimize bias?	• Equal weighting • Common score comparisons • Standard error of measurement • Best performance • Qualitative information about student	
What professional development will be offered to different groups? What do they need to know and be able to do? When will professional development be offered?	• Administrators • Teachers • Counselors • Psychologists • Parents/guardians	
What will be included in the board-approved policies?	• Identification process • Informed consent • Committee review • Student retention • Student reassessment • Student exiting • Appeals procedures	

ADVICE FOR THE SOLE PRACTITIONER

For those educators who work in small schools or rural districts, you can provide gifted education services to advanced students within your school with or without formal identification by differentiating instructional practices. Creating a classroom environment where students have opportunities to demonstrate their diverse talents and gifts is foundational to any formal identification process. Those students who are informally identified can receive services through acceleration and enrichment.

In implementing a formal identification process, the single practitioner first needs to know the state or district rules and regulations regarding identification practices. Next, information would need to be gathered regarding what the school or district is currently doing to identify gifted and talented students. After this information is gathered, the next step would be to use the plan in this chapter to determine which components are in place and which will need to be added. Using the resources at the end of this chapter and professional organizations such as the National Association for Gifted Children (www.nagc.org) and The Association for the Gifted (www.cectag.com), the sole practitioner will want to identify individuals who might help in reviewing and revising the preliminary plan. These individuals might be from nearby schools, local universities, or regional service centers. Armed with this information and support, the practitioner would develop a final draft of the plan and share it with those who might be interested. Once local educators and/or community members are ready to provide support, then this group would be ready to present the plan to the Board of Trustees for their review. Hopefully, with the support of local educators and the community, the board might be willing to implement all or some of the components of the new identification plan.

SUGGESTED RESOURCES

American Educational Research Association, American Psychological Association, & National Council on Measurement in Education. (2014). *Standards for educational and psychological testing*. Washington, DC: AERA Publications. Retrieved from http://www.apa.org/science/programs/testing/standards.aspx

These standards represent the work of three organizations (i.e., AERA, APA, and NCME) and provide guidance about testing. The standards address validity, reliability, fairness in testing, operations, and testing applications.

Johnsen, S. K. (Ed.). (2011). *Identifying gifted students: A practical guide* (2nd ed.). Waco, TX: Prufrock Press.

This book is written for practitioners who are interested in identifying gifted students and it is organized around the sequential set of steps used in the identification process. Technical information is provided for tests frequently used in gifted education.

National Association for Gifted Children. (2010). *NAGC Pre-K–Grade 12 Gifted Programming Standards: A blueprint for quality gifted education programs*. Washington, DC: Author.

These standards provide evidence-based practices and student outcomes used by schools in developing programs and services for gifted and talented students.

Standard 2 specifically addresses assessment and describes how schools might provide equal access, develop a comprehensive and cohesive identification system, and minimize bias in the identification process.

Subotnik, R. F., Olszewski-Kubilius, P., & Worrell, F. C. (2011). Rethinking giftedness and gifted education: A proposed direction forward based on psychological science. *Psychological Science in the Public Interest, 12*, 3–54.

This monograph reviews and summarizes research related to giftedness and provides directions for the field of gifted education. The authors emphasize how potential needs to be recognized early and how psychosocial variables play an essential role in its manifestation.

REFERENCES

American Educational Research Association, American Psychological Association, & National Council on Measurement in Education. (2014). *Standards for educational and psychological testing.* Washington, DC: AERA Publications. Retrieved from http://www.apa.org/science/programs/testing/standards.aspx

Binet, A. (1905). New methods for the diagnosis of the intellectual level of subnormals. *L'Année Psychologique, 12*, 191–244.

Borland, J. H., Schnur, R., & Wright, L. (2000). Economically disadvantaged students in a school for the academically gifted: A postpositivist inquiry into individual and family adjustment. *Gifted Child Quarterly, 44*, 13–32.

Coleman, L. J., & Cross, T. L. (2005). *Being gifted in school: An introduction to development, guidance, and teaching.* Waco, TX: Prufrock Press.

Coleman, M. R., & Johnsen, S. K. (Eds.). (2011). *RtI for gifted students.* Waco, TX: Prufrock Press.

Council of State Directors of Programs for the Gifted, & National Association for Gifted Children. (2013). *2012–2013 state of the states in gifted education: National policy and practice data.* Washington, DC: Author.

Daniels, V. I. (1998). Minority students in gifted and special education programs: The case for educational equity. *Journal of Special Education, 32*, 41–44.

Ford, D. Y., & Harmon, D. A. (2001). Equity and excellence: Providing access to gifted education for culturally diverse students. *Journal of Secondary Gifted Education, 12*, 141–148.

Ford, D. Y., & Harris, J. J. (1999). *Multicultural gifted education.* New York, NY: Teachers College Press.

Franklin, R. K. (2009). *A case study of a three-year pilot program on one district's attempt to increase the gifted identification of diverse elementary school students by having a talent development program* (Unpublished doctoral dissertation). Virginia Commonwealth University, Richmond, VA.

Frasier, M. M., Garcia, J. H., & Passow, A. H. (1995). *A review of assessment issues in gifted education and their implications for identifying gifted minority students.* Storrs: University of Connecticut, The National Research Center on the Gifted and Talented.

Gagné, F. (1985). Giftedness and talent: Reexamining a reexamination of the definitions. *Gifted Child Quarterly, 29*, 103–112.

Gardner, H. (1993). *Creating minds.* New York, NY: Basic Books.

Geary, D. C., & Brown, S. C. (1991). Cognitive addition: Strategy choice and speed-of-processing difference in gifted, normal, and mathematically disabled children. *Developmental Psychology, 27*, 398–406.

Guilford, J. P. (1950). Creativity. *American Psychologist, 5*, 444–454.

Harris, B., Plucker, J. A., Rapp, K. E., & Martinez, R. S. (2009). Identifying gifted and talented English language learners: A case study. *Journal for the Education of the Gifted, 32,* 368–393.

Jensen, A. R. (1980). *Bias in mental testing.* New York, NY: Free Press.

Johnsen, S. K. (2008). Identifying gifted and talented learners. In F. A. Karnes & K. R. Stephens (Eds.), *Achieving excellence: Educating the gifted and talented* (pp. 135–153). New York, NY: Merrill Education/Prentice Hall.

Johnsen, S. K. (2011a). (Ed.). *Identifying gifted students: A practical guide* (2nd ed.). Waco, TX: Prufrock Press.

Johnsen, S. K. (2011b). What do educators need to know about identifying gifted and talented students? In J. Roberts (Ed.), *The teacher's survival guide: Gifted classrooms* (pp. 38–40). Waco, TX: Prufrock Press.

Johnsen, S. K. (2012a). Best practices in the identification of gifted and talented students. *Gifted Education Communicator, 43*(2), 9–12, 42.

Johnsen, S. K. (2012b). The assessment standard in gifted education: Identifying gifted students. In S. K. Johnsen (Ed.), *NAGC Pre-K–Grade 12 Gifted Education Programming Standards: A guide to planning and implementing high-quality services* (pp. 71–96). Waco, TX: Prufrock Press.

Johnsen, S. K. (2014). Gifted programming standards. In C. M. Callahan & J. A. Plucker (Eds.), *Critical issues and practices in gifted education: What the research says* (2nd ed., pp. 281–295). Waco, TX: Prufrock Press.

Johnsen, S. K., & Ryser, G. (1994). Identification of young gifted children from lower income families. *Gifted and Talented International, 9*(2), 62–68.

Joseph, L., & Ford, D. Y. (2006). Nondiscriminatory assessment: Considerations for gifted education. *Gifted Child Quarterly, 50,* 42–51.

Kitano, M. K., & Pedersen, K. S. (2002). Action research and practical inquiry: Multicultural-content integration in gifted education: Lessons from the field. *Journal for the Education of the Gifted, 26,* 269–289.

Kurtz, B. E., & Weinert, F. E. (1989). Metacognition, memory performance, and causal attributions in gifted and average children. *Journal of Experimental Child Psychology, 48,* 45–61.

Lidz, C. S. (1991). *Practitioner's guide to dynamic assessment.* New York, NY: Guilford.

Marland, S. P., Jr. (1972). *Education of the gifted and talented: Report to the Congress of the United States by the U.S. Commissioner of Education.* Washington, DC: U.S. Government Printing Office.

McCoach, D. B., Kehle, T. J., Bray, M. A., & Siegle, D. (2001). Best practices in the identification of gifted students with learning disabilities. *Psychology in the Schools, 38,* 403–411.

Moon, T. R., Tomlinson, C. A., & Callahan, C. M. (1995). *Academic diversity in the middle school: Results of a national survey of middle school administrators and teachers* (Research Monograph 95124). Storrs: University of Connecticut, The National Research Center on the Gifted and Talented.

Morris, J. E. (2002). African American students and gifted education. *Roeper Review, 24,* 59–62.

National Association for Gifted Children. (2010a). *NAGC Pre-K–Grade 12 Gifted Programming Standards: A blueprint for quality gifted education programs.* Washington, DC: Author.

National Association for Gifted Children. (2010b). *Redefining giftedness for a new century: Shifting the paradigm* (Position statement). Washington, DC: Author.

No Child Left Behind Act, Pub. L. No. 107-110 (Title IX, Part A, Definition 22) (2002); 20 U.S.C. § 7801 (22) (2004).

Passow, A. H., & Frasier, M. M. (1996). Toward improving identification of talent potential among minority and disadvantaged students. *Roeper Review, 18,* 198–202.

Peterson, J. S., & Margolin, R. (1997). Naming gifted children: An example of unintended "reproduction." *Journal for the Education of the Gifted, 21,* 82–101.

Pierce, R. L., Adams, C. M., Speirs Neumeister, K. L., Cassady, J. C., Dixon, F. A., & Cross, T. L. (2007). Development of an identification procedure for a large urban school corporation: Identifying culturally diverse and academically gifted elementary students. *Roeper Review, 29,* 113–118.

Plata, M., & Masten, W. (1998). Teacher ratings of Hispanic and Anglo students on a behavior rating scale. *Roeper Review, 21,* 139–144.

Reis, S. M., Gubbins, E. J., Briggs, C. Schreiber, F. R., Richards, S., & Jacobs, J. (2004). Reading instruction for talented readers: Case studies documenting few opportunities for continuous progress. *Gifted Child Quarterly, 48,* 309–338.

Renzulli, J. (1978). What makes giftedness? Reexamining a definition. *Phi Delta Kappan, 60,* 80–184, 261.

Robins, J. H., & Jolly, J. L. (2011). Technical information regarding assessment. In S. K. Johnsen (Ed.), *Identifying gifted students: A practical guide* (2nd ed., pp. 75–118). Waco, TX: Prufrock Press.

Ryser, G. R. (2011a). Fairness in testing and nonbiased assessment. In S. K. Johnsen (Ed.), *Identifying gifted students: A practical guide* (2nd ed., pp. 63–74). Waco, TX: Prufrock Press.

Ryser, G. R. (2011b). Qualitative and quantitative approaches to assessment. In S. K. Johnsen (Ed.), *Identifying gifted students: A practical guide* (2nd ed., pp. 37–62). Waco, TX: Prufrock Press.

Scott, M. S., Perou, R., Urbano, R., Hogan, A., & Gold, S. (1992). The identification of giftedness: A comparison of White, Hispanic and Black families. *Gifted Child Quarterly, 36,* 131–139.

Scruggs, T., & Mastropieri, M. (1985). Spontaneous verbal elaborations in gifted and nongifted youths. *Journal for the Education of the Gifted, 9,* 1–10.

Soto, L. D. (1997). *Language, culture, and power: Bilingual families and the struggle for quality education.* Albany: State University of New York Press.

Speirs Neumeister, K. L., Adams, C. M., Pierce, R. L., Cassady, J. C., & Dixon, F. A. (2007). Fourth-grade teachers' perceptions of giftedness: Implications for identifying and serving diverse gifted students. *Journal for the Education of the Gifted, 30,* 479–499.

Sternberg, R. J. (1988). *The triarchic mind: A new theory of human intelligence.* New York, NY: Viking Penguin.

Subotnik, R. F., Olszewski-Kubilius, P., & Worrell, F. C. (2011). Rethinking giftedness and gifted education: A proposed direction forward based on psychological science. *Psychological Science in the Public Interest, 12,* 3–54.

Tannenbaum, A. (1983). *Gifted children: Psychological and educational perspectives.* New York, NY: Macmillan.

Tannenbaum, A. (2003). Nature and nurture of giftedness. In N. Colangelo & G. A. Davis (Eds.), *Handbook of gifted education* (3rd ed., pp. 45–59). Boston, MA: Pearson Education.

Terman, L. M., & Oden, M. H. (1959). *The gifted group at mid-life; Thirty-five years' follow-up of the superior child: Genetic studies of genius* (Vol. 5). Stanford, CA: Stanford University Press.

Trice, B., & Shannon, B. (2002, April). *Office for Civil Rights: Ensuring equal access to gifted education.* Paper presented at the annual meeting of the Council for Exceptional Children, New York.

U.S. Congress, Pub. L. No. 100-297, April, 1988.

U.S. Congress, Pub. L. No. 91-230, April, 1970.

U.S. Department of Education (1994). *National excellence: A case for developing America's youth.* Washington, DC: U.S. Government Printing Office.

VanTassel-Baska, J., Feng, A. X., & Evans, B. L. (2007). Patterns of identification and performance among gifted students identified through performance tasks: A three-year analysis. *Gifted Child Quarterly, 51,* 218–231.

VanTassel-Baska, J., Johnson, D., & Avery, L. D. (2002). Using performance tasks in the identification of economically disadvantaged and minority gifted learners: Findings from Project STAR. *Gifted Child Quarterly, 46*, 110–123.

Worrell, F. C. (2010, August). *Giftedness: Endowment, context, timing, development, or performance? Does it matter?* American Psychological Foundation's Esther Katz Rosen Lecture on Gifted Children and Adolescents presented at the annual convention of the American Psychological Association, San Diego, CA.

Zuckerman, H. (1977). *Scientific elite: Nobel laureates in the United States.* New York, NY: Free Press.

Chapter 5

Comprehensive Program Design

Sally M. Reis, PhD, and E. Jean Gubbins, PhD

DEFINITION

A comprehensive program design (CPD) is a thoughtful, unified service delivery plan that has a singular purpose: to identify the many, varied ways that will be used to meet the needs of high-potential students. This plan is formulated by a variety of stakeholders, including faculty, administrators, and parents. A high-quality program design takes into consideration (a) the unique learning profiles of students identified for gifted education services within a school district, (b) the level of challenge in the regular curriculum for all students, (c) the ways in which high-potential students are already being served within and outside the district, and (d) the areas in which high-potential students are lacking in services (Karnes & Bean, 2015). A thoughtfully organized CPD also provides enrichment and exploratory opportunities for students with high potential who have not yet fully realized their abilities and talents (Plucker, Burroughs, & Song, 2010). One of the most important functions of the CPD is that it incorporates educators' and community members' philosophical and theoretical beliefs as well as practical considerations into a comprehensive plan designed to meet the needs of a specific group of students. In addition, it is critical that educators who develop a CPD consider the importance of a rich and challenging curriculum for all students (Little, 2012). High-quality curriculum and meaningful objectives in the general education setting should always be the foundation for the learning activities provided in an effective gifted and talented program (Davis, Rimm, & Siegle, 2011; Renzulli, 2012; Renzulli, Gubbins, McMillen, Eckert, & Little, 2009; Tomlinson, 2005).

The process of crafting a CPD is one of consensus building and decision making regarding a community's philosophy of giftedness and how best to meet the needs of its high-potential students. A CPD seeks to resolve the following six overarching questions: (1) Who will be served (defining the population)? (2) How will students be identified (developing a defensible identification system)? (3) What program model will be used? (4) What types of learning opportunities will be provided (based on philosophy and need)? and (5) and (6) Where and When will service options (e.g., pull-out, after school, summer services such as a Governor's School) be offered across grades and content levels, both within and outside the district? The answers to these questions depend on a number of factors, including funding, the availability of trained personnel, and the level of challenge and depth of the regular curriculum.

RATIONALE

A cohesive, thoughtful, and comprehensive program design, sometimes called a service delivery model, serves a number of critical functions. First, it communicates to teachers, administrators, and parents which student needs (e.g., academic, artistic, creative, leadership, instructional, affective) will be met. Second, a clear program design provides teachers and administrators with an administrative design or plan for implementing and coordinating all aspects of a gifted program. For example, program goals and objectives are built on the foundation provided by the program design, and then are used in subsequent program evaluations to assess the effectiveness of the program plan to enhance student achievement. Finally, a comprehensive program design provides a rationale for the decision-making process about how to allocate limited program resources and best support student learning. For example, a CPD can describe available acceleration options and the process by which students may be identified for acceleration services at various grade levels.

GUIDING PRINCIPLES AND ATTRIBUTES THAT DEFINE HIGH QUALITY

A high-quality CPD is a foundational, administrative design plan on which program goals and objectives are built. Therefore, it must demonstrate linkages between what is being provided in district and school classrooms with local and state curriculum standards and gifted program guidelines and regulations (Johnsen, 2015; National Association for Gifted Children [NAGC], 2010). Moreover, a CPD must describe current program services as applied to the general education curriculum as well as to the gifted and talented curriculum and must provide opportunities for expansion of current services across all content areas and grade levels.

A CPD should take into account a broad range of talents (e.g., academic, artistic, creative, leadership) and the spectrum of talent development (e.g., latent, emerging, manifest, actualized; Burns et al., 2002). It must also consider affective (e.g., social, emotional) needs. A high-quality CPD should describe curriculum philosophy and address grouping issues (Gentry & Fugate, 2013).

Finally, a CPD must reflect a wide range of broad-based choices that will enable the talents or potential talents of a diverse group of students to be developed. These multifaceted educational opportunities can be provided not only during the school day, but also after school and in the summer, through the active participation of professional faculty and parents (Rogers, 2007; Schroth, 2014).

There are at least seven traits of a high-quality comprehensive program design. Under each of the seven traits, a series of questions is provided to illuminate the varied facets of each trait.

Derivation of the Services

- Was the CPD based on a needs assessment of the services already provided by the district in the general education classroom and gifted program?
- Has the level of existing curriculum and educational opportunities in the district been reviewed and considered?
- What are the beliefs of parents and professionals about the nature of gifts and talents and the types of services already provided in the district?

Comprehensiveness

- Does the CPD broadly define the range of services across grade levels?
- What kind of plan has been developed for how, when, and where services will be offered?
- Are academic and artistic talents and abilities considered in the CPD?
- In what ways have leadership, creativity, and students' social and emotional needs been addressed, either through programming options and a continuum of services or through targeted professional development for key constituents?
- In what ways are plans for expansion and additions to the program outlined?
- Does the CPD include opportunities from within and outside the district to enable the highest levels of talent to be developed (e.g., summer programs, community resources, online opportunities)?

Practicality

- Does the CPD appear to be reasonable, given the resources and strengths of the district?

- Can district administrators and the board of education provide the budget necessary to deliver the services specified in the comprehensive program design?
- Are program services a good fit for current and future district initiatives?

Consistency

- Does the CPD match both the definition of giftedness and the procedures for identification adopted by the district?
- Does the CPD align with the district's philosophy, mission statement, and program goals and objectives?
- Does the definition adhere to state regulations and/or policy?
- Is the CPD linked to students' learning profiles (e.g., interests, academic strengths and weaknesses, cognitive skills' strengths and weaknesses, learning style preferences)?

Clarity

- Have teachers, administrators, and parents who have not participated in the program planning and design committee reviewed the CPD to ensure that is easy to understand?
- If a diagram is used, is the diagram or description self-explanatory?

Availability

- Is the CPD readily available to principals, teachers, and parents?
- Has training been provided to teachers, specialists, and parents about their responsibilities in the process of talent development?

Continuation, Extension, and Evaluation

- Who is in charge of ensuring that the program plan is implemented?
- What policies or practices are needed to ensure the strategic implementation of the CPD?
- What type of annual report or program evaluation will provide feedback on the success of the CPD, and what types of data will be collected and analyzed? Who is responsible?
- Will the CPD be updated and extended as the program is implemented?
- Will additional resources be sought and additional program services provided over time?
- Has an advisory board been formed to monitor the progress of the CPD?
- How will new members from all constituency groups be continuously recruited for the advisory board?

EXAMPLE IN NEED OF REVISION

Plainville School District provides its gifted and talented students with a pull-out program in Grades 4 and 5 in which advanced curriculum units in science and social studies are covered. The program is provided to academically gifted students for 1 hour each week on Wednesday afternoons from 1:00 to 2:00. The top 3% of students qualify for these services based on the results of data collected from a scholastic aptitude measure, scholastic achievement measure, and teacher recommendations. Similar screening, identification, and placement strategies are not in place for middle and high school students. The only option for high-achieving students at the high school level is to enroll in Advanced Placement (AP) courses in English literature and biology.

PROCEDURES FOR IMPROVING AND ENHANCING THE COMPREHENSIVE PROGRAM DESIGN

Two years ago, a group of Plainville faculty and administrators formed a planning committee to create a new strategic plan for the school district. It took a full year for committee members to gather the requisite materials and craft a new, revised strategic plan.

Beth Bergeron, enrichment specialist for Plainville Schools, contacted former members of the Plainville Strategic Planning Committee. She asked them to help review the gifted program design and make recommendations about how to increase its alignment with the district's strategic plan, as well as to students' learning needs. To review systematically all aspects of program design, they used the six questions contained in Table 5.1 to guide their analysis.

The information contained in Table 5.1 provides readers with a guide for assessing the overall quality of any comprehensive program design and making subsequent refinements. On the left-hand side of the table are listed the six overarching questions discussed at the beginning of this chapter. The next column, Existing Practices, provides readers with a place to identify current plans and policies.

For the sake of this example, the Existing Practices column contains a description of the practices used by the Plainville School District. As you read through each question, think through what you would have done had you been Beth Bergeron, enrichment specialist in Plainville Schools. What revisions would you have made to increase the comprehensiveness and alignment between the students' learning needs and the services?

MAKEOVER EXAMPLE

Having gathered all the pertinent information and taken the time to organize and review the data, Beth Bergeron and the other committee members

Table 5.1 Example in Need of Revision

Guiding Question	Existing Practices
Who is served?	**Screening and Identification Plan** • Students scoring in the top 3% on indicators of scholastic aptitude
How are students identified?	**Identification Tools** • Measure of scholastic aptitude administered in Grade 3 • Teacher recommendation
What program model is used?	**Program Model** • No model specified
What types of learning opportunities?	**Enrichment and Differentiation Options** • Field trips • History Day • Science Fair • AP courses: English literature and biology **Acceleration Options** • *None* **Guidance and Counseling Options** • *None*
Where are services provided?	**Service Delivery Options** • Resource room • Regular classroom
When are services provided?	**Service Delivery Options** • During school (Wednesday afternoons)

were ready to begin the decision-making process based on pertinent research (Callahan & Hertberg-Davis, 2013; Plucker & Callahan, 2014) and the NAGC Pre-K–Grade 12 Gifted Programming Standards (NAGC, 2010).

Who?

At their first meeting, the group realized that the demographics of the public school population had changed since the gifted education program was designed 8 years earlier. The district had an increasing number of families from India and Sudan and, most recently, had seen an influx of Asian families who were employed at two, large, well-known resorts located in an adjacent town. The demographics of the students in the gifted program no longer matched the demographics of the town.

To increase the match between the town demographics and the demographics of the program, committee members decided to expand the number of students identified for services. They agreed to identify up to 10% of the student population using local norms.

Committee members also decided to identify academically talented students in Grades K–5 in their first year of the revised program. In the second year, they agreed to expand the identification process to include students in Grades 6–12. They also expressed a desire to identify talented children, Grades K–12, in the third year of the plan.

How?

To ensure more equitable access to the program, committee members agreed to change the procedures used to identify students. Instead of using only two measures—a standardized measure of student aptitude and a teacher recommendation—they decided that they would use a multiple-criteria approach. Equally important, all measures would have an equal weight. No longer would students need to score at least 130 on a measure of scholastic aptitude before other measures would be considered.

Committee members looked carefully at their student population and decided on several important indicators. Most important, they included student work samples and portfolios. These pieces of evidence would surely demonstrate some of the abilities and talents of their underrepresented populations. In addition, they included teacher recommendations and peer nominations. Many of the teachers were struck by how easily students identified the leaders and artists in their midst, and this validated their decision to expand the range of talents in their comprehensive program design.

What Program Model(s)?

Committee members considered several program models (VanTassel-Baska & Brown, 2015) before deciding on a blend of two: the Schoolwide Enrichment Model (SEM; Renzulli & Reis, 2014) and Study of Mathematically Precocious Youth (SMPY; Assouline & Lupkowski-Shoplik, 2012; Benbow, 2012; Kell, Lubinski, & Benbow, 2013; Lubinski, Benbow, & Kell, 2014). They chose the SEM because it included a behavioral definition of giftedness (i.e., above-average ability, task commitment, and creativity) that would provide a more inclusive approach to gifted education services, and it addressed the learning needs of all students—including those with demonstrated and potential gifts and talents—through a continuum of enrichment services (Gubbins, 2014). They also chose the SMPY model because it focused on the unique learning needs of mathematically gifted young people. The emerging learning profile of students in Plainville illuminated a population with very high potential in mathematical reasoning. Both models linked closely with students' learning needs.

What Types of Learning Opportunities?

Beth and her colleagues carefully reviewed the services that were currently offered and made two important observations. First, the number of services—three, to be exact—was very limited. Second, they concluded that current services were not aligned with students' cognitive and affective needs. They agreed to add a variety of services from all three areas: enrichment and differentiation, acceleration, and guidance and counseling. With respect to enrichment and differentiation, they recommended that each teacher be trained in and use pre-assessment in the regular classroom to provide appropriate, ongoing levels of challenge for all students, not only those with unique gifts and talents. In addition, curriculum compacting would help teachers eliminate course material for students who had already mastered large portions of curriculum content. They also decided to expand field trips and competitions so that they spanned the content areas: social studies, science, mathematics, the arts, and language arts. At the same time, they also made a clear recommendation that each field trip and competition be linked closely to and enhance the regular curriculum. Guest speakers from the community were added to the assembly program for all students to encourage and support emerging, young leaders.

Committee members made a commitment to an afterschool program, called Power Hour, one day a week that was open to all students, Grades 1–5. In the first quarter of the year, the focus of the activities was science, and in the second quarter, the focus was history, and so forth through the last quarter so that four content areas were included over the course of the school year. During each Power Hour, three teachers—from regular education classrooms and the gifted program—monitored highly motivating games and activities related to the targeted content area. Often, students were invited to select their activities. At other times, classroom teachers recommended particular activities for small groups of children based on students' interests, learning strengths, or need for review. These enrichment and differentiation activities provided for a much closer link to the academic needs of their changing population of gifted education students. In addition, the activities served as fun and engaging ways for underserved students to demonstrate and refine their not-yet-developed talents and abilities.

Finally, the committee recommended that pull-out services be reconfigured to encourage and address students' desire to complete individual and small-group independent investigations. These direct services to students had proven powerful in the past because they increased student motivation and provided ongoing levels of challenge for interested students.

Beth and her colleagues also recommended adding three acceleration options: early entrance to kindergarten, single-subject acceleration, and pre-AP and AP courses. The addition of early entrance to kindergarten was considered the most effective way to engage very young children with advanced abilities (Assouline, Colangelo, VanTassel-Baska, &

Lupkowski-Shoplik, 2015; Assouline & Lupkowski-Shoplik, 2011; Colangelo, Assouline, & Gross, 2004; Rogers, 2002). By allowing them to advance early in their school career, the committee was convinced they would better meet the cognitive and affective needs of their students and, concurrently, reduce the number of parents who requested grade skipping in subsequent grades. They decided to use the Iowa Acceleration Scale (Assouline, Colangelo, Lupkowski-Shoplik, Lipsomb, & Forstadt, 2009) to help them make important decisions about which students would be good candidates for whole-grade acceleration, K–8. Single-subject acceleration was added to serve the needs of students who demonstrated advanced abilities in one or two content areas.

Furthermore, Beth and her colleagues reviewed the current AP course offerings at the high school. Only two courses were offered. The committee agreed that at least five core AP courses should be offered as soon as possible: English literature, biology, U.S. history, calculus, and statistics. The decision to emphasize mathematics was based on the learning profile of their student population. These additions not only increased advanced-level options at the secondary level, but also had relatively low impact on the school district budget.

In addition, the committee made two other recommendations with respect to the AP program, a cornerstone of the SMPY program model. They asked Beth to explore the pre-AP courses, especially those that could be offered via vertical teaming in mathematics, science, and English; that could be offered in the middle grades; and that might be especially appropriate for students who had potential but who had not yet demonstrated strong abilities. The committee asked Beth to come back with a proposal regarding which pre-AP courses might be especially appropriate for Plainville students. The second request of Beth was to research the providers and fee structures of AP distance learning programs, such as Virtual High Schools (VHS) and Apex Learning. They asked Beth to provide the group with recommendations regarding the feasibility and budget implications for expanding their course offerings through technology.

Finally, Beth and her colleagues added two guidance and counseling services. The first consisted of small-group discussions around students' affective needs (e.g., perfectionism, stress reduction, multipotentiality, gender issues). Beth felt strongly that these discussions should be held in the resource room for cross-grade groups of interested students. The second counseling service was college counseling. These services would be offered in the resource room, begin in middle school, and culminate in a wide array of services in high school.

Where?

Plainville's reconfigured services for high-achieving students were distributed across the regular classroom and the resource room. Beth and her colleagues agreed that small-group and independent investigations, as well as the small-group discussions focused on affective and counseling issues, should be held in the resource room. They also concluded that many of the enrichment and differentiation activities could take place in the regular classroom. This made a great deal of sense to them because many of these activities were good for all children, not just those with potential or manifest abilities.

When?

As much as possible, Beth and her colleagues tried to keep their activities within the school day. This was important for Plainville students whose parents often worked on the weekends. For the Power Hour, which took place after regular school hours, they made sure that they had school buses available to drop students close to their homes.

Table 5.2 summarizes Beth and her colleagues' choices aligned with the NAGC Pre-K–Grade 12 Gifted Programming Standards, reflecting the current school culture and academic aspirations for all students.

Beth and her colleagues reviewed the principles that guided the program design process, which were included earlier in this chapter. After

Table 5.2 NAGC Pre-K–Grade 12 Gifted Programming Standards and Program Design Elements

NAGC Standards and Student Outcomes	Makeover Example: Program Design Elements
Who will be served? **Screening and Identification Plan**	
Standard 2: Assessment 2.1. *Identification.* All students in grades Pre-K–12 have equal access to a comprehensive assessment system that allows them to demonstrate diverse characteristics and behaviors that are associated with giftedness.	• < 10% (local norms) Phase in: • Year 1 Grades K–5 • Year 2 Grades 6–12 • Year 3 Grades K–12
How will students be identified? **Identification Tools**	
Standard 2: Assessment 2.2. *Identification.* Each student reveals his or her exceptionalities or potential through assessment evidence so that appropriate instructional accommodations and modifications can be provided.	• Measure of student aptitude • Student work samples • Portfolios • Teacher recommendations • Peer nominations
What program model(s) will be used? **Program Models**	
Standard 5: Programming 5.1. *Variety of Programming.* Students with gifts and talents participate in a variety of evidence-based programming options that enhance performance in cognitive and affective areas.	• Schoolwide Enrichment Model (SEM) • Study of Mathematically Precocious Youth (SMPY)

(Continued)

Table 5.2   (Continued)

NAGC Standards and Student Outcomes	Makeover Example: Program Design Elements
What types of learning opportunities? **Curricular Options**	
Standard 1: Learning and Development 1.6. *Cognitive and Affective Growth.* Students with gifts and talents benefit from meaningful and challenging learning activities addressing their unique characteristics and needs. **Standard 3: Curriculum Planning and Instruction** 3.2. *Talent Development.* Students with gifts and talents become more competent in multiple talent areas and across dimensions of learning. 3.4. *Instructional Strategies.* Students with gifts and talents become independent investigators. **Standard 5: Programming** 5.1. *Variety of Programming.* Students with gifts and talents participate in a variety of evidence-based programming options that enhance performance in cognitive and affective areas. 5.5. *Comprehensiveness.* Students with gifts and talents develop their potential through comprehensive, aligned programming and services.	• Enrichment and differentiation • Acceleration • Guidance and counseling
What types of services? **Enrichment and Differentiation Options**	
Standard 3: Curriculum Planning and Instruction 3.1. *Curriculum Planning.* Students with gifts and talents demonstrate growth commensurate with aptitude during the school year.	• Pre-assessment • Curriculum compacting • Content-related field trips and competitions • Guest speakers for assembly programs • Power Hour Grades 1–5 (content-specific afterschool program) • Pull-out services (individual and small-group independent investigations)
What types of services? **Acceleration Options**	
Standard 5: Programming 5.6. *Policies and Procedures.* Students with gifts and talents participate in regular and gifted education programs that are guided by clear policies and procedures that provide for their advanced learning needs (e.g., early entrance, acceleration, credit in lieu of enrollment).	• Early entrance to Kindergarten • Single-subject acceleration • Pre-AP courses • AP courses • AP distance learning programs (e.g., Virtual High Schools, Apex Learning)

NAGC Standards and Student Outcomes	Makeover Example: Program Design Elements
What types of services? **Guidance and Counseling Options**	
Standard 1: Learning and Development 1.8. *Cognitive and Affective Growth.* Students with gifts and talents identify future career goals that match their talents and abilities and resources needed to meet those goals (e.g., higher education opportunities, mentors, financial support). **Standard 4: Learning Environments** 4.1. *Personal Competence.* Students with gifts and talents demonstrate growth in personal competence and dispositions for exceptional academic and creative productivity. These include self-awareness, self-advocacy, self-efficacy, confidence, motivation, resilience, independence, curiosity, and risk taking. **Standard 5: Programming** 5.7. *Career Pathways.* Students with gifts and talents identify future career goals and the talent development pathways to reach those goals.	• Small-group discussions (e.g., perfectionism, stress reduction, multipotentiality, gender issues) • College counseling (middle school and high school)
Where will services be provided? **Service Delivery Options**	
Standard 5: Programming 5.1. *Variety of Programming.* Students with gifts and talents participate in a variety of evidence-based programming options that enhance performance in cognitive and affective areas. 5.2. *Coordinated Services.* Students with gifts and talents demonstrate progress as a result of the shared commitment and coordinated services of gifted education, general education, special education, and related professional services, such as school counselors, school psychologists, and social workers.	• Push-in services • Pull-out services • Distance learning • Afterschool program
When will services be provided? **Service Delivery Options**	
Standard 5: Programming 5.2. *Coordinated Services.* Students with gifts and talents demonstrate progress as a result of the shared commitment and coordinated services of gifted education, general education, special education, and related professional services, such as school counselors, school psychologists, and social workers.	• During school • After school

reviewing, they determined that they had made considerable progress. Plainville's revised program design:

- demonstrated much stronger linkages between Plainville classrooms and the NAGC standards related to program design;
- delineated services that would be delivered in the regular curriculum and the gifted education curriculum;
- targeted several areas for program expansion as it related to identification (i.e., incorporating more grade levels and additional talent areas) and program services (i.e., distance learning);
- targeted academic, artistic, and creative talents;
- included interventions to deal with students' cognitive and affective learning needs; and
- provided for multifaceted educational opportunities within the school day and after school.

The committee realized that their new program design was a beginning and that it would change over time. There were many areas where they could—even now—tweak the CPD to make it more comprehensive and/or aligned with students' learning needs. For the time being, however, the revised plan did a far better job of reflecting student needs and the school district philosophy than what had previously been in place.

ADVICE FOR GETTING STARTED: STRATEGIC PLAN FOR CREATING THE PROGRAM DESIGN

Beth and her colleagues reflected on the process they had used to create a comprehensive strategic plan for Plainville. They had met regularly for about a year and had been involved in a wide variety of tasks. Their tasks clustered into the following stages:

- **Stage 1 (3 to 6 months): Learning and Starting to Plan.** The committee read selected chapters from seminal works (Davis et al., 2011, Chapter 4; Peters, Matthews, McBee, & McCoach, 2014, Chapters 5–6; Renzulli et al., 2009, Chapters 1, 9, 13), reviewed other program design plans, visited programs, and conducted a needs assessment. The committee carefully reviewed options currently available for talented students across a broad spectrum of areas (e.g., academics, arts, guidance, social and emotional). They considered ways to involve staff in ownership and planning. They also reviewed state and national standards, such as the NAGC Pre-K–Grade 12 Gifted Programming Standards.
- **Stage 2 (6 to 9 months): Planning, Seeking Consensus, and Input.** The district-wide committee prepared a preliminary program design and presented findings from the needs assessment and background research to focus groups of faculty, parents, and board of education

members. They also gathered input and addressed budget considerations. To build the optimal conditions for consensus among diverse
members, they adopted the "80% rule." When 80% of the committee
agreed on components of the CPD, a decision would be made to
move ahead with the planning. Use of this rule would prevent them
from getting bogged down in the process.

- **Stage 3 (9 to 12 months): Developing an Initial Plan for Comprehensive Program Design.** The committee developed an initial CPD
  plan. They included what would be done over a preliminary period
  to ensure that all key constituent groups were aware of their roles
  and responsibilities.
- **Stage 4 (1 to 3 years): Revising and Modifying the CPD Based on
  Evaluation, Feedback, and Students' Needs.** The plan was implemented and progress was evaluated regularly to make decisions
  about what would be effective for gifted students' continuous progress. A program leader or administrator was identified to monitor
  what would be done over the 2- to 3-year period to ensure that all
  key constituent groups understood that program design was an
  ongoing, continuing approach with increasing levels of staff support
  and input. The committee continued to evaluate and assess faculty
  involvement and professional development to analyze progress
  toward program goals.

During the process of CPD development, the following program components
were remodeled and/or developed:

- A needs assessment was completed to gather information about the
  needs of gifted and talented students and what the school district
  was already providing.
- A district definition of talented and gifted students was adopted that
  reflected state regulations.
- Consistency was considered, because the definition of giftedness
  needed to match the identification system and the programming
  model or services provided.
- To that end, an identification system was developed that matched
  the definition and state regulations.
- Program goals matching the definition and the needs assessment
  were developed and included clearly defined services that would be
  provided to students.
- A comprehensive program design (including curriculum, program
  services for students across grade levels, grouping options, and
  teaching responsibilities) was based on the program needs assessments, definition, goals, and desired outcomes.
- Curriculum development (for students in a separate program) and
  curriculum differentiation (within both heterogeneous and homogeneous classrooms) were implemented based on the needs assessment, program goals, and design discussed above.

Figure 5.1   Flowchart for Designing a Comprehensive Program Design

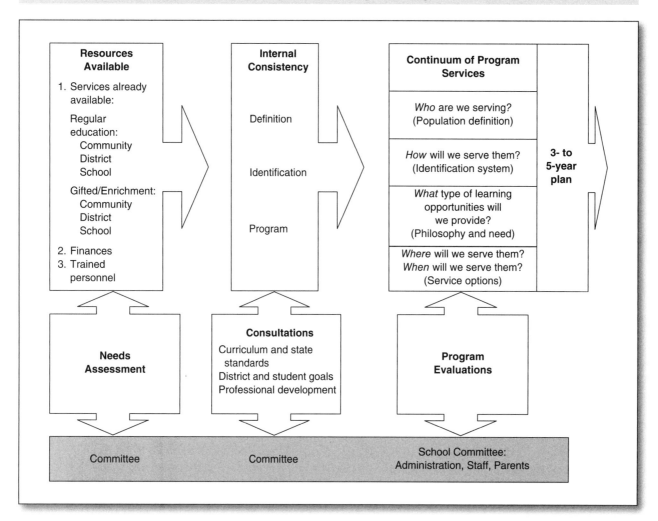

- Professional development was provided to classroom teachers, counselors, and specialists. Gifted education specialists with higher levels of background and training in gifted education were selected and trained for teaching more advanced student offerings.
- Program evaluation guided the continued development and expansion of program services for identified students.

Finally, Figure 5.1 provides a graphic representation of the process used by Beth and her colleagues to craft a comprehensive CPD. A flowchart was used to highlight the dynamic, complex process of consensus building and decision making involved in mapping out how best to meet the needs of a community's high-potential learners.

ADVICE FOR THE SOLE PRACTITIONER

Because a CPD is designed to be an all-encompassing roadmap for the development of programs and services tailored to the needs of gifted students in your district, the process of developing and implementing a CPD can seem like an overwhelming task for an individual. A sole practitioner who is interested in or charged with the responsibility for designing a comprehensive continuum of program services should consider assembling a small committee of interested faculty, staff, administrators, and parents to provide critical insight and support. The goals of this group are to arrive at a consensus about how to meet the needs of gifted and talented students and about what a comprehensive program for gifted and talented students should provide. The series of questions raised in this chapter are critical to this process and can serve to guide group discussions and decisions: Who needs special services (defining the population)? How will they be identified and selected? What types of learning opportunities will be provided (based on philosophy and need)? Where and when will the services be provided?

SUGGESTED RESOURCES

Peters, S. J., Matthews, M. S., McBee, M. T., & McCoach, D. B. (2014). *Beyond gifted education: Designing and implementing advanced academic programs.* Waco, TX: Prufrock Press.

Reflective and critical questions must be posed and answered when gifted program designs are being considered. Peters, Matthews, McBee, and McCoach raise the questions about identification, assessment, acceleration, and enrichment and provide important information to guide decision making about what types of advanced academic programs would suit students with high potential in grades K–12.

Plucker, J. A., & Callahan, C. M. (Eds.). (2014). *Critical issues and practices in gifted education: What the research says* (2nd ed.). Waco, TX: Prufrock Press.

This text provides discussions of current research from invited research experts in pertinent areas of gifted education to summarize what is known and not known. Plucker and Callahan's book provides researchers, administrators, teachers, and practitioners with needed information as elements of comprehensive program design are considered and evaluated.

Renzulli, J. S., & Reis, S. M. (2014). *The Schoolwide Enrichment Model: A how-to guide for talent development* (3rd ed.). Waco, TX: Prufrock Press.

The subtitle of *The Schoolwide Enrichment Model* is an accurate representation of the purpose of this book on talent development. Renzulli and Reis guide you through each chapter from a vision and a plan to guide the implementation of a comprehensive research-based program to investigating multiple approaches to offering challenging programming and service opportunities for all students, including students with high potential.

REFERENCES

Assouline, S. G., Colangelo, N., Lupkowski-Shoplik, A. E., Lipscomb, J., & Forstadt, L. (2009). *Iowa Acceleration Scale: A guide to whole grade acceleration K–8* (3rd ed.). Scottsdale, AZ: Great Potential Press.

Assouline, S. G., Colangelo, N., VanTassel-Baska, J., & Lupkowski-Shoplik, A. (2015). *A nation empowered: Evidence trumps the excuses holding back America's brightest students* (Vol.1). Iowa City: University of Iowa, Belin-Blank Acceleration Institute.

Assouline, S. G., & Lupkowski-Shoplik, A. (2012). The talent search model of gifted education. *Journal of Psychoeducational Assessment, 30,* 45–59.

Assouline, S. G., & Lupkowski-Shoplik, A. E. (2011). *Developing math talent: A guide to challenging and educating gifted students in math* (2nd ed.). Waco, TX: Prufrock Press.

Benbow, C. P. (2012). Identifying and nurturing future innovators in science, technology, engineering, and mathematics: A review of findings from the study of mathematically precocious youth. *Peabody Journal of Education, 87,*16–25.

Burns, D. E., Gubbins, E. J., Reis, S. M., Westberg, K. L., Dinnocenti, S. T., & Tieso, C. L. (2002). *Applying gifted education pedagogy in the general education classroom: Professional development module* (PDM02029). Storrs: University of Connecticut, The National Research Center on the Gifted and Talented.

Callahan, C. M., & Hertberg-Davis, H. L. (Eds.). (2013). *Fundamentals of gifted education: Considering multiple perspectives.* New York, NY: Routledge.

Colangelo, N., Assouline, S. G., & Gross, M. U. M. (2004). *A nation deceived: How schools hold back America's brightest students* (Vol. 1). Iowa City: The University of Iowa, The Connie Belin & Jacqueline N. Blank International Center for Gifted Education and Talent Development.

Davis, G. A., Rimm, S. B., & Siegle, D. (2011). *Education of the gifted and talented* (6th ed.). Boston, MA: Pearson.

Gentry, M., & Fugate, M. C. (2013). Cluster grouping programs and the total school cluster grouping model. In C. M. Callahan & H. L. Hertberg-Davis (Eds.). *Fundamentals of gifted education: Considering multiple perspectives* (pp. 212–225). New York, NY: Routledge.

Gubbins, E. J. (2014). Enrichment. In J. A. Plucker & C. M. Callahan (Eds.), *Critical issues and practices in gifted education: What the research says* (2nd ed., pp. 223–236). Waco, TX: Prufrock Press.

Johnsen, S. K. (2015). Gifted education programming standards. In F. A. Karnes & S. M. Bean (Eds.), *Methods and materials for teaching the gifted* (4th ed., pp. 3–41). Waco, TX: Prufrock Press.

Karnes, F. A., & Bean, S. M. (Eds.). (2015). *Methods and materials for teaching the gifted* (4th ed.). Waco, TX: Prufrock Press.

Kell, H. J., Lubinski, D., & Benbow, C. P. (2013). Who rises to the top? Early indicators. *Psychological Science, 20,* 1–12.

Little, C. A. (2012). Curriculum as motivation for gifted students. *Psychology in the Schools, 49,* 695–705.

Lubinski, D., Benbow, C. P., & Kell, H. J. (2014). Life paths and accomplishments of mathematically precocious males and females four decades later. *Psychological Science, 25,* 2217–2232.

National Association for Gifted Children. (2010). *NAGC Pre-K–Grade 12 Gifted Programming Standards: A blueprint for quality gifted education programs.* Washington, DC: Author.

Peters, S. J., Matthews, M. S., McBee, M. T., & McCoach, D. B. (2014). *Beyond gifted education: Designing and implementing advanced academic programs.* Waco, TX: Prufrock Press.

Plucker, J. A., Burroughs, N., & Song, R. (2010). *Mind the (other) gap! The growing excellence gap in K–12 education.* Bloomington: Indiana University.

Plucker, J. A., & Callahan, C. M. (Eds.). (2014). *Critical issues and practices in gifted education: What the research says* (2nd ed.). Waco, TX: Prufrock Press.

Renzulli, J. S. (2012). Reexamining the role of gifted education and talent development for the 21st century: A four-part theoretical approach. *Gifted Child Quarterly, 56,* 150–159.

Renzulli, J. S., Gubbins, E. J., McMillen, K. S., Eckert, R. D., & Little, C. A. (2009). *Systems and models for developing programs for the gifted and talented* (2nd ed.). Waco, TX: Prufrock Press.

Renzulli, J. S., & Reis, S. M. (2014). *The Schoolwide Enrichment Model: A how-to guide for talent development* (3rd ed.). Waco, TX: Prufrock Press.

Rogers, K. B. (2002). *Re-forming gifted education: Matching the program to the child.* Scottsdale, AZ: Great Potential Press.

Rogers, K. B. (2007). Lessons learned about educating the gifted and talented: A synthesis of the research on educational practice. *Gifted Child Quarterly, 51,* 382–396.

Schroth, S. T. (2014). Service delivery models. In J. A. Plucker & C. M. Callahan (Eds.), *Critical issues and practices in gifted education: What the research says* (2nd ed., pp. 577–591). Waco, TX: Prufrock Press.

Tomlinson, C. A. (2005). Quality curriculum and instruction for highly able students. *Theory Into Practice, 44,* 160–166.

VanTassel-Baska, J., & Brown, E. F. (2015). An analysis of gifted education curriculum models. In F. A. Karnes & S. M. Bean (Eds.), *Methods and materials for teaching the gifted* (4th ed., pp. 107–138). Waco, TX: Prufrock Press.

Chapter 6

Creating a Comprehensive and Defensible Budget for Gifted Programs and Services

Julie Lenner McDonald, EdD,
and Carolyn R. Cooper, PhD

> *Start by doing what's necessary, then what's possible and suddenly you are doing the impossible.*
>
> —St. Francis of Assisi

Practitioners in the field of gifted education are sensitive to the state of school and district budgets. This sensitivity is well known. In many states, the health and wealth of gifted education programs and services fluctuates with that of the local and state economy. Only 27 states in the United States fund gifted education from the state level (National Association for Gifted Children & Council of State Directors of Programs for the Gifted, 2015). Of the remaining states, local funds may be used if the citizens who reside in them value the educational benefit afforded by gifted programming and services to their community.

It follows, then, that creating a budget and being accountable for resource allocation are of paramount importance. To maintain the current level of services for the gifted, it is critical that teachers and coordinators of gifted programs understand and participate in the entire budgeting process. The budgeting process includes creating a budget and being accountable for program expenditures. When practitioners can demonstrate that tax dollars have been spent wisely—yielding student growth—they are in a much stronger position to advocate on behalf of the gifted education program and the students they serve. Funding and the budgeting process can provide accountability and support for programs and services.

DEFINITION

The budget of a gifted and talented education program is a structure that supports the program's expenses. The program budget need not be huge; however, it must contain funds for specific expenditures required to achieve the stated program goals and student outcomes. Moreover, the budget connects the program's goals and objectives, activities, timeline, evaluation scheme, and the personnel needed to implement these components. The budget is a key management tool for achieving the program's intended results, and at the same time, it can be used to demonstrate fiscal responsibility.

RATIONALE

The gifted education budget is one of the most critical components of the program. It assigns a dollar value to each goal and describes the objectives and activities to achieve the goal. Its primary role is to organize all the elements of the program for logical accounting as well as to assist in program planning. Serving as a communication tool, the budget also conveys to stakeholders efficiently, effectively, and economically how funds are both encumbered and, ultimately, expended to accomplish each program goal.

According to Standard 5 of the NAGC Pre-K–Grade 12 Gifted Programming Standards, requisite resources and materials must be provided to support the efforts of gifted education programming and services "to ensure that learners with gifts and talents receive appropriate educational services" (National Association for Gifted Children, 2010, p. 12). Just as a checkbook or online accounting system helps an individual manage his or her personal funds, so too the budget informs financial decisions that the program director must make with respect to implementing program components (Pan, Rudo, Schneider, & Smith-Hansen, 2003). The purpose of both the personal and program budgeting systems is the same: decision making for future planning.

The budget also serves as a program evaluation tool. It must be considered at the time the program administrator is planning student identification strategies, instructional services, and needed evaluation data (Davis, Rimm, & Siegle, 2011). As an evaluation tool, it reflects the program's priorities, the degree to which those priorities are addressed throughout the budget period, extenuating circumstances that interrupt the flow of priority achievement, and program decisions made to modify original plans. As a measure of program effectiveness, the gifted education budget provides ongoing direction for program decision making, the purpose of any evaluation instrument.

GUIDING PRINCIPLES AND ATTRIBUTES THAT DEFINE HIGH QUALITY

Budgets are prepared by gifted education coordinators and/or administrators to provide essential services to students in gifted education. The budgeting process will look different from district to district. Depending on district expectations, gifted coordinators and/or administrators will have different levels of involvement in the process. Due to this difference, gifted coordinators must have knowledge about all aspects of the budget process so that they can advocate accordingly. All budget expenditures are aligned to accomplish the program's goals and mission. School budget line items designated for gifted education programming reflect the program's integration with the total school curriculum, which helps with public relations, staff ownership, ensuring the equitable distribution of resources, and administrative efforts to support the program (Cooper, 2000). Last, gifted education budgets that are a part of the governing agency's budget build administrative ownership for the program (Cooper, 1995). Budget integrity leads to fiscal accountability, which must be maintained continuously.

A high-quality, defensible budget for gifted programming encompasses five key attributes: comprehensiveness, consistency, alignment, clarity, and accuracy.

Comprehensiveness

- A budget includes every type of expenditure needed to accomplish the program's stated goals and mission.
- No expenditure is too small for inclusion in the budget. Every cent allocated by the district or state must be accounted for in the program budget.

Consistency

- The budget aligns completely with the gifted program's stated goals, objectives, and services, and reflects the broader mission of the school and/or district in which it functions.
- The budget provides for an equitable distribution of resources to support the diverse needs of students participating in gifted programming.

Alignment

- All line items in the budget must be realistic and reflect federal, state, and local figures as well as vendors' current prices.
- Every line item belongs to a category with a corresponding line on the agency's master budget form for the program.

Clarity

- All line items and attendant cost designations must be easily understood.
- Only items linked directly to the program's goals are included in the budget.
- Every line item is a function of program planning, implementation, or management.

Accuracy

- A budget must be accurate from its conceptualization to its daily management.
- Any in-kind expenses must be calculated accurately and accounted for as a critical component of the total program budget.
- Fixed charges must be current and included correctly on the agency's required forms.
- Any budget items supported by grant funding must follow required procedures for allowable spending.
- Items substituted for others listed in the budget must be justified and costs modified throughout the entire budget to maintain the original budget total.
- Budget categories that carry limitations with regard to transferring funds to and/or from other categories must be respected and monitored regularly for accuracy.
- Budget accuracy makes for a cleaner audit.

STRATEGIC PLAN FOR DESIGNING A GIFTED EDUCATION PROGRAM BUDGET

The development of a high-quality gifted education program budget can be a complex process requiring careful attention to detail. The following outline provides a suggested plan for designing a budget and attending to the attributes of comprehensiveness, consistency, alignment, clarity, and accuracy.

- **Objective:** To create a gifted education program budget that is effective, efficient, economical, and defensible.
- **Evidence that the objective has been met:** A budget that is comprehensive, clear, accurate, and aligned with the program and building goals.

- **Major considerations in budget development:** Developing an effective budget for a gifted education program requires three major considerations: (1) time to construct it, (2) data to feed into it, and (3) a logical plan for organizing the data for ease in managing the budget on a daily basis. The person or team constructing the program budget must focus on each category of the budget: how it aligns with the program's goals, objectives, and activities; the components in each category that will help achieve these goals; cost of these components; and the probability of receiving in-kind contributions from the school district, individual schools, and/or other sources to help offset the overall expense of operating the gifted education program.
- **Format:** A table or spreadsheet format allows for standardized categories to be used. As decisions are made, important line items can be added to the categories to achieve the program's goals.

Step 1: Preparation

Before placing figures on the budget worksheet, the person or team constructing the budget must:

- Acquire the school and district budget process calendar from the fiscal office. Note specific dates for key submissions.
- Gather all data needed for each budget category. These data include descriptive documents, enrollment trends and projections, previous program budgets, and pay scales and/or benefits package costs for district professional and classified personnel.
- Collect all forms the school and/or district require for recording the completed budget. Have accurately spelled names and locations of personnel to whom copies of the budget must be sent.
- Review each line item of the gifted education program budget to ensure a clear understanding of its inclusion—because there will most likely be a need to present or explain the proposed budget to supervisors and/or the school board during the district's budget process.
- Become thoroughly familiar with the final program budget so as to be helpful in the event of a program or fiscal audit.

Methodical preparation for constructing the budget pays substantial dividends for the duration of the program. There is no substitute for being prepared and thorough.

Step 2: Timeline Development

With the school and/or district budget process calendar in hand, the person constructing the program budget develops a simple timeline that lists all budget construction tasks and the projected date completion.

Table 6.1 is a recommended prototype for the first months of budget preparation. Once the gifted education program's budget proposal is submitted to the appropriate administrators, there is often a brief hiatus for budget developers before the central office finalizes the district's overall budget proposal for review by the board of education and, finally, the public. Thus, the steps identified in the timeline are only the beginning of the long process, which continues until the board authorizes publication of the accepted budget for the following academic year.

Table 6.1 Budget Creation Timeline

Date	Task
Early October	• See Step 1: Preparation. • Gather necessary data on cost of consultants included in program plan, prices of equipment desired, current prices of instructional and professional materials, and information materials for parents and community members.
Mid-October	• Request meeting with building administrators to discuss upcoming budget process, changes from last year's process, and issues that may impact budget construction (e.g., total amount district has allocated to gifted education budget for the coming year). • Discuss budget priorities with small group of staff representatives. • Create a file for each budget category, and place in it every piece of information, question, or issue pertinent to that category. • Draft a worksheet form for each budget category. Use the following template to guide you.
Early December	• Prepare draft of program budget category on that category's worksheet. • Total all categories' worksheets to get a general idea of the grand total of the gifted education program's draft budget to date.
Mid-January	• Refine draft of program budget in preparation for discussing it with supervisor for suggestions. • Review draft with supervisor for modifications, if needed.
Late January/ Early February	• Modify program budget draft. Send modified draft to supervisor and attach the original he or she reviewed earlier in the process. • Make requested changes. Deliver the latest revised budget proposal to your supervisor for final approval and obtain permission to submit final budget proposal. • Provide a copy of the final proposal to your supervisor for his or her files.

TEMPLATE FOR PLANNING

The template in Table 6.2 reflects widely accepted categories of expenditures presented in a systemic manner. It is intended to remind readers about the many and varied categories of budget development so that no item is inadvertently overlooked. This template has been designed with an eye for practitioners throughout the United States with recognition that not all categories are applicable in all contexts due to available resources and legislation.

Table 6.2   Planning Template

1.0 Salaries and Wages	
1.1	Program director
1.2	Administrative assistant
1.3	Gifted education specialists (teachers, if not included in agency's personnel budget)
1.4	Gifted education specialists (central office, if not included in agency's personnel budget)
2.0 Benefits	
2.1	Social Security/state retirement system (percentage of salary)
2.2	Unemployment insurance (percentage of salary)
2.3	Worker's compensation
2.4	Insurance (health, dental, vision, life; generally in agency's master budget)
3.0 Contracted Services	
3.1	Program evaluation
3.2	Consultants
3.3	Professional development training (e.g., Advanced Placement teacher training)
3.4	Data services (for student score reports)
3.5	Regional Educational Service Center (for curriculum resources, including human, print, nonprint)
3.6	Software licenses
4.0 Supplies and Materials (include shipping and handling charges as they apply)	
4.1	General office supplies (e.g., paper, pens, business cards)
4.2	Specific office supplies (e.g., copy services, phone, technology rental; check with agency's financial officer for specifics)
4.3	Data collection materials for identification, including instruments and training materials

4.0 Supplies and Materials **(include shipping and handling charges as they apply)**	
4.4	Student materials and supplies (e.g., online advanced coursework; college-planning guides; competition/contest fees; admission fees for museums, science centers, and artistic performances; specialized supplies for student products)
4.5	Specialized teacher training materials
4.6	Parent and community resources
4.7	Professional resources (gifted education journal and magazine subscriptions, professional books and digital resources for curriculum, program models and theoretical frameworks, resources on special populations of gifted students)
4.8	Membership fees (e.g., National Association for Gifted Children, state affiliate groups)
5.0 Travel	
5.1	In state: Local mileage and tolls for routine operations (employee drives personal vehicle)
5.2	In state: Professional development trainings, meetings (employee drives personal vehicle)
5.3	Out-of-state professional development trainings, conferences, seminars (employee uses plane, train, rental car, taxi, or personal vehicle [if reasonable and approved])
5.4	Conference registration
5.5	Hotel (if travel dictates; check with agency's financial officer for policy)
6.0 Equipment	
6.1	First-time purchases for faculty or staff (e.g., computers, projectors, cameras, printers, furniture)
6.2	Replacement purchases for faculty or staff (per replacement cycle policy)
6.3	First-time purchases for students (e.g., computers, handheld devices, lab equipment)
6.4	Replacement purchases for students (e.g., per replacement cycle policy)
7.0 Miscellaneous Charges	
7.1	Honoraria for noncontracted speakers
7.2	Short-term clerical assistance
7.3	Facility rental for meetings, trainings, and so on.
7.4	Awards (e.g., certificates, plaques, gifts to speakers)
7.5	Cell phone stipend (per district policy; check with agency's financial officer)
7.6	Special printing job done outside the district
7.7	Postage (may be for private parcel shipping if agency covers general postage)
7.8	Food for meetings (per agency policy)

EXAMPLE IN NEED OF REVISION

Table 6.3 illustrates budget construction flaws within each of the five attributes of a high-quality, defensible budget: comprehensiveness, consistency, alignment, clarity, and accuracy. Review the information presented for areas in need of revision.

Table 6.3   Budget in Need of Revision

Line Item	Calculation	Program Cost	In-Kind	Total Item Cost
Salaries and Wages				
Program director	$35,000			$35,000
Administrative assistant	$10.00 per hour	40 hours		$20,800
Evaluator	$70,000	7 months	Supplies	$70,000
Contracted Services				
Consultant on differentiation	$1,500 per day	$4,500	Travel	$4,500
Conference: The Slow Learner	10 teachers at $2,500	$23,800	$1,200	$25,000
Supplies and Materials				
Books for teachers	300	$10,000	$5,000	$16,000
Buses for field trips	$135 per hour	$1,500	$1,500	$1,500
Evaluator supplies	Estimated costs	$250		$250
Office supplies	Estimated costs	$250	$100	$350
Other Charges				
Social Security	5 positions	20%		$50,000
Equipment				
New printer	$400	$400		$400
Desk and chair	$1,400	$1,000	$400	$1,400
Total				**$179,410**

MAKEOVER EXAMPLE

The corrective actions suggested in Table 6.4 can help remove the identified flaws in the example in need of revision, and substantially strengthen the gifted education program budget.

Table 6.4   Budget Attributes and Suggested Corrective Actions

Quality Attribute	Budget Flaw	Suggested Corrective Action
Comprehensiveness	• Incomplete listing of expenditures	• Add gifted specialist(s), evaluator's supplies, and the required unemployment insurance, worker's compensation, and any benefits.
Consistency	• The Slow Learner conference is not consistent with program goals. • Program goals, objectives, and activities not articulated as the introduction to the budget; alignment of budget and program goals, and so on not apparent.	• Substitute NAGC annual convention. • Specify program goals, objectives and activities with which to align gifted education program budget.
Alignment	Costs of some items are not current: • Administrative assistant salary is too low. • Evaluator's salary is inflated. • Retirement costs are not aligned. • Unemployment insurance, worker's compensations, and benefits are not listed.	• Update administrative assistant's salary. • Adjust evaluator's salary and length of contract. • Calculate retirement, unemployment, worker's compensation, and benefits costs.
Clarity	• "Program Cost" is too vague a column label. • Some item descriptions are too vague (e.g., "books for teacher"). • Administrative assistant's salary calculation is incomplete. • Length of consultant's contract not clear. • Total amounts are listed only for entire budget.	• Change to "Budgeted Amount." • Be specific about materials: 300 books on differentiation at $50 each. • Specify work period: $14.10 an hour for 40 hours for 50 weeks. • Specify terms: 3 days at $1,500 per day. • Each major category should be calculated with separate subtotals in each column.

(Continued)

Table 6.4   (Continued)

Quality Attribute	Budget Flaw	Suggested Corrective Action
Accuracy	Line items in incorrect categories and/or columns: • Evaluator is listed in Salaries and Wages. • Buses for field trips are listed in Supplies and Materials. • Evaluator's supplies are listed in In-Kind column under Salaries and Materials. • Money and other information listed in In-Kind column. • Total Item Cost column contains several errors of format and addition.	Reposition incorrectly categorized line items: • A private contractor is listed in Contracted Services. • Buses are contracted for; they should be listed in Contracted Services. • A line item can be entered only once in a budget. List all materials and supplies in Materials and Supplies category. • List only the dollar value of an item contributed by the district, school and/or others in the In-Kind column. • Line up figures for more accurate addition; record subtotal of each category; double-check by adding total of Budgeted Amount and In-Kind columns. This total must equal the Total Item Cost column.

Table 6.5 provides a revised budget in which the corrective actions highlighted in Table 6.4 have been taken.

Finally, although the budgeting process occurs on an annual cycle, practitioners must also consider long-term programming goals and overall mission as they allocate and coordinate resources. Maintaining transparency and accountability in both short- and long-term budgetary planning is the best strategy for ensuring a defensible gifted education program budget.

ADVICE FOR THE SOLE PRACTITIONER

Creating a budget for the first time can be a daunting task, especially if you are working on your own. The sole practitioner must first recognize that budgeting is a local issue and decisions are dependent on the context in which he or she is working. Therefore, it is important to meet with the school or district's financial officer to have a conversation about administrative expectations and the interface between the gifted budget and the overall school and district budget. You should view the construction of a budget proposal similarly to building a puzzle. One budget category after the next gives the budget its distinct character, and like a puzzle, it comes

Table 6.5 Revised Budget

Line Item	Calculation	Budgeted Amount	In-Kind	Total Item Cost
Salaries and Wages				
Program director	$35,000 for 12 months	$35,000		$35,000
Administrative assistant	$14.10 per hour 40 hours for 50 weeks	$28,200		$28,200
Gifted specialist	2 at $45,000 for 10 months	$90,000		$90,000
Subtotal		**$153,200**		**$153,200**
Contracted Services				
Evaluator	$70,000 for 10 months	$50,000	$20,000	$70,000
Consultant on differentiation	$1,500 per day for 3 days	$3,000	$1,500	$4,500
Buses for field trip	2 at $125 per hour for 6 hours	$750	$750	$1,500
Subtotal		**$53,750**	**$22,250**	**$76,000**
Supplies and Materials				
Teacher books on differentiation	300 at $50	$10,000	$5,000	$15,000
Evaluator supplies	$250	$250		$250
Office supplies	$1,000	$600	$400	$1,000
Subtotal		**$10,850**	**$5,400**	**$16,250**
Other Charges				
Social Security, Workers' compensation, and so on	Contact fiscal officer for most up-to-date costs			Contact fiscal officer for most up-to-date costs
Benefits (if not covered elsewhere)	Contact fiscal officer for most up-to-date costs			Contact fiscal officer for most up-to-date costs
Subtotal				
Equipment				
New printer	$400	$400		$400
Desk and chair	Desk $1,000 Chair $400	$1,000	$400	$1,400
Subtotal		**$1,400**	**$400**	**$1,800**
Total		**$219,200**	**$28,050**	**$247,250**

together in a remarkable creation. As you build your puzzle, think about meeting your students' needs first and, if you are able, reserve some funds for professional development and meeting other practitioners in adjacent districts with an eye toward building more support for yourself and your program.

SUGGESTED RESOURCES

Dereef, M. (2011). Planning to communicate: A budget companion. *School Business Affairs, 77*(3), 12–14.

This article offers advice for the creation of a plan to communicate with stakeholders during the budget process. Dereef argues that a timely and clear message can help you advocate effectively for the resources needed to meet student needs.

The Rennie Center for Education Research & Policy. (2012). *Smart school budgeting: Resources for districts.* Boston, MA: Author.

This toolkit is designed to build understanding about the budget creation process and resource decisions faced by school district personnel and policy makers. The following topics are discussed: introduction to school budget analysis, setting goals, types of budgets, strategies for analyzing spending, tools for budget analysis, and cost-saving strategies.

REFERENCES

Cooper, C. R. (1995). Integrating gifted education into the total school curriculum. *School Administrator, 52*(4), 8–9, 12–15.

Cooper, C. R. (2000). Gifted and talented education. In S. Tonnen (Ed.), *What principals should know about . . .* (pp. 27–50). Springfield, IL: Charles C Thomas.

Davis, G. A., Rimm, S. B., & Siegle, D. (2011). *Education of the gifted and talented* (6th ed.). Boston, MA: Pearson.

National Association for Gifted Children. (2010). *NAGC Pre-K–Grade 12 Gifted Programming Standards: A blueprint for quality gifted education programs.* Washington, DC: Author.

National Association for Gifted Children, & Council of State Directors of Programs for the Gifted. (2015). *2014–2015 state of the states in gifted education: Policy and practice data.* Washington, DC: Author.

Pan, D., Rudo, Z. H., Schneider, C. L., & Smith-Hansen, L. (2003). *Examination of resource allocation in education: Connecting spending to student performance.* Austin, TX: Southwest Educational Development Laboratory.

Chapter 7

Providing Programs and Services for Gifted Students at the Elementary Level

Jann H. Leppien, PhD, and Karen L. Westberg, PhD

DEFINITION

Comprehensive programs and services for gifted students at the elementary level are an integral component of a school's academic program. These programs should be comprehensive in scope; be based on ongoing, data-driven decision making; provide a continuum of services to address the varied gifts and talents among these learners; guarantee equity of access to students who are traditionally underserved; and include high-quality curriculum to provide continuous challenge and growth, while also considering the interests and affective needs of learners. Service delivery options at the elementary level include enrichment within the regular classroom, cluster classrooms, performance-grouped classes or classrooms, resource classrooms, full-time special classes, acceleration options, magnet schools, distance learning options, and mentorships. One-size-programming does not fit all—the service delivery models should match students' individual needs (and not the other way around).

RATIONALE

Most gifted students spend a majority of their time in regular classroom settings where their unique academic and social and emotional needs are difficult for classroom teachers to address. Students who perform or show the potential for performing at high levels when compared with their age peers require differentiated learning experiences. These experiences should include modifications in content and instruction as well as expectations of student performance appropriate for advanced learners.

The literature suggests that classroom teachers, due to a variety of circumstances, are not making appropriate modifications for meeting the needs of capable students (Archambault et al., 1993; Loveless, Farkas, & Duffett, 2008). For example, a teacher survey by Loveless and colleagues (2008) indicated that teachers were more likely to provide one-on-one attention to academically struggling students (80% of teachers) than academically advanced students (5% of teachers). Also, 73% of the teachers themselves acknowledged that their brightest students were bored or underchallenged, which indicates a need for specialized services. Despite the fact that little is being done to address the needs of advanced students in the classroom, teachers recognize that it is important to do more to address the needs of these students (Archambault et al., 1993; Loveless et al., 2008).

Elementary classroom teachers who are expected to modify the curriculum for gifted students are typically asked to do so without sufficient training, resources, or support necessary for tailoring their instruction (Council of State Directors of Programs for the Gifted & National Association for Gifted Children, 2013; VanTassel-Baska, 2006). Although differentiating curriculum and instruction for all students is important for effective teaching, differentiation serves as only one approach and should not exclude other services for gifted learners, such as cluster or performance-grouping models, subject or grade-level acceleration, curriculum compacting, or pull-out resource classrooms.

Researchers have studied the effects of various types of special services (e.g., acceleration, pull-out programs, homogeneous grouping) on the outcomes for gifted learners at the elementary level. In a recent research synthesis of academic acceleration options, Rogers (2015) reported positive academic gains and slight social gains for gifted students. Vaughn, Feldhusen, and Asher (1991) conducted a meta-analysis examining the outcomes from pull-out programs for gifted students in Grades 1–9 and found positive effects on achievement, critical thinking, and creativity. Although studies in kindergarten are relatively infrequent, Adelson and Carpenter (2011) examined the relationship between kindergarten students' achievement grouping and reading growth, concluding that kindergarten gifted students placed in achievement groups demonstrated greater reading growth than kindergarten gifted students who were not participating in achievement groups.

GUIDING PRINCIPLES AND ATTRIBUTES THAT DEFINE HIGH-QUALITY PROGRAMS AND SERVICES

The gifted education services provided at the elementary level must be aligned with the gifted education mission, program goals, definition of advanced learners, and identification procedures. The principles that follow are based on best practices that are reflected in several publications and the NAGC Pre-K–Grade 12 Gifted Programming Standards.

- Gifted education services must begin in kindergarten and be provided to all grades at the elementary level.
- Schools should use more than one service delivery model to meet the unique needs of capable students at the elementary level, including services for twice-exceptional and other typically underserved students.
- Educators should recognize that just selecting a service option for identified students (e.g., cluster grouping, self-contained classrooms) is not sufficient for meeting students' academic or affective needs; it is the advanced and differentiated curriculum, not the type of service, that is responsible for student growth.
- The educators delivering advanced curriculum and instruction must have training on the characteristics of gifted learners, a commitment to meeting students' individual needs, and the knowledge and skills for providing advanced curriculum and instruction.
- All faculty in a school should receive training on various aspects of gifted education, be informed about program services provided in a school, and work collaboratively to meet students' needs.
- Positive attitudes and support of the administration and faculty must be developed to impact program ownership, a situation in which everyone shares in the success of a program that meets students' needs.
- Acceleration options that address the needs of students with exceptional needs must be included among the service delivery options at the elementary level, such as early entrance to kindergarten or Grade 1, subject acceleration, and grade skipping.
- Curriculum that includes advanced depth, complexity, and advanced pacing should be selected or developed for students, and a scope and sequence for the curriculum should be established.
- The services at the elementary level should include opportunities for students to pursue their interests and strength areas through independent study, projects, or mentorships.
- Identified students must be engaged in appropriately advanced levels throughout the week and should receive ongoing daily instruction commensurate with their abilities as well as have opportunities to participate in out-of-school experiences, such as competitions and internships.

- Schools should monitor, analyze, and use performance growth data on gifted students receiving advanced services in elementary programs and should conduct ongoing evaluation of the services.

EXAMPLE IN NEED OF REVISION

Urbana is a large, metropolitan school district that provides gifted education services to formally identified students in Grades 3–6. The district identifies approximately 3% of the students using national norms on composite ability and achievement tests. Students identified for special services are assumed to have strengths in reading and mathematics because of their high scores on standardized tests. The student population is diverse regarding race, ethnicity, socioeconomic status, and country of origin. Approximately 25% of the students are English language learners, and 75% receive free or reduced-price lunch. Approximately 50% are students of color, primarily of Hispanic American, Native American, and African American backgrounds. Students who have been identified for the gifted program are largely White, non-Hispanic.

Each elementary school in Urbana is served by a part-time gifted education specialist whose primary responsibility is to provide direct services to identified students in pull-out classes in Grades 3–6 for 1 hour per week. The specialist teaches curriculum units prepared approximately 5 years ago by the district's gifted education specialists. Gifted education specialists rotate teaching the units at each grade level, including a unit on logic puzzles, a unit on China, and a unit on explorers. Four units are taught each year to each grade level. In addition to the units, the specialists in some of the schools are able to work with a small group of Grade 4 students on Destination Imagination teams during afterschool hours, but this doesn't occur at every school or consistently across the grade levels. Each specialist is assigned to five schools and rotates among them each week.

MAKEOVER EXAMPLE

The gifted education services in the Urbana school district were woefully inadequate and indefensible for a number of reasons. Services were being provided to students in only Grades 3–6, rather than including K–2, and serving only a small percentage of students. Furthermore, the students identified were not representative of the demographics of the district population. Because of the use of composite test scores, it was possible to overlook students who might have been strong in one or more academic areas. In addition to the number, age, and type of students being served, it was doubtful that the identified students' academic and social and emotional needs were being addressed in just 1 hour per week, which left approximately 25 hours a week in which students likely were not receiving daily challenge in content areas. The district had no articulated goals to guide the program services. Furthermore, what was being provided to students, in the name of curriculum, was based on the interest of teachers rather than on the identified students' strengths, interests, and academic needs.

A district-wide gifted education steering committee was formed to make changes in the elementary services to better meet the needs of high-ability students. The 10-member steering committee, composed of two principals, the gifted education coordinator, the district assessment coordinator, four classroom teachers, and two parents, began by reviewing the NAGC Pre-K–Grade 12 Gifted Programming Standards, visiting other programs, and reading recommended gifted education literature. The committee then examined student data in the district and conducted an informal needs assessment. After doing this, the committee established a mission, program goals, and definition of advanced learners. The committee also decided that the district would serve the top 6% to 8% of the students using local norms on multiple assessment measures, including aptitude and achievement tests in reading and mathematics, teacher and parent rating scales, and other curriculum-based assessments. Informal identification procedures were implemented for students in Grades K–2, and all students were tested at the end of Grade 2 for formal screening and identification.

The committee decided that a continuum of gifted education services was needed in the district, beginning with K–2 students who were involved in academic advancement and critical thinking curriculum provided by their classroom teachers who had received specialized training. Reading and math cluster classrooms were formed in Grades 3–6 with instruction delivered by their classroom teachers who received specialized training. Each grade level had one reading cluster classroom teacher and one math cluster classroom teacher. The district established acceleration procedures that addressed early entrance to school, subject acceleration, and grade acceleration for students whose academic strengths were particularly exceptional. In addition to these services, the highest scoring students from typically underserved populations (culturally and linguistically diverse as well as twice-exceptional) were identified and served in classrooms as well as in pull-out classes taught by the gifted education specialists during the daily schoolwide Response to Intervention (RTI) instructional time called WIN (What I Need). The gifted education specialist in each building also provided opportunities for students to engage in inquiry-based independent studies based on student interest. Because of the comprehensive services being offered and the need to train classroom teachers on how to differentiate their instruction for advanced learners, the district provided funding for hiring more gifted educational specialists whose responsibilities increased to support classroom teachers as they worked to provide appropriate challenges to students through differentiated instruction.

The committee was successful in convincing the school district to purchase advanced curriculum materials appropriate for gifted learners. In addition to the purchased curriculum, teachers received professional development on how to create high-level curriculum that focused on abstract ideas, essential understandings, and advanced skills of disciplines. Teachers were also provided with training on how to use curriculum-based, performance-based, product-based, and out-of-level assessments to guide their instructional decisions and document student growth.

ADVICE FOR GETTING STARTED IN DESIGNING ELEMENTARY GIFTED PROGRAMS AND SERVICES

Table 7.1 can be used with the NAGC Pre-K–Grade 12 Gifted Programming Standards (see Appendix B, page 261) to plan new or to revise existing gifted education services for elementary students.

After considering features of programming, a steering committee could use the grid in Table 7.2 (see page 98) as a tool for developing an action plan for program improvement. An example has been listed on the grid.

Developing comprehensive elementary gifted education programs and services is a daunting task that requires collaborative planning by administrators, counselors, faculty, and parents. Depending on the size of a school district and the overall structure of the district, as well as the diverse academic and social and emotional needs of gifted learners, different decisions must be made to implement an effective program. It is through these efforts that the task is doable and ensures success.

ADVICE FOR THE SOLE PRACTITIONER

The sole practitioner interested in services for high-ability students in his or her elementary school should begin by, first of all, familiarizing him- or herself with the literature on program development in gifted education. Then, he or she should ask a small group of individuals to discuss this concern, which initially could be done informally or in a Professional Learning Community (PLC). When these individuals are committed to pursuing plans for services, they should meet with their administrator to formalize a steering committee. The steering committee's first task is to become familiar with comprehensive services for high-ability students by reviewing the NAGC Pre-K–Grade 12 Gifted Programming Standards (NAGC, 2010), reading resources, and perhaps visiting other programs. Additional faculty members should be invited to participate and form a self-study group that reads and discusses a book or articles on gifted education. If the school or district does not have a formalized acceleration plan, the steering committee should develop procedures to guide early entrance to school, subject acceleration, and grade acceleration. At some point, after program goals, services, and identification procedures have been established, the committee evolves into an advisory committee. If the elementary school must operate without a gifted education specialist, a sample plan for services follows.

Table 7.1 Decision-Making Planning Guide

Program Components	Guiding Questions	Features or Options
Establish the mission, belief statements, goals, and identification for gifted education services	What will be the mission and goals for the gifted program? Who will be served, and how will they be identified?	• Establish a task force to develop plans for gifted education services. • Begin by developing a mission, belief statements, and goals for gifted education services. Consider aligning these goals with the educational goals of the school district. • Select or develop a definition of giftedness that aligns with the established program goals, reflects the demographics of the students in the district, and specifies who will be served through advanced program services. • Establish procedures for identifying students for services that include practices described in the NAGC program standards. • Use multiple assessments that measure diverse abilities, talents, and strengths that are based on current theories, models, and research. • Include program and student goal statements to guide the types of services and educational experiences that will be provided to identified students.
Budget for the gifted and talented services	What will be the annual budget allocated to the elementary gifted program services?	Examine state, local, and grant funds for supporting gifted education services. Create a preliminary budget in a variety of categories to support the overall implementation of a comprehensive gifted program. Consider the following categories: • salaries, wages, and fringe benefits for personnel dedicated to the implementation of the program (e.g., a program administrator/coordinator charged with the overall implementation of the program, gifted education specialists or teachers who provide direct services to identified students, and secretarial support for managing the daily operations of the program); • contracted services (e.g., outside evaluators, consultants for professional development, and perhaps psychologists); • supplies and materials including testing materials, office supplies, materials for a professional library, and curricular resources; • resources for providing professional development to teachers and parent support groups; and • supplementary transportation costs for supporting field trips, college tours, or competitions.

(Continued)

95

Table 7.1 (Continued)

Program Components	Guiding Questions	Features or Options
Administration of the program	Will you have a district coordinator or administrator for your gifted and talented program?	• Consider a full-time administrator for elementary gifted and talented programs. • Consider a full-time administrator for gifted and talented programs district-wide with a part-time administrator for the elementary gifted services. • Consider a full-time administrator for gifted and talented programs district-wide without an administrator for elementary gifted services. • Consider a part-time (at least 50%) administrator for elementary gifted programs in the district. • Consider a part-time (less than 50%) administrator for gifted programs in the district. • Consider a situation with no administrator for gifted services exists (e.g., a teacher leader oversees the gifted and talented services at the elementary level).
Other district-level personnel for gifted education services	Will other district-level personnel have responsibilities for supporting the gifted and talented program?	• Determine if enrichment specialists will collaborate with classroom teachers on direct and indirect services to identified students. • Consider having cluster classroom teachers provide advanced curriculum and a faster pace of instruction for identified students in core academic areas. • Consider self-contained teachers who will provide instruction to students in full-time classroom settings. • Contemplate having counselors who will provide support for personal growth, social and emotional growth, and career counseling.
Service delivery models	What combination of services will be used to provide for the academic affective needs of the identified students?	Consider more than one of the following options: • differentiated instruction that includes pre-assessment, curriculum compacting, and advanced content in the regular classroom; • cluster grouping of identified students in general education classrooms with provisions for advanced content, higher-level thinking, and faster pacing; • pull-out classes for identified students that provide advanced curriculum and opportunities to focus on students' strengths and individual interests; • special classes of homogeneously grouped identified students; • full-time school(s) for identified students; • afterschool learning opportunities (e.g., Destination Imagination, robotics clubs, Future Problem Solving, visual and performing art classes); • distance learning or online learning opportunities for advanced curriculum and instruction; • grade-level acceleration; and • subject acceleration.

Program Components	Guiding Questions	Features or Options
Ongoing professional development	What types of training do school personnel need? When will it be offered and to whom?	• Consider ongoing professional development for all teachers, administration, and counselors on several topics, including characteristics and unique learning and emotional needs of a diverse range of advanced learners; identification referrals and procedures; how to provide differentiated instruction; how to develop and provide advanced curriculum; and how to design and use assessment data. • Establish a parenting the gifted and advocacy group with the intent to promote skills and strategies for meeting the special needs of gifted learners at home and supporting them in school.
Curriculum and instruction	What content areas need advancement and greater complexity to be appropriate for capable learners? What will distinguish the curriculum for students identified for the gifted program from the general curriculum? What arrangements will be made to provide for a continuum of services throughout the school district?	• Align curriculum and instruction offered within the program to curriculum standards that address the specific needs of the identified students. • Provide opportunities for students to work with intellectual peers. • Use data to match the curriculum and instruction with students' needs (e.g., subject or group acceleration). • Ease the movement of students between grade levels to ensure a continuum of services as well as a scope and sequence of content and skills. • Provide opportunities for students to pursue individual interests and passions through independent studies, internships, and mentorships. • Purchase or develop a curriculum that (a) includes elaborative, complex, and in-depth study of major ideas, problems, and themes; (b) integrates knowledge within and across disciplines; (c) uses a conceptual approach to explore advanced content that is discipline-based; (d) pursues advanced levels of understanding beyond the general education curriculum through abstraction, depth, breadth, and complexity; (e) asks students to use methods and materials that approximate those of an expert or practicing profession; and (f) accommodate self-directed learning fueled by student interest, adjustments for pacing, and variety of instructional approaches and materials. • Develop a plan for addressing the social and emotional needs of identified students, such as creating affective seminars, collaborating with guidance counselors, and purchasing materials for addressing affective needs.
Student and program evaluation	How will you gather data about the impact of the services provided to the identified students? How will you gather data on the effectiveness and quality of various program components?	• Determine how formative, interim, and summative assessment data will be collected and used to document student growth in the academic and nonacademic areas in which students are served. • Decide what, and how, data will be used to determine future student goals and to plan for appropriate interventions. • Implement an annual evaluation that examines the success of the program goals and whether or not the activities of the program are being implemented as designed. • Consider contracting with an external program evaluator on a regular basis, such as once every 3 years, to ensure quality and longevity of the gifted education services.

97

Table 7.2 Grid for Planning or Revising Gifted Programs at the Elementary Level

Program Outcomes	What Are We Doing Now?	What Do We Want to Do?	Barriers to Implementation	Supportive Implementation Opportunities	Action Plans
Services for Grades K–2	Nothing	• Provide advanced curriculum and instruction in reading and mathematics for high-ability students. • Provide enrichment and problem-solving experiences for kindergarten students.	• Primary teachers are reluctant to group students by achievement levels. • Primary teachers do not want to label or identify students.	• Data indicating students have mastered grade-level curriculum and beyond. • Parents of primary students requesting more challenging curriculum for their children.	• Form a committee of teachers, parents, administrators, and other specialists, to explore options for K–2 services, including cluster grouping, subject acceleration, or within classroom grouping.

First, assuming the school has two or more classrooms per grade level, cluster classrooms could be implemented (5–8 students per grade level assigned to one cluster teacher). The cluster classroom teachers need to educate themselves about how to meet the needs of high-ability learners and determine the advanced curriculum that must be purchased or developed. Second, if students have demonstrated mastery of standards at their grade level and learn at an accelerated pace, they should be allowed to receive subject instruction at the next grade level, which is sometimes referred to as "walk to reading" or "walk to math." Third, the school should consider implementing enrichment clusters, a schoolwide initiative in which multiage students who share common interests participate in specialized classes aligned with their interests.

This is not the only configuration of services possible, but it is just one example of a combination of services designed to meet high-ability students' needs at the elementary level.

SUGGESTED RESOURCES

Gentry, M. (2014). *Total school cluster grouping and differentiation: A comprehensive, research-based plan for raising student achievement and improving teacher practices* (2nd ed.). Waco, TX: Prufrock Press.

This book provides information for teachers and administrators who are interested in implementing a schoolwide cluster grouping plan designed to increase the achievement of all students. The theoretical underpinnings of the model, research support for the model, and practical implementation advice are provided.

Chapters on other programming topics are also included, such as curriculum compacting, differentiation, twice-exceptional learners, affective needs, and other complementary elementary program services.

Karnes, F. A., & Bean, S. M. (Eds.). (2014). *Methods and materials for teaching the gifted* (4th ed.). Waco, TX: Prufrock Press.

This edited book provides comprehensive descriptions of strategies and resources for differentiating instruction for gifted learners. The book serves as an excellent introduction to gifted education curriculum planning, instructional unit design, evaluation, and teaching methods. Chapters in this comprehensive textbook are written by respected leaders in the field of gifted education and include information on important topics, such as differentiated curricular design, process skills development, building instructional units that challenge students, and evaluating learner outcomes. Instructional practices for use with advanced students are described, such as problem-based learning, creative teaching strategies, independent study, mentorships, and classroom simulations.

Renzulli, J. S., Gentry, M., & Reis, S. M. (2014). *Enrichment clusters: A practical plan for real-world student-driven learning* (2nd ed.). Waco, TX: Prufrock Press.

This book provides a rationale and practical plan for implementing enrichment clusters to multiage students on a schoolwide basis. Enrichment clusters are designed to be a place and time for students to engage in special classes in which they have mutual interests. The goal of enrichment clusters is to develop authentic products for real audiences.

Renzulli J. S., Gubbins, E. J., McMillan, K. S., Eckert, R. D., & Little, C. A. (Eds.). (2009). *Systems and models for developing programs and services for the gifted and talented* (2nd ed.). Waco, TX: Prufrock Press.

The second edition of this book provides descriptions of major systems and models specially developed to guide programs for the gifted. Forty-two experts in gifted education contributed to 25 chapters, and each chapter includes a discussion of the model, theoretical underpinnings, research on effectiveness, and considerations for implementation. Gifted education coordinators and practitioners involved in making decisions about gifted education programming and curricular design will become familiar with the major models developed by leaders in the field of gifted education.

Renzulli, J. S., & Reis, S. M. (2014). *The Schoolwide Enrichment Model: A how-to guide for talent development* (3rd ed.). Waco, TX: Prufrock Press.

This guidebook provides step-by-step information and procedures on how to develop a Schoolwide Enrichment Program in a school or district. The model provides a framework for student services that takes into consideration local resources, students' needs, and faculty strengths and interests. The book includes information on the underlying research of the model and provides specific resources for implementation.

REFERENCES

Adelson, J. L., & Carpenter, B. D. (2011). Grouping for achievement gains: For whom does achievement grouping increase kindergarten reading growth? *Gifted Child Quarterly, 55,* 265–278. doi:10.1177/0016986211417306

Archambault, F. X., Jr., Westberg, K. L., Brown, S. W., Hallmark, B. W., Zhang, W., & Emmons, C. L. (1993). Classroom practices used with gifted third and fourth grade students. *Journal for the Education of the Gifted, 16,* 103–119.

Council of State Directors of Programs for the Gifted, & National Association for Gifted Children. (2013). *2012–2013 state of the states in gifted education: National policy and practice data.* Washington, DC: Author.

Loveless, T., Farkas, S., & Duffett, A. (2008). *High-achieving students in the era of NCLB.* Washington, DC: Thomas B. Fordham Institute.

National Association for Gifted Children. (2010). *NAGC Pre-K–Grade 12 Gifted Programming Standards: A blueprint for quality gifted education programs.* Washington, DC: Author.

Rogers, K. B. (2015). The academic, socialization, and psychological effects of acceleration: Research synthesis. In S. G. Assouline, N. Colangelo, J. VanTassel-Baska, & A. Lupkowski-Shoplik (Eds.), *A nation empowered: Evidence trumps the excuses holding back America's brightest students* (Vol. 2, pp. 19–29). Iowa City: The University of Iowa, The Connie Belin & Jacqueline N. Blank International Center for Gifted Education and Talent Development.

VanTassel-Baska, J. (2006). A content analysis of the evaluation findings across 20 gifted programs: A clarion call for enhanced gifted program development. *Gifted Child Quarterly, 50,* 119–215.

Vaughn, V. L., Feldhusen, J. F., & Asher, J. W. (1991). Meta-analyses and review of research on pull-out programs in gifted education. *Gifted Child Quarterly, 35,* 92–98.

Chapter 8

Providing Programs and Services for Gifted Students at the Secondary Level

Joan K. Jacobs, PhD, and Rebecca D. Eckert, PhD

DEFINITION

Secondary gifted students are those learners who are attending a middle school, high school, or junior high. Typically, students in secondary settings are adolescents[1] who are grappling with issues of identity development and independence, while balancing increasing levels of academic challenge. Although gifted students experience similar developmental milestones as other secondary students, asynchronous development may result in completely different trajectories or social and emotional responses. This asynchrony further complicates secondary school experiences and creates the need for specific programs or services (Dixon & Moon, 2015; National Association for Gifted Children [NAGC], 2010; Rakow, 2011).

The decisions educators make about service delivery and program organization for high-ability students within secondary settings affects the learning environment for the entire school community. When approached strategically, these choices—including programming options, curriculum, grouping arrangements, and personnel—create a comprehensive continuum

---

[1] This includes students in the early middle grades, often referred to as *tweens*.

of services that responds to the different pace and depth of functioning of secondary gifted students and provides support for continued learning (Dixon & Moon, 2015; NAGC, 2010; Rakow, 2011).

RATIONALE FOR SPECIAL SERVICES FOR GIFTED STUDENTS AT THE SECONDARY LEVEL

Within a secondary school, the student population is focused on discovering who they are and who they will become. Regardless of their gender or cultural identities, gifted adolescents experience similar fundamental transitions and changes as do their peers: "the onset of puberty (biological), the emergence of more advanced thinking abilities (cognitive), and the transition into new roles in society (social)" (Moon & Dixon, 2015, p. 6).

This search for identity and purpose becomes paramount during the secondary school years and has the power to shape a gifted student's long-term goals and career path well into adulthood. In fact, research suggests that how adolescents fit into (or experience) a school community will influence strongly how they pursue their passions and interests, and this ultimately develops their talents (Csikszentmihalyi, Rathunde, & Whalen, 1996; Dixon & Moon, 2015). Repeated negative interactions with educators, peers, or coursework may invalidate or stifle exploration and development. However, in schools with a positive, growth-oriented climate, students are encouraged to develop both the skills (e.g., self-regulation, critical thinking) and dispositions (e.g., growth mindset, resilience, positive self-concept) that allow the pursuit of excellence in any field of study (Peterson, Assouline, & Jen, 2015).

GUIDING PRINCIPLES AND ATTRIBUTES THAT DEFINE HIGH QUALITY

For gifted students to thrive in a secondary setting requires that school personnel consider how this group of learners differs from the rest of the school population and identify potential modifications in the school environment to promote full development. Specifically, high-quality secondary programs and services for gifted students will encompass five key attributes:

1. curricular offerings and adaptations,

2. social and emotional supports,

3. transition planning and multiple pathways,

4. flexibility and responsiveness to individual needs, and

5. integrated professional development opportunities for staff.

Curricular Offerings and Adaptations

One of the cornerstones of any high-quality service or program for secondary gifted students is to provide curricular offerings that deliver challenge, choice, and engagement. There are multiple academic programs and strategies that can help ensure that gifted adolescents have opportunities to learn new information and skills every day.

Advanced Placement

One option for providing advanced curriculum is Advanced Placement (AP). Administered by the College Board (n.d.), AP was created in the 1950s to enable high school students to earn college credit by passing college-level course exams. Colleges and universities frequently offer credits or placement for each exam passed at a given level on a 5-point scale. The College Board designates field experts, including both high school and college educators, to develop a common curricular framework of skills and knowledge in each class. Additionally, the College Board audits each teacher's syllabus and reading material to ensure common expectations.

One potential advantage for high school students who participate in AP is the possibility of savings of both tuition and time in college. Some students may enter college with enough credits earned during high school to start their college education as sophomores, while others may have time to finish multiple majors and minors within 4 years. However, little consistency exists across postsecondary institutions and across disciplines within institutions on the exam score needed to earn course credit (Byrd, Ellington, Gross, Jago, & Stern, 2007).

Schools must factor in costs of AP course implementation, which can vary. At a minimum, a fee must be paid for each AP exam administered to a student. Teacher training, while optional, requires a substantial budget, especially for districts in outlying areas that require travel. Curricular materials are also available for purchase. Because AP offers discrete courses characterized by advanced curriculum rather than a comprehensive gifted program, critics have raised the concern that AP courses may not provide the best option for all students seeking additional academic challenges (Foust, Hertberg-Davis, & Callahan, 2009; Hertberg-Davis & Callahan, 2008). Only recently have some of the courses added a focus on conceptual thinking rather than accumulation of large amounts of information. Critics point out that this is one reason that AP on its own should not be considered a complete program for gifted students at the secondary level.

International Baccalaureate

Another popular advanced curricular option is the International Baccalaureate Programme (IB), developed in 1966 in response to the need of military and diplomatic families to find educational stability while changing locations frequently. The program focuses on global perspectives and currently offers curricular frameworks designed specifically for students in elementary (ages 3–12), middle (ages 11–16), and high schools (ages 16–19).

The Middle Years Programme serves students ages 11–16; these 5 years of programming can span two schools—one middle, one high—or a school could opt to provide an abbreviated program (International Baccalaureate Organization, n.d.). In this way, a middle school could offer IB programming even if the local high school does not.

The Middle Years Programme can be inclusive or academically selective, depending on the needs of the community. Eight subjects emphasize a global perspective, and the courses effectively prepare students for subsequent work in the Diploma Programme in high school, and challenging postsecondary coursework.

Students who enroll in the high school Diploma Programme are required to take Theory of Knowledge, which involves metacognition—thinking about how we know what we know—and a total of nine courses at both the Standard Level and Higher Levels. This menu offers students the ability to learn in depth in their strength areas, while still requiring a minimum level of competency in the others. Students who complete the Diploma Programme will earn a diploma not only from their high school, but also from International Baccalaureate. The Career-Related Programme represents an alternative for students at the high school level with an emphasis on experiential learning in real-world settings. Students must complete selected Diploma courses and a career-related study focused on the development of professional skills. Both programs require written examinations upon completion (International Baccalaureate Organization, n.d.). The testing fees are similar to those of AP, although the exams and requirements differ significantly. Like AP, the courses offer college credit at some higher education institutions based on exam performance (Byrd et al., 2007).

Because of its focus on common experiences for students, IB is more likely to rise to the level of a program for gifted students; it provides rigorous instruction with a culminating test in all courses. Teachers in every program (i.e., Middle Years, Diploma, Career-Related) are required to attend IB training that focuses not only on course standards but also on pedagogy. If students elect to enroll in the full Diploma Programme, their coursework will have focused on creativity, community action, independent research, and an extended essay that pulls together these various elements. Multiple benchmarks help ensure that a student, at the end of his or her experience, is able to think critically about the world through a variety of lenses, not just about one subject. Likewise, a number of these requirements necessitate an advisor, so the student works closely with a chosen mentor throughout most of the program.

The monetary investment for a school, however, can be quite substantial. Each teacher in the program (as well as administrators and media specialists) is required to attend training prior to program involvement. Additionally, schools should anticipate that their library holdings need to reflect the premise of the program. Likewise, the application costs, annual membership fees, and other expenses add up quickly.

Honors or Advanced Courses

Another way in which secondary administrators and faculty have responded to the needs of high-achieving students is through the creation of honors or advanced courses. Often these classes are designed and coordinated by a district curriculum director or teacher with content-area expertise who is responding to a stated need in the community—providing a degree of flexibility to the instruction as well as a cost-effective way to increase challenging opportunities for students.

Nevertheless, the honors designation may create much confusion, because there is little shared understanding about what an honors course is, whom it serves, or what the outcome is. In most systems, *honors* means that the school intends the course to be more difficult than the regular version of the subject, although in many cases it is left to the individual teacher to determine what makes a course difficult. Difficulty may be a result of advanced levels of conceptual understanding, more work required outside class, and/or or a more competitive classroom environment. Due to the lack of shared definitions across geographical boundaries, honors or advanced classes can result in high-quality curriculum or a means of hiding low-quality services.

Weighted Courses

Weighted courses increase a student's grade point average (GPA) based on the idea that if the student takes a more difficult course, that fact should be reflected in what the course is worth on the report card and/or school transcript. In many systems, weighted grades are offered to students participating in honors, AP, or IB courses. Typically, if a school offers a 4-point scale for grades, a weighted course would count as 5 points. Consequently, if a student earns a B in a weighted course, he or she would still have a 4.0 average (Lang, 2007).

The use of a weighting formula to calculate high school GPAs is a district-level decision and a common practice in U.S. high schools (Lang, 2007; Warne, Nagaishi, Slade, Hermesmeyer, & Peck, 2014). Some colleges and universities use the weighted credit as part of their admissions process, whereas others have the students recalculate their GPAs without the additional weight. Nevertheless, scholarly debate continues on the utility of this practice because of the potential effect on college admissions and opportunities for student financial aid (Sadler & Tai, 2007). Perspectives on weighted courses vary; although weighted courses may provide incentive for taking challenging coursework and offer some insight into student performance in advanced coursework (Sadler & Tai, 2007), critics have raised concern about the predictive value and lack of uniformity in the use of the weighted GPA (Warne et al., 2014).

Differentiated Within the General Education Classroom

In the United States, differentiation in the general education classroom is more common in elementary schools than in secondary schools. Traditionally, it has referred to adjustments made to the curriculum, assessment, and instruction for gifted students so that they would experience additional challenge, choice, and opportunities for acceleration that may be lacking in the regular curriculum in the context of the general education classroom, and there are multiple models from which to choose (Karnes & Bean, 2015; Tomlinson, 1999). In recent years, however, *differentiation* in the publishing industry has tended to focus more on supports for English language learners (ELLs) and special education populations.

Differentiation for gifted students in the general education classroom typically includes pretesting and compacting (Karnes & Bean, 2015; Reis et al., 1993); pre-assessment allows students to demonstrate mastery of content prior to instruction in a given unit or for a given lesson, and compacting refers to the practice of requiring the students to learn only the material they have not already mastered. Some districts provide the option for students to test out of a course in which they can show mastery; this may or may not result in credits earned. The use of these methods tends to be highly motivating for secondary students, who appreciate the independence and individualization afforded by these opportunities.

Given the amount of time secondary gifted students spend in the general education classroom—particularly at the middle level where heterogeneous grouping is often preferred—differentiated instructional strategies can offer one solution to promoting challenge and engagement. However, ongoing teacher training and administrative support are essential to effective implementation (Dixon, Yssel, McConnell, & Hardin, 2014; Hertberg-Davis & Brighton, 2006).

Distance Learning

Distance learning utilizes technology to enable students to take courses not typically available in their school or district. This can be a real boon for young advanced learners who are not socially ready or able to participate in high school or college courses, those in rural schools where population size does not warrant advanced levels of courses, or for schools that are in the throes of financial cutbacks and have had to eliminate whole sections of offerings, such as a particular language. In addition, the availability of free, online courses and tutorials has grown with the advent of massive open online courses or MOOCs (e.g., Khan Academy, edX). Moreover, for some adolescents, the flexibility of scheduling of distance learning can be a benefit, as it is for students whose afterschool schedules are packed with activities throughout the week.

Schools offering distance learning as one option will enhance the available selections for students, but distance learning is not a panacea. Like all other classes, distance learning is only as good as the teacher and the curricula are, and not all students will respond positively to this less-structured learning environment. Moreover, students will need devices and wireless connectivity that work regardless of the weather or other exigencies as well as staff to guide and support them. Students who thrive in this environment may appreciate the flexibility and ability it affords them to move forward as they are ready, but quality control of courses and ability to pay tuition are two important considerations when selecting this strategy for adapting curricular offerings for gifted students.

Independent Study

Independent study classes vary widely and can include a distance learning course taken by one student, a regular course that a student takes at a time of day when it isn't offered to a group, or an opportunity to pursue a unique area of interest. Many other variations exist. What independent study opportunities generally have in common is that the student works on a chosen topic under the guidance of an adult who can provide topical or procedural feedback and support. Typically, the student earns credits for this work and is able to explore areas of interest in more depth than might be possible within regular course offerings.

Independent studies require additional supervisory responsibilities, paperwork, and a need for flexibility of scheduling—often within a highly structured system and busy school day. Nevertheless, resources such as the Autonomous Learner Model or the Secondary Enrichment Triad Model can support a manageable, research-based implementation option for secondary gifted students (Renzulli, Gubbins, McMillan, Eckert, & Little, 2009).

Mentorships, Internships, and Apprenticeships

Mentorships can be another option to enable gifted students to study a topic of interest in depth—even when it is not covered by the curricular offerings in school. Mentors work individually with students; they serve as role models, help students understand methodologies professionals use, and/or assist in framing research questions. Of particular benefit to adolescents, mentors help students experience the real work of the professional in a field of interest and better understand career opportunities.

Mentorships can be especially useful when a student's deep interests have no home in the regular school curriculum. Mentors can provide feedback, as well as a way to bridge the gap between the student's abilities and the regular curriculum. Additionally, mentorships can promote self-efficacy for individuals who are traditionally underrepresented in a field or discipline (e.g., African American engineers, Latino ballet dancers). In recent years, telementoring has become a viable option, particularly for students from communities that do not have experts in the field of interest. Likewise, because gifted students may not share interests of students their age, a mentor can provide a collegial relationship and peer, by being both a professional guide and someone with whom the student can discuss mutual interests.

Grade Skipping (or Early Entrance)

Perhaps the best known form of acceleration, grade skipping, when done effectively, is unlikely to result in any negative outcomes for learners or their families (Assouline, Colangelo, Lupkowski-Shoplik, Lipscomb, & Forstadt, 2009). Yet despite research supporting its use, few schools or districts use grade skipping as a means of providing challenge for advanced learners (Colangelo, Assouline, & Gross, 2004). The Iowa Acceleration Scales (Assouline et al., 2009) make use of this body of research on grade skipping to assist districts in making well-informed decisions about when grade skipping is likely to lead to improved outcomes for learners. It posits all the various issues that may arise in the discussion about grade skipping (e.g., competitive sports, physical size of the student, social skills, timing of the grade skip) as well as intelligence, achievement, and aptitude test scores; it guides the conversation so that family members, students, and school personnel feel comfortable with the decision, either way.

Subject-Specific Acceleration

Students with an aptitude in a specific subject may benefit from being enrolled in a more advanced course than those typically offered to students at their grade level. A student skilled in math, for example, may attend middle school until the last period, when he takes an upper-level math class at the high school. Or a high school teacher may begin her day at the middle school where she teaches a trigonometry course to a small group of middle school students ready for this challenge. This type of acceleration is most easily accomplished in math and languages, in which there is a specific course sequence of skill acquisition, but can occur in any subject area. Subject-specific acceleration helps ensure continuous progress for students who may be enough out of level in a specific subject area that the school has no appropriate courses for the individual.

Concurrent Enrollment (or Dual Enrollment)

Concurrent enrollment enables secondary students to earn both high school and college credit simultaneously while taking one course in their area of strength. Students may attend college courses, or in some cases, the delivery may be at the secondary school in a dual credit course. This second type of concurrent enrollment typically requires that a high school teacher meet specific criteria according to the college providing the credits. Students pay the college tuition or the school pays the instructor, and students remain in a high school environment but earn both high school and college credit.

Concurrent enrollment has a number of different configurations, ranging from the dual credit course to enrollment in two schools simultaneously, to taking a distance learning course in the evenings. Likewise, a number of universities also offer distance programming targeted to this audience.

Quality control may be a concern with dual credit courses, in part because they are so varied in their design, but also because tuition costs and teacher requirements are highly variable. In some cases, students may receive a discounted tuition rate from the college, but if they want to attend a different postsecondary institution, the credits will not travel with them until they pay the full tuition. In addition, some colleges and universities limit the number of transfer credits accepted. Program coordinators and students need to be aware that these potentials exist; making informed decisions in advance of graduation is critical.

Early Entrance to College

Some institutions of higher education provide for the option of early entrance to college, thereby allowing high school students to attend college on a full-time basis before they have graduated from high school. Typically, this option is reserved for highly gifted students who have moved through their K–12 experience at an accelerated pace. In many cases, this is done on an individual basis; a student applies for and is accepted to begin college work at a relatively young age and takes college classes with older students.

A smaller subset of colleges, however, offers specific programs tailored to these younger students to assist in transitioning effectively to the university. The University of Iowa's Belin-Blank Center, for example, creates a residential cohort as students move from their sophomore or junior year of high school to college. Common schedules, weekly seminars, meetings with a counselor, cohort activities, and common housing all support gifted students during the transition. Likewise, Mary Baldwin College provides two programs for early entrance: one allows students ages 13–15 to enter college without requiring any time spent attending a traditional high school, while the other enables students age 16 or 17 to complete high school and college credits simultaneously. It is important to note that this type of program is residential and geared toward supporting the various social and emotional issues that tend to emerge for younger advanced learners in collegiate settings.

Early entrance programs have had good track records, primarily because they offer a complete package for the advanced student who requires more academic challenge than is available at the high school. Not every child is ready for this experience early, however. Students and families need to consider the student's prior experiences, academic performance, maturity, and academic and career goals.

Special Schools: Governor's Schools

Some states have governor's schools that provide advanced learning opportunities for secondary gifted students in a residential environment. Typically, they focus on academic, artistic, interdisciplinary, social, and/or emotional areas so that students are able to explore their potential with other students of similar ability. Their programs vary greatly in funding sources and levels, type and amount of oversight, full time versus part time, nomination and selection criteria and procedures, discipline focus (e.g., STEM, arts), and implementation. Limited spaces are typical, and currently not every state offers this option for advanced students.

Special Schools: Magnet Schools

Magnet schools generally exist in large districts or across districts within a state. They are public schools that enroll students from multiple school boundaries and often provide a thematic focus for curriculum, activities, and/or school services.

Historically, magnet schools in the United States were created to eliminate the problem of de facto segregation within schools. Because students choose magnet schools based on the focus area rather than geographical boundaries, a more diverse student population is typical. Entrants may need to meet particular qualifications prior to being accepted (in some cases entrance examinations, auditions, or interviews).

Social and Emotional Supports

Curricular offerings are only one of several important components to providing high-quality services and programs for gifted students in secondary schools (NAGC, 2010). High-quality gifted programs also attend to myriad social and emotional concerns that can result from asynchronous development, or a mismatch of a student's social, cognitive, and physical development (Webb, Gore, Amend, & DeVries, 2007). Gifted students develop unevenly relative to their peers and may, therefore, be more advanced intellectually but behind physically or emotionally, which can create additional issues. Moreover, gifted students in middle and high schools who are balancing multiple commitments (academic and extracurricular) while striving to meet high expectations can experience high levels of stress and may benefit from available social and emotional supports (Foust, Hertberg-Davis, & Callahan, 2008; Peterson et al., 2015).

"Integrating affective issues into cognitive strategies will have a great impact since gifted youth often exclude the affective domain from decision making, overvaluing cognitive processes and undervaluing emotional ones" (Greene, 2005, p. 230). High-quality gifted programs offer purposeful, coordinated opportunities such as counseling, regular communication with students and families, flexible scheduling and grouping, and discussion groups promoting self-discovery and understanding of giftedness in adolescence (Peterson et al., 2015).

A thoughtfully coordinated, high-quality gifted program includes a plan for attending to the following issues often experienced in middle and high school:

- identity formation (including but not limited to cultural, ethnic, racial, and gender identities),
- underachievement,

- multipotentiality,
- perfectionism,
- stereotype threat, and
- career development.

See Chapter 9 for additional discussion and guidance regarding social and emotional supports for gifted students.

Transition Planning and Multiple Pathways

Adolescence is characterized by change; therefore, attending to this ever-present aspect of life in secondary schools is another way to ensure high-quality services for gifted learners. Transition planning and the creation of multiple pathways to access available opportunities have numerous positive benefits for gifted students and their families and can often be achieved through a few thoughtful conversations and administrative adjustments.

Of primary concern for educators striving to ease transitions within the school system is the sharing of information about individual student talents and interests, current performance levels, goals, and achievements. Although the student is the ultimate repository of this information, a formalized system of communication between adults (at varying grades, schools, departments, and/or programs) reduces the loss of instructional time or potential for misunderstanding of appropriate responses to student characteristics. Ultimately, face-to-face meetings scheduled with enough time for participating faculty to arrive prepared with copies of student profiles, records, or Individualized Education Plans (IEPs) are ideal; however, this may not always be possible—and it still won't address the learning differences of new students within a district or school. Other methods of information sharing such as an organized electronic records transfer or correspondence between guidance offices will suffice as long as a clear procedure is established that includes guidelines for who collects and transmits the information, who receives the information, and how information is processed upon arrival. Regardless of how the information is collected and shared, the ultimate goal is to ensure its use in curricular planning and supporting student success throughout all school experiences. To be highly effective, transitional plans should include final action steps for how the shared information will be disseminated and used.

Highly effective program planning also takes into account the shift in student roles and responsibilities that occur in secondary settings. As gifted adolescents move through middle and high school toward graduation, students frequently assume more responsibility and control for academic decisions as adult influence wanes (and peer influence flourishes), thereby making self-awareness and preparation for effective self-advocacy a growing necessity for secondary school students (NAGC, 2010). Gifted students benefit when they are afforded regular opportunities to develop a full understanding of their unique gifts and talents as well as corresponding learning differences. Seminars, discussion groups, advisory sessions, or other learning opportunities that allow students to engage with a like-minded peer group and increase in understanding of giftedness can also promote the exploration of various career paths and societal roles (Peterson, Betts, & Bradley, 2009).

Finally, due to shifting schedules, changing interests, and emerging issues in secondary settings, high-quality services provide multiple entrances and pathways for gifted students to develop their talents and access guidance from supportive adults. For example, a student who cannot find a way to fit a gifted seminar into his 10th-grade schedule may still relish the opportunity to work with a local physicist on the weekends, or a seventh grader may prefer to participate only in honors math classes this year (and not honors English) because of her prior struggles with creative writing. Decisions like these can have long-term effects on how a gifted student's talent develops so careful attention must be paid to the guidance and opportunities provided, especially during transitional periods for students.

Flexibility and Responsiveness to Individual Needs

As gifted students move through secondary schools, asynchrony and developmental changes may require schools to think about individualizing of programming and interventions to better meet student needs. All schools need to consider how they respond to students who have characteristics that may require individualized interventions or curricular adaptations. One size does not fit all; therefore, practitioners striving to create a high-quality secondary gifted program must consider proactively the multiple ways that they can support talent development and promote positive, engaging learning environments for all students. Moreover, they must ensure that gifted adolescents are aware that supports exist and how to take advantage of these resources to develop their talents and skills fully.

A host of concerns that affect gifted adolescents speak to the need to approach course scheduling at the secondary level with flexibility and a willingness to individualize rather than making assumptions about what course is next in the sequence. Students who must navigate the realities of meeting district requirements for graduation, pursuing their existing passion areas that could potentially garner scholarships in college, and pursuing possible new interests within the limitations of the school day may face impossible choices that they do not have experience to handle. Schools must be equipped to help gifted adolescents consider the implications of their decisions.

Professional Development Opportunities for Staff

Providing services to gifted students must be an integrated effort across school personnel rather than the responsibility of a few individuals.

Therefore, high-quality programs must provide ongoing, coordinated training and professional growth opportunities for all members of a secondary school staff (Dixon et al., 2014; NAGC, 2010). Counselors, teachers, and administrators should share responsibility for ensuring an appropriate level of academic challenge and support for gifted students when social and emotional issues present themselves. Teachers may assume that a class designated as honors, gifted, or AP comprises an inherently homogeneous class of students, yet secondary schools rarely provide staff development to recognize and address the wide range of learners in every classroom. To optimize learning, teachers must develop pedagogical tools to support student differences through effective differentiation strategies.

Support for the unique social and emotional needs of all secondary students is critical. Counselors and teachers of gifted students need to understand how differences may, on occasion, present unique challenges in the social realm for gifted students or may present emotional challenges for them. Moreover, educators should be provided the tools to know when to refer or how to intervene. Therefore, a high-quality program must attend to the learning of middle and high school faculty and staff as well as gifted students. (See Chapter 12 for additional guidance.)

EXAMPLE IN NEED OF REVISION

During the spring of her first year as the enrichment coach at Kitville Middle School, Jenny Edwards contacted the head guidance counselor at the high school to learn more about next year's programming options for the eighth-grade students. Her goal was to provide some specific guidance for families concerned about making a smooth transition from the middle school environment where small teams of teachers and the enrichment coach are able to plan for students' individual learning differences to the larger, departmentalized high school where students are responsible for advocating for themselves.

The counselor, Zach Miller, responded promptly and thanked Jenny for reaching out for more details. "Like many schools in the state, we've been working hard for the past decade to provide a wider variety of AP classes for our students at Kitville High—even offering two for qualifying freshman. It's a great way to help our families save some college tuition money. Why don't I send you the link to find this information in our course catalog?"

"That would be a great start," responded Jenny. "I know that our district budget doesn't allow for an enrichment coach at the high school, but are there any student groups or enrichment opportunities that I should let my students know about?"

"Well, at least the district is still investing in art and music instruction, so there are many different options for gifted students interested in those areas as well as tons of extracurricular activities. We've got a championship Quiz Bowl team, and I think the chess team is doing pretty well this year. With a little initiative, your students will be able to find something to keep them busy, I'm sure." Zach looked at his watch and thought of the recommendation letters he had to send out before he could head home for the evening. "Is there anything else you need from me?"

On the other end of the line, Jenny shook her head. "No, I think I've got a pretty clear picture of the options for the incoming gifted students. Thanks for your time."

This conversation was an example of a first step in attending to transitional issues for secondary gifted students. Nevertheless, additional attention to planning for gifted students moving into a new system will enhance opportunities for talent development and provide greater support for students and their families. Investing time now developing the transitional plan for all students will make the process easier to manage in the future.

Unfortunately, what Jenny recognized quickly in her conversation with Zach was that no actual program or coordinated group of services existed for gifted students at Kitville High School: Discrete AP courses and a few afterschool options do not, by themselves, make a program, particularly without the focused attentions of at least one adult who has knowledge and background in the characteristics of gifted students and appropriate service options. Within any secondary school's gifted population, there is great diversity; some students may find advanced coursework engaging and sufficient while others yearn for additional challenges and to study a topic in greater depth. Others may find navigating within a new system difficult, and still others are creative and do not fit neatly within the prescribed limits of the high school.

Likewise, Jenny still does not know if there are any faculty or counselors at the high school with expertise or interest in working with gifted students and their families. Without a gifted specialist or recognized contact person in the school, it will be challenging for some students to identify and access available learning opportunities aligned with individual skill sets and interests.

MAKEOVER EXAMPLE

Sighing, Jenny hung up the phone and thought about what to do next. She realized that coherence existed in some places, and she was worried about Kacy, who was already 3 years ahead in math and taking his third language besides English. She decided to call one of her friends from graduate school for advice. Melissa, who worked for a large district as the gifted facilitator, surely would have advice.

"Of course we have a transition plan!" exclaimed Melissa. "I'm happy to share it with you. First, we have a spreadsheet with all the students and their individual characteristics that suggest modifications in their program would serve them well, whether in the academic, social and emotional, or medical areas. That helps the high school counselors and teachers know what to prepare for."

"I could imagine a similar spreadsheet system could ease the transition from multiple elementary schools into our middle school program. And our sixth-grade teams would love that information as well," Jenny chimed in.

Melissa continued, "We also have a meeting with parents so that if they think their children will benefit from something beyond the usual program options—a course not in the typical sequence, for example—we have that request well enough in advance that those responsible for scheduling can put the student into the mix so that they know how many sections or what accommodations they'll need.

"In the past 5 years, I've been working to make sure that each high school has a gifted facilitator, whose job it is to get to know the students and advocate for them. Sometimes it's a full-time enrichment specialist, but in our smaller schools the specialist may be a dedicated staff member with training and a list of educators in the district to whom he or she can reach out for help or suggestions. Each high school also has a counselor with gifted training who can meet with students concerning schedules or other issues that may arise, so all the gifted students on our roll are assigned to that counselor.

"We created a menu of course offerings, as well as those that are distance learning options so that students could see the full array of what they may want to aim for as they move through the school.

"Finally, we have training every year about gifted pedagogy and communication within our middle and high schools so that teachers know what's available, best practices, and where to go if they see a problem or potential that isn't being addressed. Our administrators are also really great about encouraging data teams, and we are careful to focus on the needs not only of students who aren't successful, but also of those who are."

Jenny thought about these options and decided to get started making a positive difference in her own backyard.

ADVICE FOR GETTING STARTED

The first step in creating or enhancing services for gifted students in secondary schools is to determine what is already happening for this group. It is helpful to think of secondary gifted services as a menu of current options. Beginning with this kind of list of discrete elements that are already in place will help individuals charged with this important task recognize where the gaps are and consider creative—yet workable— solutions for providing optimal learning environments for gifted students in middle and high schools. In addition, there are numerous resources available from scholars and professional organizations—in print, online, or in person—to assist you in the strategic development and organization of services and program options.

Table 8.1 is a template designed to aid in the process of data gathering and to guide conversations of a strategic planning group or task force as

Table 8.1 Template to Jump-Start Your Thinking About Secondary Programs and Services

Trait	Focusing Question	What Are We Doing Now?	What Do We Want to Do?
Curricular offerings and adaptations	What options exist for gifted students to encounter advanced and/or more complex content (e.g., AP, IB, honors, dual enrollment, acceleration)?		
	What resources and supports exist for teachers to differentiate instruction and provide appropriate levels of challenge for gifted students throughout the school day?		
	What barriers exist in our school district for middle or high school students who have particular skill sets or who want to pursue an area of interest or advanced study?		
	What additional opportunities for talent development, acceleration, and exploration exist within the community (e.g., distance learning, mentorships, summer programs, extracurricular activities)?		
	Who is responsible for coordinating and aligning curricular offerings and tracking student participation?		
Social and emotional support	What evidence do we have to suggest that our students feel comfortable in expressing their gifts and talents in our secondary school(s)?		
	What opportunities exist for secondary students to develop self-understanding and effective self-advocacy skills?		
	What dispositions and habits of mind prepare gifted students for college and career (e.g., growth mindset, self-regulation, grit)? How do secondary students develop these at school?		
	What opportunities for cross-grade learning are afforded for gifted students to collaborate and communicate with peers of similar abilities and interests?		
	What plans exist to address issues that may arise for gifted adolescents including identity formation (e.g., gender, cultural, ethnic), multipotentiality, creativity, perfectionism, and underachievement?		
Transition planning and multiple pathways	How is information about gifted students shared within the school system to foster effective transitions (e.g., between grades, schools, departments, faculty)?		

Trail	Focusing Question	What Are We Doing Now?	What Do We Want to Do?
Transition planning and multiple pathways (cont.)	Who is responsible for maintaining student profiles, records, and/or Individualized Education Plans (IEPs)? How frequently are these items collected and updated?		
	How are curricular adaptations (e.g., independent study, mentorships, acceleration) proposed and coordinated? How have we informed students and parents regarding these alternate learning pathways?		
	What opportunities are provided for gifted students to explore and plan for new societal roles and professions?		
	What mentorship opportunities exist to help students discover their strengths, passions, and skills for future careers?		
Flexibility and responsive to individual needs	How are academic schedules and class selection organized? What options exist for cross-checking advanced course scheduling and addressing conflicts?		
	Who is responsible for helping secondary students access and/or navigate opportunities for appropriate challenge? What information is needed to effectively meet individual student needs?		
	How are secondary students included in the planning for and coordination of program and/or service delivery options?		
Professional development opportunities for staff	Who is responsible for the health and welfare of all the gifted students in the school building? Does each individual know specific strategies to use with this population?		
	What training exists in the special needs of gifted students for the gifted facilitator, counselors, and others who work with this population?		
	Have we identified institutions of higher learning that may offer coursework, endorsements, or certificates in gifted education for our teachers? What do we do to encourage all teachers to participate?		
	Who is available locally to assist with professional development for faculty and staff?		

they work to design or revise a coordinated program for gifted students in secondary schools.

Although this chapter provides advice for creating or improving programming and service delivery for gifted secondary students, it is important to consider how to ensure that your thoughtful, comprehensive implementation plan can continue long after the work of a task force (or fearless leader) has ended. As is emphasized in several other chapters in this text, developing a program that will last requires that it be codified in writing as part of school board policy. The policy should address who is served, for how long, under what conditions, the program focus, training needed on the parts of professionals, and other key details to ensure smooth transitions and positive learning environments for gifted students at all levels in the district, including secondary settings. Recurring short visits from students who have benefitted from your program planning are likely to help the school board and community members recognize the needs of gifted secondary students and the program as being a positive presence in your school.

ADVICE FOR THE SOLE PRACTITIONER

Often in secondary schools there may be no espoused or coordinated gifted program. Practitioners who find themselves in such a scenario should consider that there might still be bright spots in the landscape. First, assess what is already in place: advanced courses, academic clubs, summer programs that appeal to this population, training on the parts of certain faculty and staff members, and communication with parents, for example. Analyze what is already present, and determine where the holes are: What do we need to do better to ensure that our high-ability learners can make the most of their opportunities within the school? It may be that what is most lacking in your school or system is the coordination and planning that allow students to navigate the existing system and experience positive, growth-oriented learning opportunities. Seek the support of a sympathetic or encouraging administrator before designing or implementing changes, and remain open to joining school efforts or committees (e.g., data teams, curriculum reviews) that may yield opportunities for collaboration and idea sharing in the long run.

Although opportunities for connecting with colleagues at your school are limited now, there are benefits to seeking out others interested in gifted education at the secondary level. Many professional organizations and universities offer professional development and networking opportunities that can be pursued in person or online. In addition, neighboring schools and communities may be able to offer some examples of what has—and hasn't—worked in their middle and high schools, so you wouldn't need to reinvent every aspect of the program. Thinking beyond the school walls may also be a source of support in the planning and implementation process. Consider joining forces with community leaders, parents, students, and other interested individuals to help you plan program modifications so that you have buy-in on a larger level.

Finally, remember that change—particularly thoughtful positive change—takes time; a small, focused success may do more to win over fellow advocates and spur on continued positive growth than a massive overhaul with several stumbles and setbacks. So give yourself permission to break your plans down into smaller, more manageable steps while you build momentum and goodwill.

SUGGESTED RESOURCES

Dixon, F. A. (2008). *Programs and services for gifted secondary students: A guide to recommended practices.* Waco, TX: Prufrock Press.

Written as a companion reference to *The Handbook of Secondary Gifted Education*, this book is tailored for practitioners, administrators, and coordinators of gifted education programs seeking additional guidance on service and program options. The first section provides suggestions for academic, personal/social, and career exploration best practices for gifted adolescents. The next section describes various programmatic offerings in depth, and the third section offers an innovative vision for secondary gifted education practices.

Dixon, F. A., & Moon, S. M. (Eds.). (2015). *The handbook of secondary gifted education* (2nd ed.). Waco, TX: Prufrock Press.

Leading scholars have assembled research concerning major considerations of educating students in secondary settings in this service publication of the National Association for Gifted Children. Each of the 24 chapters address a range of issues, including social and emotional development of adolescents, identity and career development, effective programming options, components of effective curriculum and talent development for gifted secondary students, and extracurricular activities, as well as recommendations for staff development.

Olszewski-Kubilius, P. (2010). *Gifted adolescents.* Waco, TX: Prufrock Press.

Part of the Practical Strategies Series in Gifted Education, concise volumes focused on providing practical answers to common questions in gifted education, this text focuses on talent development in adolescence, critical issues for gifted students in secondary settings, and implications for educational practice and parenting.

Rakow, S. (2011). *Educating gifted students in middle school: A practical guide* (2nd ed.). Waco, TX: Prufrock Press.

This text is particularly valuable for readers seeking advice and insights specifically tailored to the middle grades. Rakow provides practical information about meeting the needs of gifted middle school students through program development, classroom practices, and research-based curricular adaptations. Each of the 11 chapters focuses on topics unique to the middle school experience, including chapters on Response to Intervention, middle school boys and other special populations, changing middle grade configurations, and differentiation strategies.

REFERENCES

Assouline, S., Colangelo, N., Lupkowski-Shoplik, A., Lipscomb. J., & Forstadt, L. (2009). *The Iowa Acceleration Scale: A guide for whole-grade acceleration K–8* (3rd ed.). Scottsdale, AZ: Great Potential Press.

Byrd, S., Ellington, L., Gross, P., Jago, C., & Stern, S. (2007). *Advanced Placement and International Baccalaureate: Do they deserve gold star status?* Washington, DC: Thomas B. Fordham Institute.

Colangelo, N., Assouline, S. G., & Gross, M. U. M. (2004). *A nation deceived: How schools hold back America's brightest students* (Vol. 1). Iowa City: The University of Iowa, The Connie Belin & Jacqueline N. Blank International Center for Gifted Education and Talent Development.

College Board. (n.d.). *AP course audit.* Retrieved from http://www.collegeboard .com/html/apcourseaudit/faq.html

Csikszentmihalyi, M., Rathunde, K., & Whalen, S. (1996). *Talented teenagers.* Cambridge, England: Cambridge University Press.

Dixon, F. A., & Moon, S. M. (Eds.). (2015). *The handbook of secondary gifted education* (2nd ed.). Waco, TX: Prufrock Press.

Dixon, F. A., Yssel, N., McConnell, J. M., & Hardin, T. (2014). Differentiated instruction, professional development, and teacher efficacy. *Journal for the Education of the Gifted, 37,* 111–127.

Foust, R. C., Hertberg-Davis, H., & Callahan, C. M. (2008). "Having it all" at sleep's expense: The forced choice of participants in Advanced Placement Courses and International Baccalaureate Programs. *Roeper Review, 30,* 121–129.

Foust, R. C., Hertberg-Davis, H., & Callahan, C. M. (2009). *Students' perceptions of the social/emotional implications of participation in Advanced Placement and International Baccalaureate programs* (RM09238). Storrs: University of Connecticut, The National Research Center on the Gifted and Talented.

Greene, M. J. (2005). Teacher as counselor: Enhancing the social, emotional, and career development of gifted and talented students in the classroom. *Gifted Education International, 19,* 226–235. doi:10.1177/026142940501900305

Hertberg-Davis, H. L., & Brighton, C. M. (2006). Support and sabotage: Principals' influence on middle school teachers' responses to differentiation. *Journal of Secondary Gifted Education, 17,* 90–102.

Hertberg-Davis, H., & Callahan, C. M. (2008). A narrow escape: Gifted students' perceptions of Advanced Placement and International Baccalaureate programs. *Gifted Child Quarterly, 52,* 199–216.

International Baccalaureate Organization. (n.d.). *Programmes.* Retrieved from http://www.ibo.org/en/programmes/

Karnes, F. A., & Bean, S. M. (Eds.). (2015). *Methods and materials for teaching the gifted* (4th ed.). Waco, TX: Prufrock Press.

Lang, D. M. (2007). Class rank, GPA, and valedictorians: How high schools rank students. *American Secondary Education, 35*(2), 36–48.

Moon, S. M., & Dixon, F. A. (2015). Conceptions of giftedness in adolescence. In F. A. Dixon & S. M. Moon (Eds.), *The handbook of secondary gifted education* (2nd ed., pp. 5–34). Waco, TX: Prufrock Press.

National Association for Gifted Children. (2010). *NAGC Pre-K–Grade 12 Gifted Programming Standards: A blueprint for quality gifted education programs.* Washington, DC: Author.

Peterson, J. S., Assouline, S. G., & Jen, E. (2015). Responding to concerns related to the social and emotional development of gifted adolescents. In F. A. Dixon & S. M. Moon (Eds.), *The handbook of secondary gifted education* (2nd ed., pp. 65–90). Waco, TX: Prufrock Press.

Peterson, J. S., Betts, G., & Bradley, T. (2009). Discussion groups as a component of affective curriculum for gifted students. In J. L. VanTassel-Baska, T. L. Cross, & F. R. Olenchak (Eds.), *Social-emotional curriculum with gifted and talented students* (pp. 289–317). Waco, TX: Prufrock Press.

Rakow, S. (2011). *Educating gifted students in middle school: A practical guide* (2nd ed.). Waco, TX: Prufrock Press.

Reis, S. M., Westberg, K. L., Kulikowich, J., Caillard, F., Hébert, T., Plucker, J., . . . Smist, J. M. (1993). *Why not let high ability students start school in January? The curriculum compacting study* (RM93106). Storrs: University of Connecticut, The National Research Center on the Gifted and Talented.

Renzulli, J. S., Gubbins, E. J., McMillan, K. S., Eckert, R. D., & Little, C. A. (Eds.). (2009). *Systems and models for developing programs and services for the gifted and talented* (2nd ed.). Waco, TX: Prufrock Press.

Sadler, P. M., & Tai, R. H. (2007). Weighting for recognition: Accounting for Advanced Placement and honors courses when calculating high school grade point average. *NASSP Bulletin, 91*(1), 5–32.

Tomlinson, C. A. (1999). *The differentiated classroom: Responding to the needs of all learners.* Alexandria, VA: Association for Supervision and Curriculum Development.

Warne, R. T., Nagaishi, C., Slade, M. K., Hermesmeyer, P., & Peck, E. K. (2014). Comparing weighted and unweighted grade point averages in predicting college success of diverse and low-income college students. *NASSP Bulletin, 98*, 261–279.

Webb, J. T., Gore, J. L., Amend, E. R., & DeVries, A. R. (2007). *A parent's guide to gifted children.* Tucson, AZ: Great Potential Press.

Chapter 9

Services That Meet the Social and Emotional Needs of Gifted Children

Maureen Neihart, PsyD

DEFINITION

Social and emotional needs are psychosocial conditions that must be met to ensure well-being and high achievement. These needs influence all other aspects of development and involve intrapersonal and interpersonal competencies, self-esteem, self-regulation, and self-beliefs. Meeting social and emotional needs involves more than guidance and counseling services or affective activities in the classroom. It is a comprehensive approach to supporting gifted students so that they experience well-being and develop their talents to the highest possible level. It is an approach that develops psychosocial competencies as an integrated part of talent development (Bloom, 1985; Cross & Cross, 2011; Dweck, 2012; Frederickson & Branigan, 2005; Neihart, 2016; Subotnik, Olszewski-Kubilius, & Worrell, 2011).

RATIONALE

Social and emotional needs are at the heart of well-being and are the foundation for achievement. A large literature exists about the unique psychological issues of the gifted (see Neihart & Yeo, 2016, for a review).

Studies suggest that although gifted children as a group generally demonstrate good adjustment, many such children need targeted assistance to cope with their peer relationships, perfectionism, asynchronous development, situational stressors, and postsecondary planning. We also know that the attitudes, competencies and beliefs necessary for well-being and talent development can be systematically strengthened through targeted interventions and experiences (Becker & Luthar, 2002; Blackwell, Trzesniewski, & Dweck, 2007; Chua, 2014; Ericsson, Charness, Feltovich, & Hoffman, 2006; Miller et al., 2012). In addition, the academic success of twice-exceptional children is often connected to their social and emotional development (Foley-Nicpon, 2016). They typically face greater academic, social, and emotional challenges in school due to the large discrepancies in their abilities. Therefore, any gifted or talent development program aiming to promote well-being and high achievement must include systematic and targeted efforts to address students' social and emotional needs and develop their psychosocial competencies.

GUIDING PRINCIPLES AND ATTRIBUTES THAT DEFINE HIGH QUALITY

There are three guiding principles for developing services to meet the social and emotional needs of gifted students in the research. The first is that there is *no substitute for challenge in the curriculum and interactions with others with similar interests, ability, and drive* (e.g., true peers). These two provisions are essential for well-being and high achievement among high-ability students. A good counselor or well-developed classroom affective activities will not compensate for the negative impact caused by lack of challenge and little access to true peers (Neihart, Pfeiffer, & Cross, 2016a; Plucker, 2015). Truly exemplary services and programs ensure opportunities for high-ability students at all levels to work with similar peers during some of the school day. There are many ways to provide these opportunities, but flexible grouping arrangements for learning, subject and grade acceleration, multiage learning activities, and across-grade-level classrooms are a few well-known examples (Horvat & Lewis, 2003).

The second guiding principle is that *one approach does not fit all*. Gifted children are a widely diverse group, which means that a variety of interventions and supports must be provided to meet their social and emotional needs. Accommodations must be differentiated to address variations related to ability, gender, domain of talent, age, culture, and socioeconomic status. Such accommodations may be differentiated along a continuum, ranging from classroom guidance activities and parent meetings to focus groups, chat groups, online seminars or discussion groups, and individual and family counseling. Both electronic and face-to-face approaches should be provided.

The third principle is that *provisions must be designed systematically and purposively and based on the best available evidence* (Neihart, Pfeiffer, & Cross,

2016b). All stakeholders should be involved in collaborative efforts to determine policies and practices that are grounded in the best science whenever possible. (See Chapter 17 regarding scientifically based research practices.)

These three guiding principles set the backdrop for our thinking about school-based approaches to meeting the social and emotional needs of highly able young people. The next step is to consider a vision for high-quality provisions in the classroom and within the larger school community. Exemplary services share six attributes.

- Services are informed by the *best possible evidence* base. This means evaluating the best available research and integrating it with practitioner expertise and with the needs and characteristics of gifted students in the school. Policies and practices should also be determined in ways that are congruent with the organizational and community context.

- Services should be *culturally and contextually relevant*. The psychosocial skills and attitudes needed for well-being and achievement are consistent across many cultures and contexts; however, there is evidence of some important distinctions regarding emotional expression, self-beliefs, and mental health across some cultural groups (Markus & Kitayama, 1991; Peters & Williams; 2006). Moreover, social and emotional needs can vary across socioeconomic levels, gender, ethnicity, and culture. Services should be developed with these variables in mind. Services must be sensitive to cultural differences in needs, characteristics, and values. Diversity can be often addressed by using flexible grouping practices, by leveraging technology, and by ensuring that resources and materials are culturally sensitive.

- Exemplary programs support *provisions for different forms of acceleration*, including subject acceleration, grade skipping, and early entrance to school or college when appropriate. Subject or grade acceleration is not appropriate for all high-ability students, but extensive research concludes that these two practices are the most effective intervention for some high-ability children when they are carefully selected (Colangelo, Assouline, & Gross, 2004; Neihart, 2007). Therefore, exemplary programs have written policies that describe how such decisions are made and implemented. The best practices use objective and norm-referenced measures such as the Iowa Acceleration Scale (Assouline, Colangelo, Lupkowski-Shoplik, Lipscomb, & Forstadt, 2009) to assist with the decision making about grade acceleration.

- Services should be *systematic and integrated* across grade levels. In other words, there should be a clearly articulated plan for services across the school district that is consistent, well ordered, and efficient. Students should not encounter gaps in services when they move from one level to another or from one school to another.

- Services should also be *developmental.* They should be matched to the particular developmental needs and characteristics of children of various ages, and they should reflect a progression that builds on earlier learning and developmental milestones and anticipates future needs.
- Services have a *schoolwide emphasis.* All school personnel working with high-ability students are prepared to address their social and emotional needs.

EXAMPLE IN NEED OF REVISION

As you read the following example of Wellspring School District, reflect on your own school system. Compare your provisions for the social and emotional needs of gifted children with those described here. In what ways are your services similar? In what ways are they different?

Wellspring School District strongly believes in the importance of inclusion and equality for all students. Their motto is "Together we achieve." They are widely recognized in the region for their commitment to supporting children with special needs as well as those with special gifts or talents. They are committed to mixed-ability classrooms and offer a weekly pull-out program for identified gifted students at both the elementary and middle school levels. The district has no written policy on acceleration and no child has ever been grade skipped. Since the implementation of the Common Core State Standards Initiative (CCSS), the district has set a policy prohibiting within-classroom ability grouping (Plucker, 2015). Middle school principals will allow subject acceleration when parents insist, but elementary principals do not allow it. At the high school, a wide range of advanced courses is offered, including Advanced Placement (AP) classes. These classes tend to have few students from minority groups, although they comprise 19% of the student body. There is no affective curriculum for the high school other than what is taught through health classes. Advanced students do not receive any targeted instruction on psychosocial skills needed to develop their talent. Although there are no formalized opportunities for enrichment at the high school, there is a mentorship program run by the guidance office for interested students (Subotnik, Edmiston, Cook, & Ross, 2010).

The elementary counselors spend half their time conducting developmental guidance activities in the regular classrooms and the other half running small groups and individual counseling. No differentiated guidance services are provided for high-ability students. At the middle school, the school counselor works with the gifted resource teacher to provide affective activities in the classroom and also runs a few small counseling groups for high-ability students (Peterson, 2008). High school counselors focus mostly on college advising for college-bound students and on intervention counseling for students at risk or in crisis.

Schoolwide professional development on the social and emotional needs of gifted children has never been offered, but training on differentiated instruction was provided 3 years ago. The district does provide financial support for interested teachers to take specialized courses or workshops. Recently, 15 teachers completed a master's degree in gifted education at a local university. There are also many opportunities for informal updates for interested personnel. Teachers may attend the annual state conference and are provided with information updates through short presentations at faculty meetings, optional afternoon meetings, and an internal Listserv. The district also has an internal website devoted to special needs education that includes pages devoted to meeting the needs of gifted students. In addition, the district has begun to build capacity with Professional Learning Communities (PLCs).

Parents of high-ability children volunteer as aides in both the elementary classrooms and the middle school pull-out program. A few parents serve as mentors to individual secondary students, and there is an online parent newsletter that usually addresses one social or emotional topic in each issue. Four times a year, large group meetings are held for parents of high-ability children.

PROCEDURES FOR REVISION

How does your school's services compare to Wellspring's provisions? Wellspring's approach is common. Several changes could be made to meet the social and emotional needs of high-ability students more effectively.

First, the district should ensure that acceleration options are available to qualified students. To be most effective, teachers and administrators need training that builds understanding that acceleration options such as grade skipping, subject acceleration, early entrance, and concurrent enrollment are effective means for promoting high achievement and healthy adjustment for qualified students. The district should develop a brief written policy that describes the procedures parents and teachers are to follow when they wish to recommend a student for acceleration options. They might use the Iowa Acceleration Scale (Assouline et al., 2009) to use with parents and child-study teams when making decisions about acceleration.

Further, the district should evaluate whether students have adequate access to learn with others with similar interests, abilities, and motivation. There should be provision for grouping arrangements that facilitate this access to true peers so that students spend time working at their edge of competence, developing their talent as well as the attitudes, beliefs, and interpersonal skills needed for high performance and well-being. This will require a coordinated effort by teachers, school guidance teams, and administrators.

In addition, opportunities for enrichment should be provided district-wide so that all students have opportunities to demonstrate abilities that may be hidden. Enrichment can take many forms, including mini-courses; apprenticeships; online workshops, classes, or courses; independent studies;

small group investigations; or Saturday programs. Enrichment can also be provided within the classroom through instructional strategies that leverage technology to support differentiated learning and students' interests (Reis, McCoach, Little, Muller, & Kaniskan, 2011).

There is a clear need for expanded and differentiated guidance services at all levels, but especially at the high school where the counselors are engaged predominantly in college planning with older students. Interested counselors who understand the social and emotional development of gifted children and the psychosocial skills necessary for talent development could be encouraged to provide targeted intervention, workshops, or counseling groups and to consult with teachers regarding systematic strategies they can use to strengthen the psychosocial competencies needed to develop talent. There should be particular emphasis on developing the psychosocial skills necessary for high performance, such as regulation of emotion and motivation, goal setting, and managing stress or anxiety (Calderon & Subotnik, 2007; Church, Elliot, & Gable, 2000; Delisle & Galbraith, 2003; Grant & Dweck, 2003; Luzzo & Gobet, 2011; Midgley, Kaplan, & Middleton, 2001; Neihart, 2008, 2016; Preuss & Dubow, 2004; Subotnik et al., 2011).

MAKEOVER EXAMPLE

Individuals interested in enhancing the services provided to meet the social and emotional need of gifted students formed a task force to conduct a needs assessment among all stakeholders. The assessment included where and how specific psychosocial skills needed for high achievement were being taught and developed throughout the district. Based on data that were gathered, the task force prioritized needs and proposed an action plan to address them. The plan was approved by the administration, sanctioned by the board of education, and implemented over 2 years.

Recognizing that ensuring challenge in the curriculum is foundational to talent development and well-being for high-ability students, a team of Wellspring practitioners met to craft a policy for grade and subject acceleration and to determine provisions that could be made related to acceleration and ability grouping district-wide. They gathered examples of policies from other districts (e.g., Ohio Department of Education, 2006) and used the National Workgroup on Acceleration Guidelines (Colangelo et al., 2010) to craft a written policy to guide parents, teachers, and administrators in making effective decisions about various options. They recommended the use of the Iowa Acceleration Scale (Assouline et al., 2009) as part of evaluation procedures for students being considered for grade skipping in particular.

In an effort to improve its identification of students with hidden talents, the district expanded enrichment opportunities for all students by instituting mini-courses and enrichment clusters at the elementary and middle school levels and by providing ongoing training in a wide variety of classroom enrichment strategies for all teachers (Tomlinson, 2014; Winebrenner, 2012).

One counselor at the high school was identified as a specialist in guidance services for talented students and was provided with additional training. She offers one seminar or workshop for a group of interested students each quarter. In addition, a middle school counselor collaborates with teachers to provide exploratory college and career activities. He also offers a focus group on college/career planning each semester for interested students and families. At all levels, there is increased collaboration between the school counselor and those teachers who work with high-ability students. The counselors provide mini-workshops on topics such as stress and time management, effective goal setting, developing optimal mindsets, bullying, and healthy competition (Pargman, 2006; Pekrun, Elliot, & Maier, 2009).

The following broad, affective goals were agreed on for the district's high-ability students:

- Students at all levels will explore enrichment opportunities.
- Students will be able to describe in their own words ways that persons with high ability may be similar to and different from others.
- Students in Grade 3 and higher will be able to identify six psychosocial skills needed for talent development and well-being.
- Students will be able to demonstrate strategies for strengthening the psychosocial skills needed to develop their talent and maintain well-being. Such skills might include strategies for managing anxiety, maintaining rest and recovery routines, improving flexibility, developing more optimistic thinking, coping with setbacks, and managing perfectionism.
- All secondary gifted students will be able to advocate for their learning needs with classroom teachers.
- Beginning in the middle school, gifted girls, gifted students of color, and disadvantaged gifted students will evaluate potential conflicts that may arise for them that stem from mixed messages about achievement and belonging.
- Students will explore postsecondary options relevant to their interests, goals, and values.
- Parents of gifted students will be able to explain the ways that the development and education of high-ability children differs from those of other children.
- Parents will encourage and support their children in appropriate self-advocacy at school.

At least three objectives for each goal were determined for elementary, middle, and high school gifted students. The district now has more of a scope and sequence for affective curriculum within services for gifted students. For example, here are objectives for Goal 4 at the middle school level:

- Students will compare and contrast three strategies for rest and recovery and determine which one is more effective for their individual use.
- Students will demonstrate three different strategies for managing anxiety and be able to document which strategy works best for them in different kinds of situations.
- Students will evaluate personal self-beliefs that are adaptive and maladaptive and demonstrate at least one strategy they can use to strengthen adaptive self-beliefs.

The district designed a method for evaluating the impact of these changes every 3 years. A stratified sample of students, teachers, and parents is asked annually to complete a short questionnaire about student achievement and psychosocial progress. A small number of randomly selected students and their parents are also invited every 2 years to be interviewed about the program's impact on the students' social and emotional needs and achievement.

ADVICE FOR GETTING STARTED

The strategic plan provided below can be used to jump-start the process of revising or creating gifted programming and service options to meet the social and emotional needs of high-ability students more effectively.

- **Objective:** To develop or improve school services that address the social and emotional needs of high-ability students.
- **Evidence:** A menu of documented supports, interventions, and policies that support the social and emotional needs of gifted students in Wellspring School District.
- **Tasks:** Conduct a survey of current provisions, identify priorities for improvement, and develop an action plan for making improvements.

Table 9.1 on the next page shares an example plan by month highlighting actions, the person responsible, and evidence that indicates the actions are successful.

Finally, the assessment scale in Table 9.2 (page 131) is offered as a tool to begin the evaluation of services to meet the social and emotional needs of high-ability students in a district. Each item is scored on a 4-point scale; the higher the rating, the more likely it is that the district has exemplary services to support gifted students. Very low and very high ratings on individual items illuminate weaknesses and strengths, respectively.

ADVICE FOR THE SOLE PRACTITIONER

Sole practitioners can be encouraged. There is robust evidence that small changes can have a big impact on children's overall adjustment. Relationships are central to both well-being and talent development, so

Table 9.1   Action Plan by Month

Date	Action	Person Responsible	Evidence
Month 1	Meet with guidance personnel to identify services provided for gifted students	Gifted coordinator	List of services by school
Month 1	Create online, anonymous survey for teachers	Advisory committee chair	Electronic survey
Month 2	Circulate survey to all teachers to identify provisions, gaps, and priorities	Building administrator	Electronic survey results
Month 2	Review electronic survey results	Advisory committee chair	Short, narrative summary of key findings with list of priorities
Month 3	Formulate online, anonymous parent survey	Parent and gifted teacher	Electronic questionnaire
Month 3	Invite parents to complete online questionnaire	Chair of parent advisory group	Summary of electronic results
Month 4	Summarize questionnaire results	Chair of parent advisory group	List of key findings and priorities
Month 4	Create anonymous, online student questionnaire	Advisory committee chair	Finished questionnaire
Month 4	Select stratified sample of students	Director of technology	List of student names with their homeroom teacher
Month 5	Students complete online questionnaire during homeroom	Building administrator	Electronic survey results
Month 6	Review results of student questionnaires	Advisory committee chair	List of key findings and priorities; selected examples of student comments
Month 6	Identify top three priorities for services and staff development	Advisory committee chair	List of priorities
Months 7–8	Write action plan to address priorities	Gifted coordinator	Written action plan

Table 9.2   Assessing Services to Meet the Social and Emotional Needs of High-Ability Students

1. All personnel have had training in the social and emotional needs of gifted students and the psychosocial skills necessary for talent development.	1	2	3	4
2. All high-ability students have frequent access to others with similar interests, ability, and drive.	1	2	3	4
3. All high-ability students are challenged in the regular classroom.	1	2	3	4
4. A range of acceleration options is available.	1	2	3	4
5. There is a written policy for acceleration.	1	2	3	4
6. The differentiated needs of high-ability students from culturally diverse backgrounds are recognized and addressed.	1	2	3	4
7. Guidance personnel work collaboratively with teachers of high-ability students to address social and emotional needs and to strengthen psychosocial skills needed to develop talent.	1	2	3	4
8. Differentiated guidance services are offered for high-ability students at the elementary level.	1	2	3	4
9. Differentiated guidance services are offered for high-ability students at the middle school level.	1	2	3	4
10. Differentiated guidance services are offered for high-ability students at the high school level.	1	2	3	4
11. Parents regularly receive information related to the social and emotional needs and psychosocial skills of their high-ability children.	1	2	3	4
12. There is district-wide agreement concerning desired psychosocial outcomes for high-ability students.	1	2	3	4
13. Broad goals for meeting social and emotional needs of high-ability students have been identified at the elementary level.	1	2	3	4
14. Broad goals for meeting social and emotional needs of high-ability students have been identified at the middle level.	1	2	3	4
15. Broad goals for meeting social and emotional needs of high-ability students have been identified at the high school level.	1	2	3	4
16. There is an identified curriculum to develop and strengthen psychosocial skills necessary for talent development and well-being with a scope and sequence across grade levels.	1	2	3	4

Note: 1 = Not at all; 2 = To a limited extent; 3 = Satisfactory; 4 = Exemplary

anything and everything that sole practitioners can do to support and strengthen the relationships high-ability children have with adults and peers will be helpful. Providing interested teachers and school counselors with succinct, practical information about specific strategies to improve well-being and develop the psychosocial skills needed to develop talent will increase the number of adults who can effectively respond to gifted students in a variety of contexts throughout the school day (Cross & Cross, 2011; Dweck, 2012; Neihart, 2008; Neihart et al., 2016a).

In addition, educating parents about the social and emotional characteristics and needs of their children, as well as the psychosocial skills needed for high achievement, will help them be better advocates and stronger partners with their child's school.

If sole practitioners have time to conduct guidance activities themselves, they will find many useful resources to guide them (e.g., Cross & Cross, 2011; Neihart, 2008, 2016; Peterson, 2008; Pfeiffer & Burko, 2016; Seligman, 1995, 2011). In addition, it can be helpful to team with the school counselor to offer psychoeducational or support groups for gifted students. This approach enhances the awareness of the counselor about the needs and issues of gifted students and enhances the guidance skills of the sole practitioner. Taking active steps to strengthen relationships with school guidance personnel will facilitate learning from one another.

Finally, there will be times when sole practitioners find that they are the only ones available to provide direct guidance to gifted students or their families. At those times, practitioners need to be prepared with referral information regarding local specialists, national information centers, and reliable websites to access the information and support that they need. Taking a small amount of time up front to prepare a list of locally accessible specialists and centers will enable single practitioners to dispense high-quality referrals and recommendations efficiently. A list of websites and organizations will prove equally valuable.

SUGGESTED RESOURCES

Cross, T. L., & Cross, J. R. (Eds.). (2011). *Handbook for counselors serving students with gifts and talents: Development, relationships, school issues, and counseling needs/interventions.* Waco, TX: Prufrock Press.

This is a comprehensive resource for school counselors working with gifted students. It combines theory with practical application. Topics include underachievement, suicide, perfectionism, peer relationships, and gender-specific issues, among many others.

Neihart, M., Pfeiffer, S. I., & Cross, T. L. (Eds.). (2016). *The social and emotional development of gifted children: What do we know?* (2nd ed.). Waco, TX: Prufrock Press.

This tightly organized text provides concise summaries of the empirical literature from the past 15 years on 22 topics related to the social and emotional development of gifted children, including gender differences, bullying, counseling, twice-exceptionality, depression, and areas of risk. A section on psychosocial factors associated with talent development details what we know about specific attitudes, self-beliefs, and psychosocial skills needed for high performance.

Peterson, J. S. (2008). *The essential guide to talking with gifted teens: Ready-to-use discussions about identity, stress, relationships and more.* Minneapolis, MN: Free Spirit.

This book explains how to conduct discussion groups that support social and emotional development for gifted teens; it includes a CD with corresponding printable resources. The book is organized around six areas of focus: identity, stress, relationships, feelings, family, and the future. Within each of these are additional subtopics, including bullying, cyber-aggression, sexuality, divorce, and loss. The book meets standards of the American School Counselor Association.

REFERENCES

Assouline, S. G., Colangelo, N., Lupkowski-Shoplik, A. E., Lipscomb, J., & Forstadt, L. (2009). *Iowa Acceleration Scale: A guide to whole grade acceleration K–8* (3rd ed.). Scottsdale, AZ: Great Potential Press.

Becker, B. E., & Luthar, S. S. (2002). Social-emotional factors affecting achievement outcomes among disadvantaged students: Closing the achievement gap. *Educational Psychologist, 37,* 197–214.

Blackwell, L. S., Trzesniewski, K. H., & Dweck, C. S. (2007). Implicit theories of intelligence predict achievement across an adolescent transition: A longitudinal study and an intervention. *Child Development, 78,* 246–263.

Bloom, B. (Ed.). (1985). *Developing talent in young people.* New York, NY: Ballantine.

Calderon, J., & Subotnik, R. (2007). Focus on the psychosocial dimensions of talent development: An important potential role for consultee-centered consultants. *Journal of Educational and Psychological Consultation, 17,* 347–367.

Chua, J. (2014). Dance talent development: Case studies of successful dancers in Finland and Singapore. *Roeper Review, 36,* 249–263.

Church, M. A., Elliot, A., & Gable, S. (2000). Perceptions of classroom environment, achievement goals, and achievement outcomes. *Journal of Educational Psychology, 93,* 43–54.

Colangelo, N., Assouline, S. G., & Gross, M. U. M. (2004). *A nation deceived: How schools hold back America's brightest students* (Vol. 1). Iowa City: The University of Iowa, The Connie Belin & Jacqueline N. Blank International Center for Gifted Education and Talent Development.

Colangelo, N., Assouline S., Marron, M. A., Castellanos, J., Clinkenbeard, P., Rogers, K., . . . Smith, D. (2010). Guidelines for developing an academic acceleration policy. *Journal of Advanced Academics, 21,* 180–203.

Cross, T. L., & Cross, J. R. (Eds.). (2011). *Handbook for counselors serving students with gifts and talents: Development, relationships, school issues, and counseling needs/interventions.* Waco, TX: Prufrock Press.

Delisle, J., & Galbraith, J. (2003). *When gifted kids don't have all the answers: How to meet their social and emotional needs.* Minneapolis, MN: Free Spirit.

Dweck. C. S. (2012). Mindsets and malleable minds: Implications for giftedness and talent. In R. F. Subotnik, A. Robinson, C. M. Callahan, & E. J. Gubbins (Eds.), *Malleable minds: Translating insights from psychology and neuroscience to gifted education* (pp. 7–18). Storrs: University of Connecticut, The National Research Center on the Gifted and Talented.

Ericsson, K. A., Charness, N., Feltovich, P. J., & Hoffman, R. R. (Eds.). (2006). *The Cambridge handbook of expertise and expert performance*. New York, NY: Cambridge University Press.

Foley-Nicpon, M. (2016). The social and emotional development of twice-exceptional children. In M. Neihart, S. I. Pfeiffer, & T. L. Cross (Eds.), *The social and emotional development of gifted children: What do we know?* (2nd ed., pp. 103–118). Waco, TX: Prufrock Press.

Frederickson, B. L., & Branigan, C. (2005). Positive emotions broaden the scope of attention and thought-action repertoires. *Cognition and Emotion, 19*, 313–332.

Grant, H., & Dweck, C. (2003). Clarifying achievement goals and their impact. *Journal of Personality and Social Psychology, 85*, 541–553.

Horvat, E. M., & Lewis, K. S. (2003). Reassessing the "Burden of Acting White": The importance of peer groups in managing academic success. *Sociology of Education, 76*, 265–280.

Luzzo, D., & Gobet, F. (2011). The neglected importance of emotions. *Talent Development & Excellence, 3*, 85–87.

Markus, H. R., & Kitayama, S. (1991). Culture and the self: Implications for cognition, emotion, and motivation. *Psychological Review, 98*, 224–253.

Midgley, C., Kaplan, A., & Middleton, M. (2001). Performance-approach goals: Good for what, for whom, under what circumstances, and at what cost? *Journal of Educational Psychology, 93*, 77–86.

Miller, E. M., Walton, C. M., Dweck, C. S., Job, V., Trzesniewski, K. H., & McClure, S. M. (2012). Theories of willpower affect sustained learning. *PLoS ONE, 7*(6), e38680.

Neihart, M. (2007). The socioaffective impact of acceleration and ability grouping: Recommendations for best practice. *Gifted Child Quarterly, 51*, 330–341.

Neihart, M. (2008). *Peak performance for smart kids.* Waco, TX: Prufrock Press.

Neihart, M. (2016). Psychosocial factors in talent development. In M. Neihart, S. I. Pfeiffer, & T. L. Cross (Eds.), *The social and emotional development of gifted children: What do we know?* (2nd ed., pp. 159–171). Waco, TX: Prufrock Press.

Neihart, M., Pfeiffer, S. I., & Cross, T. L. (2016a). *The social and emotional development of gifted children: What do we know?* (2nd ed.). Waco, TX: Prufrock Press.

Neihart, M., Pfeiffer, S. I., & Cross, T. L. (2016b). What have we learned and what should we do next? In M. Neihart, S. I. Pfeiffer, & T. L. Cross (Eds.), *The social and emotional development of gifted children: What do we know?* (2nd ed., pp. 283–298). Waco, TX: Prufrock Press.

Neihart, M., & Yeo, L. S. (2016). Psychological issues unique to the gifted. In S. I. Pfeiffer (Ed.), *Handbook of giftedness and talent.* Washington, DC: American Psychological Association.

Ohio Department of Education. (2006). *Model student acceleration policy for advanced learners.* Retrieved from http://www.fairborn.k12.oh.us/Downloads/accelerationpolicy[1].pdf

Pargman, D. (2006). *Managing performance stress: Models and methods.* New York, NY: Taylor & Francis.

Pekrun, R., Elliot, A. J., & Maier, M. A. (2009). Achievement goals and achievement emotions: Testing a model of their joint relations with academic performance. *Journal of Educational Psychology, 101*, 115–135.

Peters, H. J., & Williams, J. M. (2006). Moving cultural background to the foreground: An investigation of self-talk, performance, and persistence following feedback. *Journal of Sport Psychology, 18*, 240–253.

Peterson, J. S. (2008). *The essential guide to talking with gifted teens: Ready-to-use discussions about identity, stress, relationships and more.* Minneapolis, MN: Free Spirit.

Pfeiffer, S. I., & Burko, J. (2016). Counseling the gifted. In M. Neihart, S. I. Pfeiffer, & T. L. Cross (Eds.), *The social and emotional development of gifted children: What do we know?* (2nd ed., pp. 243–258). Waco, TX: Prufrock Press.

Plucker, J. A. (2015). *Common Core and America's high-achieving students.* Washington, DC: Fordham Institute. Retrieved from http://edexcellence.net/publications/common-core-and-americas-high-achieving-students

Preuss, L. J., & Dubow, E. F. (2004). A comparison between intellectually gifted and typical children in their coping responses to a school and a peer stressor. *Roeper Review, 26,* 105–111.

Reis, S. M., McCoach, D. B., Little, C. A., Muller, L. M., & Kaniskan, R. B. (2011). The effects of differentiated instruction and enrichment pedagogy on reading achievement in five elementary schools. *American Education Research Journal, 48,* 462–501.

Seligman, M. (1995). *The optimistic child.* New York, NY: HarperPerennial.

Seligman, M. (2011). *Flourish: A visionary new understanding of happiness and well-being.* New York, NY: Free Press.

Subotnik, R. A., Edmiston A. M., Cook, L., & Ross, M. D. (2010). Mentoring for talent development, creativity, social skills, and insider knowledge: The APA catalyst program. *Journal of Advanced Academics, 21,* 714–739.

Subotnik, R. A., Olszewski-Kubilius, P., & Worrell, F. (2011). Rethinking giftedness and gifted education: A proposed direction forward based on psychological science. *Psychological Science in the Public Interest, 12,* 3–54.

Tomlinson, C. A. (2014). *The differentiated classroom: Responding to the needs of all learners* (2nd ed.). Alexandria, VA: ASCD.

Winebrenner, S. (2012). *Teaching gifted kids in the regular classroom: Strategies and techniques every teacher can use to meet the academic needs of the gifted and talented.* Minneapolis, MN: Free Spirit.

Chapter 10

Attending to the Needs of Twice-Exceptional Learners

Megan Foley-Nicpon, PhD,
Alissa Doobay, PhD, and Soeun Park

What does it mean to have twice-exceptional students in your classroom? What are their needs? How are they similar to or different from any other student? In this chapter, we provide answers to these questions so educators can help these youth thrive in their academic and personal environments. We discuss identification and provision of support service challenges and provide strategies for educators to respond to students' concerns while enhancing their academic experiences.

WHAT IS TWICE-EXCEPTIONALITY?

Over the last 30 years, twice-exceptional students, or those who possess exceptional abilities as well as disabilities, have received greater attention in the field of gifted education. The history of the twice-exceptional movement is well documented in a recent issue of *Gifted Child Today* (Baldwin, Baum, Pereles, & Hughes, 2015), and readers quickly become aware of the great foundational contributions of scholars in the field (e.g., Baum, 1984; Baum & Owen, 1988, 2004; Brody & Mills, 1997; Neihart, 2000; Silverman, 1989; Yewchuk & Lupart, 1988). These scholars continue to make contributions to the expanding body of knowledge about twice-exceptional learners today.

The growing population of twice-exceptional students is estimated to be close to 400,000 (Foley-Nicpon & Cederberg, 2015), a figure that does not account for all those children who are served by a 504 Plan or who receive no special educational or accommodation services. Professionals, teachers, and parents have acknowledged the unique challenges that twice-exceptional students encounter in their academic and social lives, but many have limited knowledge about how to address and support this population (Foley-Nicpon & Assouline, 2015; Reis, Baum, & Burke, 2014).

Despite a practical need for clarity, defining twice-exceptionality is complicated (Foley-Nicpon, Allmon, Sieck, & Stinson, 2011). Generally stated, twice-exceptional students show talent in one or more domains and, at the same time, experience learning, social and emotional, or behavioral challenges (National Education Association, 2006). Some students may demonstrate artistic and leadership talent, but also experience social and emotional concerns, while others may attain high academic achievement in one area and manifest disabilities in another (Foley-Nicpon & Assouline, 2015). The multiple combinations of one or more gifted domains and disabilities create a variety of manifestations that obfuscate the assessment and identification of twice-exceptional students (National Education Association, 2006; Reis et al., 2014).

The complexity of twice-exceptionality can lead to what is commonly referred to as the *masking effect*, which impacts the provision of appropriate interventions (Foley-Nicpon et al., 2011). The National Twice-Exceptional Community of Practice (2E CoP) emphasized the masking effect in their recent agreement on the definition of twice-exceptionality:

> Twice exceptional (2e) individuals evidence exceptional ability and disability, which results in a unique set of circumstances. Their exceptional ability may dominate, hiding their disability; their disability may dominate, hiding their exceptional ability; each may mask the other so that neither is recognized or addressed. (Baldwin, Omdal, & Pereles, 2015, p. 218)

Once identified, twice-exceptional students commonly show discrepancies between their potential and actual achievement (Foley-Nicpon & Assouline, 2015; Morrison & Rizza, 2007). Thus, more emphasis should be placed on finding their specific areas of exceptionality to establish effective accommodations and interventions (Morrison & Rizza, 2007). In accordance with this consideration, Reis and colleagues (2014) proposed a new operational definition deriving from a professional symposium on twice-exceptional students:

> Twice-exceptional learners are students who demonstrate the potential for high achievement or creative productivity in one or more domains such as math, science, technology, the social arts, the visual, spatial, or performing arts or other areas of human productivity AND who manifest one or more disabilities as defined by federal or state eligibility criteria. These disabilities include specific learning disabilities; speech and language disorders; emotional/

behavioral disorders; physical disabilities; Autism Spectrum Disorders (ASD); or other health impairments, such as Attention Deficit/Hyperactivity Disorder (ADHD). These disabilities and high abilities combine to produce a unique population of students who may fail to demonstrate either high academic performance or specific disabilities. Their gifts may mask their disabilities and their disabilities may mask their gifts. (p. 221)

These comprehensive definitions are what guide this chapter's focus. It is essential to look at specific types of twice-exceptionality more closely, which is the focus of the next section where gifted and talented students with ASD, ADHD, Specific Learning Disabilities (SLD), and emotional and behavioral disturbances are briefly discussed. These specific disabilities were chosen because they are the ones most discussed in the previous literature (Foley-Nicpon, Assouline, & Colangelo, 2013) and are covered in the contemporary definitions created by experts in the field (Baldwin, Omdal et al., 2015; Reis et al., 2014).

Gifted Students With ASD

Common features of ASD include social impairment, a limited range of interests, and repetitive patterns of behaviors and activities (American Psychiatric Association [APA], 2013). High-ability students with ASD will present with the core symptoms required for diagnosis to varying degrees, but it can be challenging to understand the dichotomies separating high intellectual functioning from poor social skills (Foley-Nicpon et al., 2011; Foley-Nicpon & Assouline, 2015). These students may experience additional symptoms of depression, attention problems, and difficulties adjusting to change, but their lack of insight into coexisting problems leads them to underreport their challenges, which further complicates the assessment and identification process (Foley-Nicpon, Doobay, & Assouline, 2010).

Recent investigations of gifted students with ASD have provided insight into their academic and cognitive profiles (Assouline, Foley-Nicpon, & Dockery, 2012; Foley-Nicpon, Assouline, & Stinson, 2012). For instance, in Foley-Nicpon, Assouline, and Stinson's (2012) sample, students demonstrated high verbal ability with relatively worse short-term memory and significant deficits in processing speed. In addition, Assouline and colleagues (2012) suggested that lower-order thinking skills, such as working memory and processing speed, positively correlate with the students' academic achievements. These findings point to gaps between the potential and achievement of gifted students with ASD and the need for comprehensive assessments coupled with individualized interventions for this population.

Gifted Students With ADHD

Coexistence of giftedness and ADHD has been well documented in the literature (Antshel et al., 2008; Antshel et al., 2007; Foley-Nicpon et al.,

2011), where individuals exhibit high ability in one or more domains along with hallmark ADHD symptoms of inattention, hyperactivity, and impulsivity (APA, 2013). Because of these cognitive and behavioral challenges, gifted students with ADHD may undergo performance issues and emotional lability (Foley-Nicpon & Assouline, 2015). Their high ability may be underidentified or not noticed at all because it often is more pressing for teachers and parents to treat the students' inattention and hyperactivity symptoms than to program for their high-achieving domains (Foley-Nicpon at al., 2011; Reis at al., 2014). Yet, for those with high ability and ADHD, it is crucial to discover their outstanding abilities hidden by other exceptionalities. For example, Fugate, Zentall, and Gentry (2013) found gifted students with ADHD tend to show higher levels of creativity as well as poorer working memory than their undiagnosed counterparts. The authors proposed that creativity measures should be incorporated in the identification process to help include this group of learners in talent development opportunities (Fugate et al., 2013).

Gifted Students With SLD

Students with high cognitive ability can have coexisting difficulties in academic domains, such as reading, mathematics, and writing. However, students identified for special education services are not likely to be considered for gifted programming, even if it is educationally appropriate. For example, in Barnard-Brak, Johnsen, Pond Hannig, and Wei's (2015) recent study, only 11.1% of the 330 students in special education who had at least one score above the 90th percentile were enrolled in gifted programming. Why are these students underidentified as gifted? One reason may be the failure to operationalize what it means to have high ability and learning disabilities (Lovett & Sparks, 2011). That is, how high ability or giftedness is defined varies significantly (e.g., the multiple screening and identification criteria vary by school, school district, and state), as does how learning difficulties are identified (e.g., the difference between a student's ability and achievement scores, Response to Intervention [RTI] and curriculum-based assessment strategies, comprehensive assessment). Furthermore, this group of students are sometimes underidentified and underserved because the selection processes for gifted programs and special education are commonly mutually exclusive (Foley-Nicpon et al., 2011). That is, until very recently, that children could have both talent in math and a disability in writing was considered an impossibility. Because their performance often is at grade-level expectations, any challenges may be perceived as inconsequential to their academic success (Baum, Owen, & Dixon, 1991; Foley-Nicpon & Assouline, 2015). This can lead to frustration and confusion for students when academic output is not consistent with their advanced reasoning skills (Barnard-Brak et al., 2015). Finally, due to the masking effect, students with high abilities can mask their learning and processing difficulties, and vice versa (McCoach, Kehle, Bray, & Siegle, 2001; Pfeiffer, 2015).

Researchers have proposed it is crucial to focus on the expected potential and actual performance of gifted students with SLD, rather than emphasizing only their grade-level achievements (Assouline & Whiteman, 2011; Foley-Nicpon et al., 2011; Reis et al., 2014). Assouline, Foley-Nicpon, and Whiteman (2010) suggested the Wechsler family of tests provide a General Ability Index (GAI), which can be a better indicator of high academic abilities than a Full Scale IQ because it focuses on the student's higher-order thinking skills, such as cognitive comprehension, conceptualization, and reasoning. An evaluator may adopt a holistic approach including cognitive, academic, and psychosocial assessment data supplemented with contextual background information to better document the unique profiles of this population (Foley-Nicpon et al., 2011). Once identified, additional assessment to "confirm" profiles is a fruitless effort that distracts professionals from providing interventions in the students' areas of talent and academic difficulty (Wormald, Rogers, & Vialle, 2015).

Gifted Students With Emotional/Behavioral Concerns

Although most research findings have emphasized the academic challenges twice-exceptional individuals experience (Peterson & Morris, 2010), it is reasonable to assume that this population of students may encounter emotional challenges and gaps between their academic and social and emotional development (Foley-Nicpon et al., 2013). Twice-exceptional students are likely to experience lower than average self-esteem and self-concept, life satisfaction, and psychosocial functioning (Barber & Mueller, 2011; Foley-Nicpon, Rickels, Assouline, & Richards, 2012), which is often observed by parents and teachers, but not the students themselves (Assouline et al., 2010; Foley-Nicpon, Assouline, & Fosenburg, 2015). That is, twice-exceptional students may not be aware of or report their emotional and behavioral challenges; thus, a more in-depth look into their lives including their peer relationships, family background, attitudes and behaviors in different settings, and observations from multiple resources is necessary (Foley-Nicpon & Assouline, 2015).

Assessment of Twice-Exceptionality

Answering the question, "How do I identify a twice-exceptional student?" is challenging. Ostensibly, it requires gathering data from multiple sources, because talent domains are almost always identified in schools, and mental health disabilities or diagnoses are almost always identified outside of schools. This need for collaboration between two different professions (education and mental health) is easier said than done for a multitude of reasons, including sometimes different training and philosophical views, or different physical locations (e.g., a school or a mental health clinic) and goals for the child. The issue is further complicated by the changing landscape of how learning disabilities are identified in schools. In reaction to the deficiencies of the ability-achievement discrepancy model (difference between the student's cognitive abilities and scores on academic achievement tests), RTI, which is a tiered approach to intervention that is grounded in scores from curriculum-based assessments, has received additional momentum as a method of identifying students' educational difficulties in schools (McCallum et al., 2013; Ofiesh, 2006). In their discussion of gifted students with SLD, Assouline and Whiteman (2011) suggested that the discrepancy model, which focuses on the difference between students' expected and actual outcomes, may discover underserved gifted students with SLD who might not have been identified through a curriculum-based screening procedure. For instance, some students with gifted verbal ability may show lower reading achievement, indicating specific reading disabilities. This intra-individual approach enables educators to look into the students' strengths and weaknesses more closely and find their unique learning needs (Assouline et al., 2010). However, the discrepancy model also has many flaws, including failing to focus on the psychological processes involved in learning and the reliance on significantly discrepant numbers that may or may not adequately represent the rationale for the student's academic struggles (Ofiesh, 2006).

The RTI approach has been increasingly used in school systems to identify a student's potential strengths and weaknesses through an ongoing assessment and intervention format (Fuchs, Mock, Morgan, & Young, 2003; McCallum et al., 2013). Assouline and others (2010) raised concerns about this model, suggesting it will miss some twice-exceptional students who perform at or above grade level academically, which is significantly below their ability. The discussion on how to adjust an RTI model for this special population of students has just begun (McCallum et al., 2013). For instance, McCallum and colleagues (2013) proposed the use of liberal criteria of academic strengths and areas for growth during the screening phase to include a broader pool of potential twice-exceptional students. Yet the RTI approach also disregards the measurement of psychological processes that underlie academic difficulties, ignoring the reality that multiple origins can lead to the same outcome (Ofiesh, 2006).

Because of the deficits in the sole use of discrepancy model or RTI in identification of students with disabilities, including twice-exceptional students, many experts have recommended the use of comprehensive or holistic assessment approaches (Flanagan, Fiorello, & Ortiz, 2010; Foley-Nicpon et al., 2011; Hale et al., 2010; McCallum et al., 2013; Ofiesh, 2006). The comprehensive assessment procedure should include diverse forms of assessment, such as standard measures of achievement, ability, psychosocial functioning, executive functioning, cognitive processing, and clinical interviews to better understand contextual information about a student (Foley-Nicpon & Assouline, 2015; Hale et al., 2010). Furthermore, for students with disabilities to receive accommodations in college, a comprehensive evaluation is often required (Ofiesh & McAfee, 2000). Not only do we need to identify our twice-exceptional students' talent domains and their areas for growth for their time in K–12 education, but also information about cognitive processes is crucial to successfully transition into postsecondary settings. Students' disability status and legal protections must be in place so they can soar in their talent domains (Ofiesh, 2006).

GUIDING PRINCIPLES AND ATTRIBUTES THAT DEFINE HIGH QUALITY

To adequately identify and serve twice-exceptional students in schools, the following high-quality deliverables should be in place:

- **Comprehensive, collaborative identification methods.** This first deliverable has been discussed at length in the previous section. These methods should include information from achievement, cognitive, and psychosocial domains, along with parent and teacher reports of psychosocial factors that influence performance.
- **Service provision for talent domains.** As previously discussed, there are likely students identified for special education services who are not being equally considered for programming opportunities in their talent domains (Barnard-Brak et al., 2015). Therefore, taking an individual differences approach where the comprehensive data gathered for each student is analyzed not only for difficulties but also for strength domains is crucial. Once identified, accelerative and/or enrichment opportunities should be provided in the student's talent domain, depending on the individual student's needs. Acceleration can be a useful tool with twice-exceptional students (Foley-Nicpon & Cederberg, 2015), particularly in smaller schools (Schultz, 2012) because it provides an inexpensive and effective means of exposing twice-exceptional students to advanced content (Assouline, Colangelo, VanTassel-Baska, & Lupkowski-Shoplik, 2015). Additionally, emerging evidence is also pointing to the psychosocial benefits of summer enrichment programming for twice-exceptional students (Cederberg, Foley-Nicpon, & Park, 2015), which is an additional way to meet the student's specific talent development needs.
- **Service provision for special needs.** It should not be unusual for a student to be placed in the gifted or advanced section for English or math, yet at the same time visit the learning center to receive supports for organization and time management. Gone should be the days where we scratch our heads when we see a student identified for the extended learning or gifted program also belong to the friendship group at lunch. In 2008, Crim, Hawkins, Ruban, and Johnson, after examining more than 1,000 Individualized Education Plans (IEPs), discovered that no one was identified for gifted and talented or acceleration services, even though 112 had an ability score in the High Average range or above. As already noted, Barnard-Brak and colleagues (2015) had similar results. This practice must stop so that we realize a student with an IEP can also have

talent in one or more domains. Furthermore, if a student is identified for services in his or her talent domain, accommodations typically are still required (Schultz, 2012).

- **Promotion of self-understanding and self-advocacy skills.** Twice-exceptional students want to be successful not only in their K–12 education but also in their life after school. Emphasis should be paid to understanding what it means both to be high ability and to have a disability. Learning how to advocate for one's needs is a key feature to reaching success (Speirs Neumeister, Yssel, & Burney, 2013; Willard-Holt, Weber, Morrison, & Horgan, 2013), and these skills should be taught once the student reaches an appropriate developmental age (e.g., middle and high school).

EXAMPLE IN NEED OF REVISION

Jack's parents approached his third-grade teacher to discuss some concerns they had been having about his performance at school. They shared their perception that he is a bright and hardworking child who seems to struggle with writing tasks and has difficulty staying focused on his work. This leads to regular battles over homework at home. In addition, they feel that, despite his efforts, his performance at school does not reflect the intellect and drive for learning that he shows in conversations and other everyday interactions with them. His current performance is also discrepant from their expectations based on his precocious language development during his early years. He did not qualify for the school's talented and gifted program this year due to his performance on statewide assessments, which came as a surprise to them. They recalled that he had some early challenges learning to read, for which he briefly received Title I reading services, and they asked his teacher whether she thought he might have learning challenges in need of further intervention. Jack's teacher assured his parents that she would review Jack's educational records and discuss their concerns with the special education teacher and the school administrator.

In reviewing his classroom work, Jack's teacher found that he typically showed average to above average performance in comparison to his peers, and his third-grade DIBELS performance was slightly above the benchmark goal. His scores on statewide examinations similarly depicted him as a student with consistently average to above average academic abilities (reading: 64th percentile, writing skills: 49th percentile, math: 89th percentile, science: 82nd percentile, and social studies: 70th percentile). Jack's teacher reviewed these results with the special education teacher and school administrator, who all agreed that Jack was a well-behaved and responsible student who was performing at the expected level in school. Jack's teacher sent an e-mail to his parents explaining that Jack was doing well in school, was viewed as a joy to have in class, and that there was no need for his parents to be concerned.

Comments: This example illustrates how easily the learning needs of twice-exceptional students can be misunderstood when decisions are based solely on typical progress monitoring methods used within the schools. The relationship between the parents and teacher was positive and respectful, and the teacher appropriately involved other staff members, but there was insufficient information available to determine whether Jack had learning needs that differed from those of his peers. As a result, she was unintentionally dismissive of this family's concerns, and no changes were made to Jack's educational plan. Involving the school psychologist and the gifted and talented coordinator may have resulted in further testing being conducted to better elucidate Jack's learning profile and academic needs.

MAKEOVER EXAMPLE

Jack's parents approached his third-grade teacher to discuss some concerns they had been having about his performance at school. Following this conversation, Jack's teacher assured his parents that she would review Jack's educational records and discuss their concerns with the special education teacher, gifted education teacher, and the school administrator. Although all parties agreed that Jack's scores appeared to be consistent with those of a typical third-grade student, the gifted education teacher explained how learning and attention disorders can have a masking effect on a child's abilities. She described how a student with high cognitive abilities may be able to compensate for learning and attention challenges to such a degree that their performance does not fall below grade level, particularly during the elementary years, but that their learning challenges also limit them from demonstrating their potential. She recommended referring Jack for a comprehensive evaluation with the school psychologist, to which the rest of the team agreed.

The school psychologist completed a comprehensive assessment of cognitive, academic, and psychosocial functioning with Jack. His intellectual ability was assessed using the Wechsler Intelligence Scale for Children (5th ed.). He was found to have verbal reasoning ability in the Extremely High range (99.7th percentile), and he performed in the Very High range with regard to visual-spatial ability (95th percentile) and fluid reasoning ability (94th percentile). His working memory skills were in the High Average range (82nd percentile). However, he showed a weakness in processing speed, with a score in the Low Average range (18th percentile). His performance in this area was significantly impacted by fine motor difficulties. The results of academic testing using the Wechsler Individual Achievement Test (3rd ed.) were variable. He showed strong oral language (96th percentile) and mathematics (95th percentile) ability. In fact, his math skills were advanced for a fourth-grade student. He obtained an overall reading score at the 58th percentile, and an overall written language score at the 45th percentile. Although these latter two scores indicate that Jack has academic skills consistent with this grade level, they are significantly discrepant from his very superior verbal intellectual ability. Statistically, the discrepancy between Jack's verbal intellectual skills and his academic performance in the written language and reading domains occurs in less than 5% of the population. No significant challenges with executive functioning were noted on parent and teacher rating scales (Behavior Rating Inventory of Executive Function), and Jack's performance was within normal limits on the Conners Continuous Performance Test (2nd ed.). However, it was noted that he had greater difficulty sustaining his focus on reading and writing tasks due to his learning challenges. Psychosocial screening measures revealed that Jack was experiencing mild anxiety and low self-concept related to his academic challenges, but he appeared to be a generally well-adjusted child. Based on these results, the school psychologist diagnosed Jack with Specific Learning Disorder in the areas of reading and written expression.

The results of the evaluation were shared with Jack's parents, along with the school psychologist's recommendation that academic services and supports be initiated for addressing Jack's academic challenges and his areas of talent. Jack's parents participated in an additional meeting with the school team to develop an academic plan for meeting Jack's needs. Key outcomes following this meeting included the development and implementation of accommodations and supportive services through a 504 Plan within the school setting that included provision of additional time and a reduced-distraction environment to complete tests and quizzes, use of a computer and/or voice recognition software to complete written assignments, note-taking services, occupational therapy for fine motor challenges, and behavioral supports to improve focus while completing challenging academic tasks (e.g., reducing environmental distractions, having work chunked into short segments, providing frequent breaks, having an educator check his understanding of assignments before expecting him to work independently, providing rewards for demonstration of good effort). In addition, he was placed in the gifted and talented program at the school where he participated in enrichment activities and advanced-level problem-solving tasks. After working through the Iowa Acceleration Scale (Assouline, Colangelo, Lupkowski-Shoplik, Lipscomb, & Forstadt, 2009) with his educational team, Jack was accelerated 1 year in his math and science courses. Further recommendations were provided for enrichment programs in the community that matched Jack's interests and abilities, and Jack began receiving private tutoring to help build his reading and writing skills.

Several months later, Jack's parents again met with his teacher to express their appreciation for assisting them in better understanding and meeting their son's educational needs. They shared their perceptions that he was thriving in the gifted and talented program, and he was developing greater confidence in language arts. Jack's mother described the experience of having Jack evaluated as "empowering" due to being provided comprehensive information about his abilities and a wide range of options for addressing his learning needs. She shared, "We feel like we now have so much opportunity and so many tools to address his needs."

ADVICE FOR GETTING STARTED

Most professionals outside gifted education have limited to no awareness of the twice-exceptional phenomenon (Foley-Nicpon et al., 2013). Therefore, it is likely best to begin with professional development. Those familiar with the needs of the population are encouraged to talk to school administrators about providing professional development opportunities to increase the knowledge, awareness, and skills necessary for stakeholders, such as school psychologists, administrators, RTI teams, school counselors, and other mental health professionals to understand this population. If outside training is not available, we suggest training be created in-house using resources that outline this information from a research-based perspective. All materials must be grounded in research so that recommendations are helpful, not harmful. That is, some interventions not grounded in research (e.g., facilitated communication for students with autism spectrum disorders) can instill false hope for "cures," which is unethical and potentially harmful to families.

The second step is to form a collaborative group of professionals charged with identifying and supporting twice-exceptional students. The members of this group would vary depending on the school constellation, but should at a minimum include educators of the gifted, special educators, school counselors, and general education teachers. Given that twice-exceptional students do not present the same as gifted students without a disability, the team will need to be creative in terms of how assessment data are utilized. For example, using a composite score on a standardized achievement test as a screening method for further testing is likely not effective because twice-exceptional students commonly show peaks and dips in their assessment data, making composite scores misrepresentative. Establishing a formal process for identification that is sensitive to diverse students' needs and presentation is crucial. This formal process must consider results from multiple measures and multiple informants, where the screening step casts a broad net (McCallum et al., 2013).

The third step is generating both general and specific programming guidelines for the identified twice-exceptional students. As already mentioned, this means attending to the students' ability and disability domains. Because of the heterogeneity of how students will present, it is challenging to provide specific recommendations because they will vary depending on the student's talent domain(s) and areas for growth. Although time-consuming, taking an individual differences approach where the team considers the needs of the particular student is recommended.

ADVICE FOR THE SOLE PRACTITIONER

Although the team approach to educational planning is touted as ideal, it is not always an option, particularly for those working in small school districts or rural communities. If a school's population is small, this also means the educator may have many fewer twice-exceptional students in his or her building, which makes it more challenging to find resources. Positively, the sole practitioner can sometimes have more flexibility in his or her approach and consider students who present outside the box a bit more readily. At the same time, we recommend educators be a part of a wider network of practitioners through Listservs, state associations for the gifted, or national-level gifted education communities, such as the National Association for Gifted Children, so that ideas can be shared.

SUGGESTED RESOURCES

Assouline, S. G., Foley-Nicpon, M., & Fosenburg, S. (2013). *The paradox of twice-exceptionality: Packet of information for professionals—2nd edition (PIP-2)*. Iowa City: The University of Iowa, The Connie Belin & Jacqueline N. Blank International Center for Gifted Education and Talent Development. Retrieved from http://www2.education.uiowa.edu/belinblank/clinic/pip2.pdf

This document provides information for educators and staff working with twice-exceptional children (specifically, high-ability children with ADHD, ASD, and SLD) in summer program settings. There are helpful tips that can be applied to academic year educational settings, such as how to enhance talent domains and compensate for social, language, and behavioral difficulties.

Foley-Nicpon, M., Assouline, S. G., Colangelo, N., & O'Brien, M. (2008). *The paradox of giftedness and autism: Packet of information for families*. Iowa City: The University of Iowa, The Connie Belin & Jacqueline N. Blank International Center for Gifted Education and Talent Development. Retrieved from http://www2.education.uiowa.edu/belinblank/pdfs/pif.pdf

This document provides information for families of high-ability children with ASD who will be attending summer programs for gifted children. There are helpful tips about disclosing information to staff, discussing the program with one's child, avoiding potential behavior problems, attending to medication needs, approaching unstructured time, and orienting the child to the summer program.

National Association for Gifted Children. (2009). *Twice-exceptionality*. Washington, DC: Author. Retrieved from http://www.nagc.org/sites/default/files/Position%20Statement/twice%20exceptional.pdf

This white paper provides an overview of twice-exceptionality that can be distributed to educators and parents to help describe the nuances involved identifying and working with this population.

The Twice-Exceptional Newsletter (http://www.2enewsletter.com)

This is an online resource for families, educators, and mental health professionals who work with twice-exceptional students. There are numerous resources, including newsletters on specific topics within twice-exceptionality, a blog and e-mail briefing, a provider database, and much more.

REFERENCES

American Psychiatric Association. (2013). *Diagnostic and statistical manual of mental disorders* (5th ed.). Arlington, VA: American Psychiatric Publishing.

Antshel, K., Faraone, S. V., Maglione, K., Doyle, A., Fried, R., Seidman, L., & Biederman, J. (2008). Temporal stability of ADHD in the high-IQ population: Results from the MGH Longitudinal Family Studies of ADHD. *Journal of the American Academy of Child & Adolescent Psychiatry, 47,* 817–825.

Antshel, K., Faraone, S. V., Stallone, K., Nave, A., Kaufmann, F. A., Doyle, A., . . . Biederman, J. (2007). Is Attention Deficit Hyperactivity Disorder a valid diagnosis in the presence of high IQ? Results from the MGH Longitudinal Family Studies of ADHD. *Journal of Child Psychology and Psychiatry, 48,* 687–694.

Assouline, S. G., Colangelo, N., Lupkowski-Shoplik, A. E., Lipscomb, J., & Forstadt, L. (2009). *Iowa Acceleration Scale: A guide to whole grade acceleration K–8* (3rd ed.). Scottsdale, AZ: Great Potential Press.

Assouline, S. G., Colangelo, N., VanTassel-Baska, J., & Lupkowski-Shoplik, A. (Eds.). (2015). *A nation empowered: Evidence trumps the excuses holding back America's brightest students* (Vols. 1–2). Iowa City: The University of Iowa, The Connie Belin & Jacqueline N. Blank International Center for Gifted Education and Talent Development.

Assouline, S. G., Foley-Nicpon, M., & Dockery, L. (2012). Predicting the academic achievement of gifted students with autism spectrum disorder. *Journal of Autism and Developmental Disorders, 42,* 1781–1789. doi:10.1007/s10803-011-1403-x

Assouline, S. G., Foley-Nicpon, M., & Whiteman, C. (2010). Cognitive and psychosocial characteristics of gifted students with written language disability. *Gifted Child Quarterly, 54,* 102–115. doi:10.1177/0016986209355974

Assouline, S. G., & Whiteman, C. S. (2011). Twice-exceptionality: Implications for school psychologists in the post–IDEA 2004 era. *Journal of Applied School Psychology, 27,* 380–402. doi:10.1080/15377903.2011.616576

Baldwin, L., Baum, S., Pereles, D., & Hughes, C. (2015). Twice-exceptional learners: The journey toward a shared vision. *Gifted Child Today, 38,* 206–214. doi:10.1177/1076217515597277

Baldwin, L., Omdal, S. N., & Pereles, D. (2015). Beyond stereotypes: Understanding, recognizing, and working with twice-exceptional learners. *Teaching Exceptional Children, 47,* 216–225. doi:10.1177/0040059915569361

Barber, C., & Mueller, C. T. (2011). Social and self-perceptions of adolescents identified as gifted, learning disabled, and twice-exceptional. *Roeper Review, 33,* 109–120. doi:10.1080/02783193.2011.554158

Barnard-Brak, L., Johnsen, S. K., Pond Hannig, A., & Wei, T. (2015). The incidence of potentially gifted students within a special education population. *Roeper Review, 37,* 74–83. doi:10.1080/02783193.2015.1008661

Baum, S. M. (1984). Meeting the needs of learning disabled gifted students. *Roeper Review, 7,* 16–19.

Baum, S. M., & Owen, S. V. (1988). High ability/learning disabled students: How are they different? *Gifted Child Quarterly, 32,* 321–326.

Baum, S. M., & Owen, S. V. (2004). *To be gifted and learning disabled: Strategies for helping bright students with LD, ADHD, and more.* Mansfield Center, CT: Creative Learning Press.

Baum, S. M., Owen, S. V., & Dixon, J. (1991). *To be gifted and learning disabled: From identification to practical intervention strategies.* Melbourne, Australia: Hawker Brownlow Education.

Brody, L. E., & Mills, C. J. (1997). Gifted children with learning disabilities: A review of the issues. *Journal of Learning Disabilities, 30,* 282–296.

Cederberg, C., Foley-Nicpon, M., & Park, S. (2015, November). *Evaluating a summer enrichment program's impact on academic self-efficacy of gifted and twice-exceptional students.* Paper presented at the meeting of the National Association for Gifted Children, Phoenix, AZ.

Crim, C., Hawkins, J., Ruban, L., & Johnson, S. (2008). Curricular modifications for elementary students with learning disabilities in high-, average-, and low-IQ groups. *Journal of Research in Childhood Education, 22,* 233–245.

Flanagan, D. P., Fiorello, C. A., & Ortiz, S. O. (2010). Enhancing practice through application of Cattell-Horn-Carroll theory and research: A "third method" approach to specific learning disability identification. *Psychology in the Schools, 47,* 739–760. doi:10.1002/pits.20501

Foley-Nicpon, M., Allmon, A., Sieck, R., & Stinson, R. D. (2011). Empirical investigation of twice-exceptionality: Where have we been and where are we going? *Gifted Child Quarterly, 55,* 3–17. doi:10.1177/0016986210382575

Foley-Nicpon, M., & Assouline, S. G. (2015). Counseling considerations for the twice-exceptional client. *Journal of Counseling & Development, 93,* 202–211. doi:10.1002/j.1556-6676.2015.00196.x

Foley-Nicpon, M., Assouline, S. G., & Colangelo, N. (2013). Twice-exceptional learners: Who needs to know what? *Gifted Child Quarterly, 57,* 169–180. doi:10.1177/0016986213490021

Foley-Nicpon, M., Assouline, S. G., & Fosenburg, S. (2015). The relationship between self-concept, ability, and academic programming among twice-exceptional youth. *Journal of Advanced Academics, 26,* 1–18. doi:10.1177/1932202X15603364.

Foley-Nicpon, M., Assouline, S. G., & Stinson, R. D. (2012). Cognitive and academic distinctions between gifted students with autism and Asperger syndrome. *Gifted Child Quarterly, 56,* 77–89. doi:10.1177/0016986211433199

Foley-Nicpon, M., & Cederberg, C. (2015). Acceleration practices with twice-exceptional students. In S. G. Assouline, N. Colangelo, J. VanTassel-Baska, & A. Lupkowski-Shoplik (Eds.), *A nation empowered: Evidence trumps the excuses holding back America's brightest students* (Vol. 2, pp. 189–198). Iowa City: The University of Iowa, The Connie Belin & Jacqueline N. Blank International Center for Gifted Education and Talent Development.

Foley-Nicpon, M., Doobay, A. F., & Assouline, S. G. (2010). Parent, teacher, and self perceptions of psychosocial functioning in intellectually gifted children and adolescents with autism spectrum disorder. *Journal of Autism and Developmental Disorders, 40,* 1028–1038. doi:10.1007/s10803-010-0952-8

Foley-Nicpon, M., Rickels, H., Assouline, S. G., & Richards, A. (2012). Self-esteem and self-concept examination among gifted students with ADHD. *Journal for the Education of the Gifted, 35,* 220–240. doi:10.1177/0162353212451735

Fuchs, D., Mock, D., Morgan, P. D., & Young, C. L. (2003). Responsiveness-to-intervention: Definitions, evidence and applications for the learning disabilities construct. *Learning Disabilities Research and Practice, 18,* 157–171.

Fugate, C. M., Zentall, S. S., & Gentry, M. (2013). Working memory and creativity in gifted students with and without characteristics of ADHD: Lifting the mask. *Gifted Child Quarterly, 57*, 234–246. doi:10.1177/0016986213500069

Hale, J., Alfonso, V., Berninger, V., Bracken, B., Christo, C., Clark, E., . . . Yalof, J. (2010). Critical issues in response-to-intervention, comprehensive evaluation, and specific learning disabilities identification and intervention: An expert white paper consensus. *Learning Disabilities Quarterly, 33*, 223–236.

Lovett, B. J., & Sparks, R. L. (2011). The identification and performance of gifted students with learning disability diagnoses: A quantitative synthesis. *Journal of Learning Disabilities, 46*, 304–316. doi:10.1177/00222194121810

McCallum, R. S., Bell, S. M., Coles, J. T., Miller, K. C., Hopkins, M. B., & Hilton-Prillhart, A. (2013). A model for screening twice-exceptional students (gifted with learning disabilities) within a response to intervention paradigm. *Gifted Child Quarterly, 57*, 209–222. doi:10.1177/0016986213500070

McCoach, D. B., Kehle, T. J., Bray, M. A., & Siegle, D. (2001). Best practices in the identification of gifted students with learning disabilities. *Psychology in the Schools, 38*, 403–411. doi:10.1002/pits.1029

Morrison, W. F., & Rizza, M. G. (2007). Creating a toolkit for identifying twice-exceptional students. *Journal for the Education of the Gifted, 31*, 57–76. doi:10.4219/jeg-2007-513

National Education Association. (2006). *The twice-exceptional dilemma*. Washington, DC: Author.

Neihart, M. (2000). Gifted children with Asperger's syndrome. *Gifted Child Quarterly, 44*, 222–230. doi:10.1177/001698620004400403

Ofiesh, N. (2006). Response to intervention and the identification of specific learning disabilities: Why we need comprehensive evaluations as a part of the process. *Psychology in the Schools, 43*, 883–888. doi:10.1002/pits.20195

Ofiesh, N. S., & McAfee, J. A. (2000). Results of a nationwide survey on using psychoeducational evaluations for LD service delivery in postsecondary settings. *Journal of Learning Disabilities, 33*, 14–25.

Peterson, J. S., & Morris, C. W. (2010). Preparing school counselors to address concerns related to giftedness: A study of accredited counselor preparation programs. *Journal for the Education of the Gifted, 33*, 311–336.

Pfeiffer, S. I. (2015). Gifted students with a coexisting disability: The twice-exceptional. *Campinas, 32*, 717–727. doi:10.1590/0103-166X2015000400015

Reis, S. M., Baum, S. M., & Burke, E. (2014). An operational definition of twice-exceptional learners: Implication and applications. *Gifted Child Quarterly, 58*, 217–230. doi:10.1177/0016986214534976

Schultz, S. M. (2012). Twice-exceptional students enrolled in Advanced Placement classes. *Gifted Child Quarterly, 56*, 119–133.

Silverman, L. K. (1989). Invisible gifts, invisible handicaps. *Roeper Review, 12*, 171–178.

Speirs Neumeister, K., Yssel, N., & Burney, V. H. (2013). The influence of primary caregivers in fostering success in twice-exceptional children. *Gifted Child Quarterly, 57*, 263–274.

Willard-Holt, C., Weber, J., Morrison, K.L., & Horgan, J. (2013). Twice-exceptional learners' perspectives on effective learning strategies. *Gifted Child Quarterly, 57*, 246–262.

Wormald, C., Rogers, K. B., & Vialle, W. (2015). A case study of giftedness and specific learning disabilities: Bridging the two exceptionalities. *Roeper Review, 37*, 124–138. doi:10.1080/02783193.2015.1047547

Yewchuk, C., & Lupart, J. L. (1988). Gifted handicapped: A desultory duality. In K. A. Heller, F. J. Mönks, & A. H. Passow (Eds.), *International handbook of research and development of giftedness and talent* (pp. 709–725). London, England: Pergamon Press.

Chapter 11

Promoting Opportunity, Rigor, and Achievement for Underrepresented Students

Meg Easom Hines, PhD, Brittany Nicole Anderson, and Tarek Cy Grantham, PhD

Kids show you their potential, but they don't show you all of their gifts. It is our job as an educator, as a teacher, as a mentor to help bring those gifts to fruition.

—Mary M. Frasier

Gifted children can be found in all cultural groups and at every socioeconomic level; however, attempts to identify them have been and continue to be an issue (Ford, 2013; Frasier, 1991; Passow & Frasier, 1996; Torrance, 1974). In the field of gifted education, scholars and practitioners alike have raised awareness of the underrepresentation of culturally and linguistically diverse (CLD) students and those from low-income households (National Association for Gifted Children [NAGC], 2010; VanTassel-Baska & Stambaugh, 2007). Students from low-income households typically do not have access to traditional preschool enriching learning activities at home (Barton, 2003), which in turn contributes to underachievement (Sirin, 2005) and underrepresentation (Ford, 1995). The majority of children in low-income and poor families are children of color, particularly Black and Hispanic students, and these students face the additional burden of racial discrimination (Kitano, 2007). Eligibility for these students using traditional intelligence measures may not allow for their abilities or talents to be captured. For educators working with low-income students, it is of great importance that we approach identification from a strengths-based perspective rather than a deficit one, including appropriate assessments for identification (Ford & Grantham, 2003; Olszewski-Kubilius & Clarenbach, 2012).

This chapter (a) defines the population of high-potential students who are underrepresented in gifted and advanced programs, including students from low-income backgrounds; (b) discusses the contextual elements that exist for these students; and (c) provides guidelines and examples of programs and services that might be used to help reverse the issues around underrepresentation.

DEFINITION OF UNDERREPRESENTATION

Ford (2014) recommended that educators use the Relative Difference in Composition Index (RDCI) to compute underrepresentation for a racial or cultural group. *Underrepresentation* refers to a negative discrepancy when the total percentage of gifted program enrollment of a student group is less than the group's actual percentage in the school enrollment. The key question is: What is the difference between the composition (percentage) of students in gifted education compared to the composition of students in general education? When using the RDCI approach to examine underrepresentation, educators are permitted to compare disproportionality of and among various groups. The RDCI for underrepresentation is computed as

$$\frac{[(\text{Composition (\%) of Group A in gifted education}) - (\text{Composition (\%) of Group A in general education})]}{(\text{Composition (\%) of Group A in general education})} * 100.$$

For example, the 2009 percentage of African American students in public schools represented 16.7%, but only 9.9% of the population of gifted education programs. Using the RDCI formula, African American students were underrepresented by almost 41%. Recent trends in gifted education enrollment statistics nationwide suggest that African American students tend to be more severely underrepresented than Hispanic students in gifted education programs as indicated in Table 11.1.

$$\frac{9.9 - 16.7}{16.7} * 100 = -41$$

Table 11.1 Example Calculation of the RDCI for Student Enrollment in U.S. Gifted Education

Ethnicity	2009 Percentage National Enrollment			2011 Percentage National Enrollment		
	School	Gifted	UR	School	Gifted	UR
African American/ Black	16.7	9.9	–41	19	10	–47
Hispanic/Latino	22.3	15.4	–31	25	16	–36

Source: U.S. Department of Education Office for Civil Rights (2009, 2011).

Note: UR = Underrepresentation

According to Ford (2014), "a discrepancy would be considered significant when underrepresentation exceeds a threshold determined legally or by decision and policy makers" (p. 145). (For a more detailed discussion on determining thresholds using Ford's Equity Index, see Ford, 2014.)

Underrepresentation is a complex phenomenon that is impacted by many issues, particularly income level (Olszewski-Kubilius & Clarenbach, 2012; VanTassel-Baska & Stambaugh, 2007). Poverty is a recursive problem that is tied to underrepresentation of CLD students in gifted education, and we have not adequately met the needs of low-income students by means of identification, programming, and sustainability. According to the U.S. Department of Education, *high-poverty schools* are defined as public schools where more than 75.0% of the students are eligible for free or reduced-price lunch (FRPL), and *low-poverty schools* are defined as public schools where 25.0% or fewer of the students are eligible for FRPL (Kena et al., 2015). Underrepresentation is most severe in low-income schools, and greater effort is needed to improve enrollment trends and best address students' needs.

RATIONALE

> The greater the incongruence between the culture of the home, the community, and the school, the more difficult and negative will be students' educational experiences.
>
> —Donna Ford (2013, p. 17)

Identifying potential and talent in underrepresented populations has been a concern in gifted education for decades. Much of the literature around underrepresented gifted and talented students has explored the risk of underachievement, issues with identification (eligibility and assessment measures), funding disparities, and types of interventions that have shown effectiveness in meeting the needs of underserved students (Ford, Grantham, & Whiting, 2008). However, too often in the gifted education literature, the characteristics of underrepresented students are overgeneralized and viewed as monolithic in nature. This narrow view does not take into account how income intersects with culture, ethnicity, geographic location, family values, and the larger society.

Due to these structural and cultural disconnects between educators and families that occur in many Title I schools, the primary concern among teachers and administrators has centered on raising the achievement of the lowest-performing students and closing the achievement gap among subpopulations at the basic level rather than developing the talent of all youth they serve. It has been suggested that focusing on basic levels of cultural competence in underrepresented students who perform low on tests and that raising expectations for achievement may indirectly affect the academic growth in school (Ford & Whiting, 2008). Due to the fact that a teacher's time and attention, our most critical educational resource, has been focused solely on struggling students (Olszewski-Kubilius & Clarenbach, 2012), we are faced with missing the mark on developing students with talent and high potential in these schools. The challenges presented demonstrate a lack of focus on social justice for underrepresented gifted students in our low-income schools. According to Bell (2007), "social justice is a vision of the world where the rights of all are valued, respected, and accepted and when access to the opportunities and resources necessary to be your best self is unrestricted" (p. 1). Therefore, as educators, we must be diligent in our quest for *just* classrooms where students with gifts and talents are valued regardless of their background, environment, and influences.

Identifying factors contributing to the underrepresentation of CLD students continues to stymie educators, administrators, and practitioners. Contextual influences such as economic status, culture, and language impact learning and how we view our students. Some students readily demonstrate their gifts, but for others, the demonstration of their gifts and talents may not be recognized in a traditional sense or easily observed (Ford, 2013). Without proper training or awareness of how contextual influences impact learning, teachers and counselors may potentially miss or overlook students for identification. If educators continue to exclude contextual factors from the equation of identifying students, underrepresentation of students who are culturally, linguistically, and ethnically diverse will continue to persist.

STUDENT PORTRAITS

To get a better sense of what underrepresented gifted students from low-income and/or culturally and linguistically different schools might be like, let us take a look at Todrick and Emilia.

Todrick

Todrick is a fourth-grade, nine-year-old African American male who lives in a single-parent, low-income household. He has two older siblings (middle and high school) and attends a Title I elementary school with students from predominantly low-income families. His stature is solid, but he is reserved in many respects. He is somewhat laid-back in that he goes with the flow of the classroom and responds to teacher directions well, and he also has excellent manners. He works exceptionally well with his peers in small-group settings, but seems to be frustrated or distracted when working with a whole group or classroom.

Todrick's high-potential traits, aptitudes, and behaviors might go unnoticed or not be observed because he struggles in reading. However, by taking a closer look, one can observe a great deal. Although somewhat reserved, when Todrick speaks, he takes the command of his audience much like a leader. He uses inflection and captures the attention of the students or teachers around him. A small group suits his learning preferences better because he is able to negotiate the attention of his peers. In fact, he tends to shut down in the general classroom setting or when others reject or downplay his ideas; and, at times, he resists the direction of the classroom teacher. He always is able to add excellent responses to questions that are both relevant and logical. For example, when studying issues related to disease, he connected the discussion to the current issue of Ebola and raised thought-provoking questions for the class. He sometimes stumbles when he is not able to convey his complex thinking or rationale to others when tackling a problem situation. For example, he proposed a rather abstract idea to a small group of students who were not able to understand or make the leap in the direction he was going, and then his peers mocked him. He was extremely frustrated and shut down.

Todrick has exceptional insight, is able to draw inferences, and is keenly observant in both academic subjects and in the context around him. Torrance (1974; Torrance & Torrance, 1978) recognized that to motivate students from underserved groups and promote their engagement in advanced programs, an emphasis on community and culture can accompany the development of creative problem-solving skills that undergird a future orientation. In a Community Problem Solving (CmPS) Program setting, Todrick was able to sense problems within the context of the area of concern. This was a sophisticated skill that many of the bright students in the group were unable to do. He was able to problematize the health risks and safety concerns about his community. Most of his peers headed straight into solution generation, but he was able to sense the problems in the situation. He enjoys thinking and working creatively. When given a task in idea generation, Todrick contributes ideas that are both useful and novel. During the preparation of a collaborative rap about bullying in his CmPS group, Todrick suggested, "I think that it might be good to use 'treat others like you want to be treated' to represent how kids should act about bullying." This insightful connection to the golden rule was a perfect fit for the rap and in keeping with the overall project on bully prevention. When participating in a task around nutrition, he devised a creative way to get children his age more active by creating a school competition involving Wii Fit games, complete with a reward system.

Todrick's classroom placement lacks an environment where creativity and higher-level thinking are encouraged. In a school where there is a predominant focus on intervention, he struggles to enjoy school or find a place to exhibit these traits, aptitudes, and behaviors. He has, however, found a place in his CmPS group where he can use his creative and leadership talents. Most recently, he led the group in the delivery of the proposed action plan to the principal who responded with a resounding, "Absolutely!" Without this small-group environment, Todrick could certainly be missed in any formal referral processes or nomination for gifted education programming. To identify students like Todrick, who often fly under the radar, schools can follow the guiding principles for serving high-potential, low-income students so that we might capitalize on the talents of all high-potential students in these schools.

Emilia

Emilia is a six-year-old student attending a school with a highly diverse, mixed-income population. Her school sits adjacent to a local university, and many of the students who attend this school have parents who came to the United States to attend graduate school. Emilia was originally from Guatemala, and she arrived speaking almost no English. Emilia received services from the English as a Second Language (ESL) program at her school where she began to rapidly pick up English. When gifted referral season opened at the school, Emilia's ESL teacher persistently advocated for her, citing that she was a student with an incredible memory, a thirst for learning, and high motivation.

Emilia is small and quiet with big brown eyes. She keeps very much to herself and is reserved most times in class. However, when a special program began in her first-grade classroom, other adults began to see similar high-ability attributes observed by the ESL teacher. In this same year that she moved to the school, her class participated in a university-community partnership program centered on creativity. Every week, doctoral students came in to facilitate experiences using creativity strategies through the content areas. This unique opportunity has allowed Emilia's teacher to sit back and observe her strengths as the guest teacher facilitates the creativity lessons. Emilia's teacher quickly began to see her ability to think flexibly and come up with original responses. In addition, she describes Emilia as highly creative, being able to produce many ideas and make connections in her learning that age-mates are not able to.

Never before had her teacher been able to recognize Emilia's keen sense of humor, likely because of the language barrier; but with these specialized lessons, her teacher began to see her use humor and whimsy and make connections between ideas in ways that she had not yet observed.

For example, her teacher commented that

> in a recent lesson highlighting force fit, or metaphorical thinking, Emilia connected the idea of the character Wimberly from Kevin Henkes's book *Wimberly Worried* with the idea of a hurricane (weather) currently being studied in science. Emilia shared an artistic response to the lesson noting that Wimberly was like a hurricane because at first she was so worried and nervous, like the swirling of a hurricane, and then feeling more peaceful, like the calm after the storm. No one in my room was able to make this creative leap.

This opportunity to observe students really allowed the teacher to better understand Emilia. In fact, her observations prompted her to connect with the school art teacher and ESL teacher to see if they had similar experiences with Emilia in class and what their thoughts were regarding her abilities. The whole program experience allowed a group of teachers to come together to recognize traits, aptitudes, and behaviors in Emilia in a way that had not been seen before. Without this experience and the advocacy from a variety of teachers in her setting, Emilia's gifts might have gone unrecognized.

GUIDING PRINCIPLES AND ATTRIBUTES THAT DEFINE HIGH QUALITY

A high-quality program promotes equitable practices and grants access to opportunities that otherwise would not be available for students from underrepresented populations. Moreover, all personnel within the school (e.g., administrators, specialists, classroom teachers, counselors, paraprofessionals) share the responsibility of collaborating and working with community members to identify and develop talents of underrepresented students like Todrick and Emilia in culturally responsive ways. Ford, Moore, and Milner (2005) identified testing issues, teacher referral issues, social issues, and issues surrounding policies and procedures as contributing variables to the underrepresentation of minorities in gifted programs.

Dr. Mary Frasier (1997), researcher and advocate for identifying and developing talents of CLD students and those from economically disadvantaged backgrounds, developed a system to address barriers that circumvent talent development. We are borrowing from Frasier's (1991) Four A's framework—*attitude, access, assessment*, and *accommodations* (which we are calling *adaptations*)—as a foundation to counter concerns of inequitable practices within a district to fit the needs of underserved students.

Attitude

The attitude of an individual as well as the collective sentiment in the local community or society can influence dramatically how gifted students experience school, making attitude the most crucial component of Frasier's framework. *Attitude* refers to the mental position, feeling, or emotion toward a low-income or CLD student. To truly recognize the potential of under-represented students, particularly those from low-income backgrounds, educators must combat negative assumptions and stereotypes about different communities and families (Ford & Grantham, 2003). Rather than focusing on student deficits or what is lacking, those working in high-quality gifted programs shift the focus toward uncovering and supporting student potential that manifests in culturally different ways (Torrance, 1974). As noted in the NAGC Pre-K–Grade 12 Gifted Programming Standards, educators are encouraged to engage in helping students developing identities supportive of achievement through positive learning environments.

Remaining open and flexible is key because potential manifests in different ways, and the manifestation of talent in underrepresented students from low-income and CLD backgrounds will more than likely differ from that of White and middle-class populations. To promote equitable classrooms and programming, it is imperative to focus on the strengths of students.

In high-quality programs and services, the following principles affect attitudes in positive ways:

- Educators are responsible for shifting attitudes from a deficit thinking paradigm to a strengths-based perspective and promoting this mindset for all students throughout the community.
- Administrators and teachers recognize that demonstrations of potential traits, aptitudes, and behaviors such as humor, creativity, reasoning, and problem solving may be revealed in a positive or negative manner in low-income and CLD students. It is of great importance that negative displays of potential not be overlooked.
- Teachers and administrators need to engage families (nuclear, blended, and extended) representing the school community, as well as groups such as afterschool care, churches, and neighborhoods about what it means to identify and develop talent in students with high potential.
- Schools need to retain and train effective equity-minded educators of gifted education programs, particularly in Title I schools. Building and sustaining relationships between and among the faculty, administration, students, and families in support of equity for underrepresented students in gifted and talented education programs is critical to the overall success of high-potential students.

Access

Recognizing gifted potential among underrepresented groups does not happen in a vacuum; several factors must intersect for students to develop their talent, and it begins with prioritizing access for all students to appropriately challenging and engaging learning opportunities. Frasier (1997) posited that there are several factors that limit access of low-income and CLD students for gifted programming and services: (a) low academic expectations held by educators and others, (b) low rates of referrals, (c) the inability of educators to recognize gifted behaviors when exhibited by low-income and CLD students, and (d) the lack of regard given to the influence of culture and environment on the manifestations of gifts and talents in different racial and ethnic groups and the effects this has on teacher referrals in the identification process.

The NAGC Pre-K–Grade 12 Gifted Programming Standards urge gifted education professionals to grant equal access to a comprehensive assessment system that allows all students, including CLD students, to demonstrate diverse characteristics and behaviors that are associated with giftedness. If students cannot gain access to services through a referral, they cannot be assessed for services.

In settings where CLD and low-income students have equal access to gifted programming and services, the following hold true:

- Educators take into consideration how the structural and institutional barriers (e.g., racism, elitism) and cultural factors of the school and community influence how services and programming will be perceived.
- Schools and districts provide a variety of coordinated professional development opportunities for educators to recognize and nurture high-potential learners within the community. The teacher development effort is ongoing and focuses on continual growth in understanding and supporting the local population of underserved low-income students with talent (including changes in enrollment trends).
- Educators continually analyze the local barriers that may exist for students in their school by combating underlying assumptions of the students, families, and community and by strategizing plans to overcome those barriers. They conscientiously examine and use local data to develop innovative plans when state policies focused on state and national trends limit capacity for underrepresented students to gain access to gifted education services.

Assessment

Underrepresentation of Black, Hispanic, Native American, and English language learners in gifted and talented programs and Advanced Placement (AP) courses continues to be a reoccurring and pervasive problem in schools (Ford, 1998; Ford & Grantham, 2003; Olszewski-Kubilius & Clarenbach, 2012). Expanding access to gifted programs and services is intimately linked to the way in which student abilities and talents are evaluated and identified through the assessment process. For decades, gifted education has supported a broader, expanded conception of giftedness (Gardner, 1983; Renzulli, 1978; Sternberg, 1985; Torrance, 1974, 1977), and very few researchers and theorists continue to accept an isolated IQ or achievement test score based on national norms as a valid measure of a student's capacity for doing well over the course of a lifetime (Renzulli &

Reis, 2012). Nevertheless, in many schools, identification for gifted programs is still heavily tied to performance on intelligence and/or achievement tests (Cross & Dockery, 2014; Renzulli & Reis, 2012).

A high-quality program should institute multiple criteria (e.g., creativity, leadership, achievement, mental ability, motivation), multiple measures to assess each criterion, and multiple pathways to determine eligibility for gifted program participation (Frasier, 1997). Why? Giftedness and talent are multidimensional constructs that manifest differently in racially, culturally, and linguistically different groups. Renzulli and Reis (2012) asserted that IQ or achievement scores can be used as one of a number of criteria, but should not form the entire basis in the decision-making process for identification of gifted programs and services, particularly for underrepresented students. (See Chapter 4 for additional guidance on constructing identification procedures.)

The tests used for gifted identification and services have been widely criticized and blamed for the underrepresentation of culturally, linguistically, and ethnically diverse students. There have been several recommendations to help the field develop better identification systems that promote equitable practices and not allow IQ or achievement tests to act as smokescreens or "gatekeepers" (Ford, 2013; Renzulli & Reis, 2012). The use of local norms (i.e., calculated by school and grade level) has been recommended as an identification system to compare students who share similar background characteristics or learning opportunities (Lohman, 2005; Renzulli & Reis, 2012), essentially comparing apples to apples. The use of nonverbal assessments has also been a widely recommended method to identify underrepresented students (Naglieri, 2008; Naglieri & Ford, 2003). It also has been recommended to use alternative or nontraditional instruments believed to measure the same construct (e.g., creativity; Baldwin, 2011; Torrance, 1971), as well as using a range of scores to increase the representation of culturally, linguistically, and ethnically diverse students (Ford, 2011). Educators must be equipped with and trained to use the district and state policies designed to foster equity in gifted education assessment programming and services (NAGC, 2010). Additionally, students with identified needs must represent diverse backgrounds and reflect the total school population of the district.

In high-quality programs and services, the following apply:

- School and district administrators consider the population they serve; they commit to understanding the strengths and limitations of the instruments used, and select a variety of instruments that are appropriate for low-income and CLD students in their community.
- Teachers and other persons eligible to make referrals receive professional development or workshop training on the identification process and how traits, aptitudes, and behaviors may manifest in culturally, linguistically, and ethnically different groups.
- Educators use multiple criteria or alternative assessments such as portfolios and performance-based tasks, taking into account local norms (e.g., by race, gender, language, income level) as a standard.

Adaptations

When identification and access to services are expanded, adjustments must also be made in curriculum and teaching so that learning opportunities within and beyond the gifted program reflect and support the culturally and linguistically different group of students it serves. In a high-quality gifted program, educators use and adapt program design and curriculum experiences by way of creating opportunities for students to mirror ways in which potential manifests in the community (Ford, 2013). Stimulating, engaging classrooms and programs where students have the opportunity to explore their community, take risks, problem solve, and think critically and constructively about their community provide the necessary learning experiences for students to be considered for and thrive within gifted education programming (NAGC, 2010). Community engagement is an important pathway for CLD students to bridge gaps between home and school culture and to develop competencies that support success in academically rigorous advanced courses and programs. Adaptations for underrepresented students must include a focus on principles of culturally responsive education, empowerment, and cultural competence (Ford, 2013; Ford & Whiting, 2008), preparing CLD students to emerge from barriers to equity that our diverse nation presents (Grantham, 2012). Ford and Whiting (2008) advocated that we must ask of all students, particularly gifted and advanced CLD:

- Are students aware of and sensitive to cultural differences?
- How comfortable are they in working with classmates who come from cultural backgrounds that differ from their own?
- Are gifted students sensitive to and interested in social justice and equity issues? (p. 105)

To cultivate a school climate that embodies the aforementioned traits, administrators and teachers must embrace the community and include culturally relevant curriculum, alternative programming, and possible university-school partnerships that support the objectives of the district, emphasizing achievement, rigor, and creativity (Grantham, Hines, Anderson, Catalana, & Luckey, 2015), which can in turn set the precedence of excellence for all students, creating equitable opportunities. Adapting environments and instructional activities that encourage students to express their diverse characteristics and behaviors are critical to meeting curriculum-planning and instruction standards (NAGC, 2010).

In high-quality programs and services, the following apply:

- Educators adapt traditional curriculum with culturally responsive approaches. It is of great importance that stakeholders understand the cultural differences in learning preferences and how underrepresented students demonstrate learning.
- Schools and districts use alternative programs to focus on talent development in lieu of programs only for identified students. These programs should be crafted based on the context and population of the school.

- Schools and districts should provide affective education (social and emotional development) focused on identity, self-concept, self-efficacy, peer interactions, and teacher-student relationships that takes into account cultural issues such as race, ethnicity, language, and gender background of individuals.
- Educators position creativity as a common language in schoolwide programming to motivate, engage, and build opportunity for all students, particularly underrepresented groups, to demonstrate their learning and connect school and community environments.

EXAMPLE IN NEED OF REVISION

Samantha Frost has been a teacher of the gifted at a predominantly low-income, Black, intervention-focused school for the past 5 years. She has provided services for from 4 to 15 Black students, depending on the year (approximately 1% to 3% of the total student population). The district in which Samantha teaches serves approximately 14,000 students and, of that population, there are about 1,600 identified students for the gifted program, most of whom are White, although the total district is majority Black. Calculating the percentage of students identified in the district at 11%, one can easily see how low the identified gifted students are at Samantha's elementary school.

Over time, Samantha has developed a system of using products and portfolio assessment to help identify gifted students, but increasingly she has found that teachers are nominating fewer and fewer students each year. Additionally, due to the transience of the community, it has been difficult to build and sustain the number of students in the gifted program or to develop relationships with family members. Finally, the model that her administrative team required for the program, with so few students identified, was that she would "push-in" to classrooms and serve as an intervention specialist. This is because there is typically only one gifted student per classroom, if any. Although the pressure to find and identify gifted students is large, the ability to try new things to achieve that objective is small.

MAKEOVER EXAMPLE

Challenged by the expectations, and feeling that her efforts are falling short in building programs for high-ability students at her school, Samantha decided to reach out to the administrative team for guidance and support. Working together, they used Frasier's (1997) four attributes (attitude, access, assessment, adaptations) as a framework to assist in reconceptualizing gifted programming to provide more equitable opportunities for the school's students.

Thinking about the attitude of the teaching staff and the tendency to focus on deficits in a high-stakes environment, the principal recommended contacting faculty at the local university to collaborate and problem solve. Eagerly, the faculty from the university committed to working with Samantha and a small group of teachers who were willing to step outside the school culture and think outside the box. The first initiative that the partnership established was an on-site class where students from the university would come to the school to participate as enrichment specialists helping implement creativity lessons that were embedded in the content areas.

Samantha quickly realized that the effort to engage more faculty members was gaining speed now that a small cadre of interested teachers was developing insight and expertise around teaching students with high potential. Other teachers at the school were interested in designing services to help meet the needs of the students, and there was an undercurrent of attention on the issues Samantha had struggled so much to get faculty to understand. Teachers were aware and interested to learn more about how to focus on strengths and adjust their teaching to better meet the needs of students with high ability in their classrooms. With this gradual but important shift in attitude, practices that expanded access to programming and services also grew. Samantha was able to begin more individual conversations with teachers about particular students and how they wanted to refer them for formal testing. What began as conversations about how to formally nominate students, next translated to conversations about what the teacher could do within the classroom to help meet the needs or develop the talent within a particular student.

Recognizing an opportunity to expand access further and refine their assessment process, the principal worked with Samantha to organize schoolwide professional learning with the university faculty on how to observe and address the traits, aptitudes, and behaviors of students from economically and culturally diverse populations. Teachers in all grade levels began to buy into this dynamic thinking and were inspired to also begin using the creativity strategies in their classrooms. Even though Samantha bought into the dynamic thinking mindset, she surprised herself to find that she, too, still let deficit thinking creep in and had to continually check her own assumptions. Eventually, these experiences led a group of interested teachers to consider what adaptations needed to be made in gifted programming and general education settings to better engage and challenge the many low-income and CLD students in the school.

From those initial experiences around developing and designing lessons using creativity, Samantha helped establish a CmPS team with some fourth graders, an accelerated math program for fifth graders, an afterschool leadership program for second and third graders, and a science lab for kindergarten students using creativity and critical thinking. Each of these programs grew organically from the work Samantha and the grade-level teachers began, shifting the engagement and motivation for students. What had historically been an intervention-focused school was now changing to a school that found ways to weave achievement, rigor, and creativity into the daily instruction and experiences of the students.

Serendipitously, what Samantha began to see was the embedded professional development that happened in the different programs that were established in the school. Teachers who hosted university students with creativity lessons began to ask how they could use more creativity strategies in their own teaching, while other faculty members sought more information about working with students from culturally, linguistically, and economically diverse populations. Over the summer, several teachers plan to attend a summer institute at the university digging deeper into the work of creativity and how to integrate it into the curriculum and services at the school.

The hope is that with continued collaboration and attention to the attributes of attitude, access, assessment, and adaptations, students from culturally, linguistically, and economically diverse backgrounds will have equal opportunity to reach their full potential.

ADVICE FOR GETTING STARTED

The following list of questions is designed to aid in the process of data gathering and to guide conversations of a strategic planning group or task force as they work to design or revise a program for high-potential students from culturally and linguistically different backgrounds and who may come from low-income families and communities.

Attitude

- How do we shift the thinking among school faculty to one of student potential (dynamic thinking) versus what students cannot do (deficit thinking)?
- How do we help teachers understand their important role in the identification process as the nominator and advocate for a student from CLD and/or low-income backgrounds?
- How do we help educators understand what high potential is, what it looks like, and how it manifests in a school where most students come from high-poverty homes?
- What are the ways we can help the family and community understand the needs of and be engaged in the development of our high-potential students from culturally and linguistically different backgrounds?

Access

- In what ways can we help our faculty members increase the academic expectations they have for our students from low-income or CLD backgrounds?
- How can we provide ongoing professional development for our faculty members that enables them to recognize high-potential behaviors from our student population by race, language, and the like?
- What are ways that we can acknowledge the influence of culture and environment on teachers', parents', and students' willingness to refer underrepresented students for gifted services and programming?

Assessment

- How do we help teachers better understand the identification process through the lens of a multiple criteria and how each of those areas is evaluated in light of the trends in eligibility for underrepresented groups?
- By analyzing the current identification process, where do we see places for assessing problem solving in culturally relevant ways? What and where are our pitfalls in the process of evaluation that adversely impact underrepresented groups, and what are the necessary steps to improve the process? For example, are there alternative instruments that may be used? Or is there professional learning that might be given to teachers focusing on selecting appropriate instruments and interpreting results for underrepresented students using local norms?
- Working backward, how do we use programs and services to provide learning experiences that enhance the talents of our underrepresented groups and set them up for a better identification experience? For example, if creativity is a criterion for formal identification, how are we using creativity in the school and classroom context to build creative thinking and skills in underrepresented or low-income students?
- Have the instruments used for formal testing been fielded for strengths and limitations (e.g., by race, class, gender, language differences) related to underrepresented groups?

Adaptations

- How do we best address the differences in culturally, linguistically, and economically disadvantaged students within curriculum and programming designs that appeal to predominantly White middle-class populations?
- How do we shift educators' thinking from trying to make students fit into the dominant structure of our school system and society to more strengths-based initiatives?
- How do we help our faculty honor students' culture and adapt programs and services to develop their self-identity, achievement, and talent?

ADVICE TO THE SOLE PRACTITIONER

Designing a more equitable and robust program for high-potential students involves a high level of commitment, sensitivity, flexibility, and ability to problem solve. As a sole practitioner, you will need to enlist a team dedicated to building capacity for talent development at your school; no one person can do it alone. Connecting with others in your community and school will take time, but this investment in relationship building will yield benefits and greater support for both you and your students. A key ingredient to the success of innovative programming and services at your school begins with educating your administration on the issues and asking them to help you meet the targets for your school.

Establishing relationships with other gifted teachers or school personnel in similar positions at "like" schools can also be a source of support. Supporting each other as allies in the trial and error of implementing innovative programs and services can be extremely useful and supportive. Last, understand your role as the sole practitioner. You are likely the expert at your school on doing this work. Constantly challenge yourself, your support team, your administration, and your school to do this work and help provide the tools for which to do it. Asking the questions associated with attitude, access, assessment, and adaptations will help guide the work you do. Design, negotiate, and implement pilots of innovative services that will allow students from low-income schools to actively participate in the equitable services that should be made available to them. Create programs and services that appeal to the strengths of students in your school by working with your support team, administration, parents, and student stakeholders to complete a needs assessment.

SUGGESTED RESOURCES

Ford, D. Y. (2013). *Recruiting and retaining culturally different students in gifted education.* Waco, TX: Prufrock Press.

In this book, Ford focuses on how to screen, refer, and/or assess culturally different students, and well as methods and strategies to retain them. Ford provides information on (a) colorblindness and cultureblindness and how these views affect Black and Hispanic students, (b) underrepresentation and equity formulas, (c) implications of deficit thinking, and (d) gifted programs and psychosocial environments.

Frasier, M. M. (1997). Gifted minority students: Reframing approaches to their identification and education. In N. Colangelo & G. A. Davis (Eds.), *Handbook of gifted education* (2nd ed., pp. 498–515), Boston, MA: Allyn & Bacon.

Frasier advocates for the need for schools and programs to utilize multiple criteria to identify minority students. Frasier also addresses problems affecting the identification and education of gifted minority students: access, assessment, accommodation, and attitudes. Frasier challenges the assessment procedures used and offers methods for reframing this process. This chapter is important for educators because it provides a synthesis of information undergirding the work that informs contemporary work on underrepresentation.

Olszewski-Kubilius, P., & Clarenbach, J. (2012). *Unlocking emergent talent: Supporting high achievement of low-income, high-ability students.* Washington, DC: National Association for Gifted Children.

In this special NAGC report, Olszewski-Kubilius and Clarenbach provide an overview of the state of low-income, high-ability students in our nation. The authors identify barriers low-income, high-ability students face, as well as best practices for identification, services, programs, and supportive school cultures.

REFERENCES

Baldwin, A. Y. (2011). Understanding the challenge of creativity among African Americans. In T. C. Grantham, D. Y. Ford, M. S. Henfield, D. A. Harmon, M. F. Trotman Scott, S. Porcher, & C. Price (Eds.), *Gifted and advanced Black students in school: An anthology of critical works* (pp. 73–80). Waco, TX: Prufrock Press.

Barton, P. (2003). *Parsing the achievement gap.* Washington, DC: Educational Testing Service.

Bell, L. A. (2007). Theoretical foundations for social justice education. In M. Adams, L. A. Bell, & P. Griffin (Eds.), *Teaching for diversity and social justice* (2nd ed., pp. 1–14). New York, NY: Routledge.

Cross, J. R., & Dockery, D.D. (2014). *Identification of low-income gifted learners: A review of recent research.* Lansdowne, VA: Jack Kent Cooke Foundation.

Ford, D. Y. (1995). Desegregating gifted education: A need unmet. *Journal of Negro Education, 64,* 52–62.

Ford, D. Y. (1998). The underrepresentation of minority students in gifted education: Problems and promises in recruitment and retention. *Journal of Special Education, 32,* 4–14.

Ford, D. Y. (2011). *Multicultural gifted education* (2nd ed.). Waco, TX: Prufrock Press.

Ford, D. Y. (2013). *Recruiting and retaining culturally different students in gifted education.* Waco, TX: Prufrock Press.

Ford, D. Y. (2014). Segregation and the underrepresentation of Blacks and Hispanics in gifted education: Social inequality and deficit paradigms. *Roeper Review, 36,* 143–154.

Ford, D. Y., & Grantham, T. C. (2003). Providing access for culturally diverse gifted students: From deficit to dynamic thinking. *Theory Into Practice, 42,* 217–225.

Ford, D. Y., Grantham, T. C., & Whiting, G. W. (2008). Culturally and linguistically diverse students in gifted education: Recruitment and retention issues. *Exceptional Children, 74,* 289–306.

Ford, D. Y., Moore, J., III, & Milner, H. R., (2005). Beyond cultureblindness: A model of culture with implications for gifted education. *Roeper Review, 27,* 97–103.

Ford, D. Y., & Whiting, G. W. (2008). Cultural competence: Preparing gifted students for a diverse society. *Roeper Review, 30,* 104–110.

Frasier, M. M. (1991). Disadvantaged and culturally diverse gifted students. *Journal for the Education of the Gifted, 14,* 234–245.

Frasier, M. M. (1997). Gifted minority students: Reframing approaches to their identification and education. In N. Colangelo & G. A. Davis (Eds.), *Handbook of gifted education* (2nd ed., pp. 498–515), Boston, MA: Allyn & Bacon.

Gardner, H. (1983). *Frames of mind.* New York, NY: Basic Books.

Grantham, T. C. (2012). Eminence-focused gifted education: Concerns about forward movement void of an equity vision. *Gifted Child Quarterly, 56,* 215–220.

Grantham, T. C., Hines, M. E., Anderson, B. A., Catalana, S. M., & Luckey, J. (2015). *University-school partnerships for achievement, rigor, and creativity (Project U-SPARC): A framework for promoting school improvement and gifted potential.* Technical Report. Athens: The University of Georgia, The Torrance Center for Creativity and Talent Development.

Kena, G., Musu-Gillette, L., Robinson, J., Wang, X., Rathbun, A., Zhang, J., . . . Dunlop Velez, E. (2015). *The condition of education 2015* (NCES 2015-144). Washington, DC: U.S. Department of Education, National Center for Education Statistics. Retrieved from http://nces.ed.gov/pubsearch

Kitano, M. K. (2007). Poverty, diversity, promise. In J. VanTassel-Baska & T. Stambaugh (Eds.), *Overlooked gems: A national perspective on low-income promising learners* (pp. 31–34). Washington, DC: National Association for Gifted Children.

Lohman, D. F. (2005). The role of nonverbal ability tests in identifying academically gifted students: An aptitude perspective. *Gifted Child Quarterly, 49,* 111–138.

Naglieri, J. A. (2008). Traditional IQ: 100 years of misconception and its relationship to minority representation in gifted programs. In J. VanTassel-Baska (Ed.), *Alternative assessments with gifted and talented students* (pp. 67–88). Waco, TX: Prufrock Press.

Naglieri, J. A., & Ford, D. Y. (2003). Addressing underrepresentation of gifted minority children using the Naglieri Nonverbal Ability Test (NNAT). *Gifted Child Quarterly, 47,* 155–160.

National Association for Gifted Children. (2010). *NAGC Pre-K–Grade 12 Gifted Programming Standards: A blueprint for quality gifted education programs.* Washington, DC: Author.

Olszewski-Kubilius, P., & Clarenbach, J. (2012). *Unlocking emergent talent: Supporting high achievement of low-income, high-ability students.* Washington, DC: National Association for Gifted Children.

Passow, A. H., & Frasier, M. M. (1996). Toward improving identification of talent potential among minority and disadvantaged students. *Roeper Review, 18,* 198–202.

Renzulli, J. S. (1978). What makes giftedness? Re-examining a definition. *Phi Delta Kappan, 60,* 180–184.

Renzulli, J. S., & Reis, S. M. (2012). Defensible and doable: A practical multiple-criteria gifted program identification system. In S. L. Hunsaker (Ed.), *Identification: The theory and practice of identifying students for gifted and talent education services* (pp. 25–56). Waco, TX: Prufrock Press.

Sirin, S. R. (2005). Socioeconomic status and academic achievement: A meta-analytic review of research. *Review of Educational Research, 75,* 417–453.

Sternberg, R. (1985). *Beyond IQ: A triarchic theory of human intelligence.* Cambridge, England: Cambridge University Press.

Torrance, E. P. (1971). Are the Torrance Tests of Creative Thinking biased against or in favor of "disadvantaged" groups? *Gifted Child Quarterly, 15,* 75–80.

Torrance, E. P. (1974). Differences are not deficits. *Teachers College Record, 75,* 471–487.

Torrance, E. P. (1977). *Discovery and nurturance of giftedness in the culturally different.* Reston, VA: Council for Exceptional Children.

Torrance, E. P., & Torrance, J. P. (1978). Future problem solving: National Interscholastic competition and curriculum project. *Journal of Creative Behavior, 12,* 87–89.

U.S. Department of Education Office for Civil Rights. (2009). *Elementary and secondary school civil rights survey (Select 2009).* Retrieved from http://ocrdata.ed.gov

U.S. Department of Education Office for Civil Rights. (2011). *Elementary and secondary school civil rights survey (Select 2011).* Retrieved from http://ocrdata.ed.gov

VanTassel-Baska, J., & Stambaugh, T. (Eds.). (2007). *Overlooked gems: A national perspective on low-income promising learners.* Washington, DC: National Association for Gifted Children.

Chapter 12

Designing a Professional Development Plan

Marcia B. Imbeau, PhD,
and Jennifer G. Beasley, EdD

DEFINITION

An effective professional development plan enables educators to increase their effectiveness in meeting the needs of all students, including those of high-ability learners, in their charge. Mizell (2010) suggested that "effective professional development requires thoughtful planning followed by careful implementation with feedback to ensure it responds to educator's learning needs" (p. 10). The plan may use a variety of formats and include input from a broad range of stakeholders; however, Guskey (2014) reminded us that "the effectiveness of any professional learning activity, regardless of its content, structure or format, depends mainly on how well it is planned" (p. 10).

RATIONALE

At the heart of why it is important to design a clear plan for professional development activities is educator common sense: "None of us can do what we don't know." How can teachers respond to the needs of particular learners who fall outside their realm of experience and knowledge base without opportunities to learn important knowledge and skills? Targeted professional learning regarding the diverse needs and issues of high-ability students along with practical suggestions for how teachers might effectively respond to those learner needs is likely to be more positively received when the information is relevant and adds to educator effectiveness. This is especially important because a recent report concerning gifted education across different states indicates that limited information concerning appropriate instructional strategies for engaging and challenging gifted students is included in teacher preparation programs (National Association for Gifted Children [NAGC] & Council of State Directors of Programs for the Gifted, 2015). So what are specific considerations that should guide those who have responsibilities for developing a professional development plan?

Learning Forward (2011), an international organization dedicated to quality professional development, outlined seven standards for effective adult learning that include:

1. **Learning Communities:** Professional learning that increases educator effectiveness and results for all students occurs within learning communities committed to continuous improvement, collective responsibility, and goal alignment.

2. **Leadership:** Professional learning that increases educator effectiveness and results for all students requires skillful leaders who develop capacity, advocate, and create support systems for professional learning.

3. **Resources:** Professional learning that increases educator effectiveness and results for all students requires prioritizing, monitoring, and coordinating resources for educator learning.

4. **Data:** Professional learning that increases educator effectiveness and results for all students uses a variety of sources and type of student, educator, and system data to plan, assess, and evaluate professional learning.

5. **Learning Designs:** Professional learning that increases educator effectiveness and results for all students integrates theories, research, and models of human learning to achieve its intended outcomes.

6. **Implementation:** Professional learning that increases educator effectiveness and results for all students applies research on change and sustains support for implementation of professional learning for long-term change.

7. **Outcomes:** Professional learning that increases educator effectiveness and results for all students aligns its outcomes with educator performance and student curriculum standards.

All these standards are intended to bolster educator effectiveness and also increase student learning. These goals also support professional learning that is "interactive, relevant, sustained, and embedded in everyday practice. The [professional learning standards] require professional learning that contributes to educators' expertise and the quality of their professional practice, regardless of their role in the education workforce" (Learning Forward, 2011, p. 17). Attention to these essentials of planning and implementation can also have lasting effects on an entire learning community. In a survey of more than 1,000 teachers, Garet, Porter, Desimone, Birman, and Yoon (2001) found that intentionally planned professional development increases the likelihood that change will take place.

Another consideration planners of professional learning should focus on is the specific goals of the work. Guskey (2014) cautioned planners about the "Activity Trap." He explained this idea is similar to a teacher who plans her lesson based on what she wants her students to do and what resources she will need rather than focusing on the learning objectives she wants the students to reach by engaging in the activities. If professional learning planners discuss their plans in terms of what kinds of activities they will use with their teachers (such as job-embedded and contextually relevant), the goals that the professional learning should accomplish regarding improved educator practice and student achievement are too easily lost. Effective professional development designers plan backwards, deciding first where you want to end (learning outcomes), then deciding how you will get there (learning activities). Guskey noted the following decisions guide "professional development planning: (1) student learning outcomes, (2) new practices to be implemented, (3) needed organizational support, (4) desired educator knowledge and skills, and (5) optimal professional learning activities" (p. 13).

GUIDING PRINCIPLES AND ATTRIBUTES THAT DEFINE HIGH QUALITY

Several principles of quality professional learning have been published by education agencies, state departments of education, and professional organizations to offer guidance for schools and districts responsible for planning and delivering professional learning. For example, the Massachusetts Department of Education (2012) suggested the following guiding principles:

1. High Quality Professional Development is intentional.

2. High Quality Professional Development is a process.

3. High Quality Professional Development is evaluated for effectiveness.

4. High Quality Professional Development requires strong leaders that:

    a. Strengthens the structure and organization of professional development

    b. Guarantees follow-up to professional development

    c. Promotes a culture of high expectations. (p. 3)

The Department of Education and Training (2005) further elaborated on these ideas. They offered these principles:

- Professional learning is focused on student outcomes (not just individual teacher needs).
- Professional learning is focused on and embedded in teacher practice (not disconnected from the school).
- Professional learning is informed based on the best available research on effective teaching and learning (not just limited to what they currently know).
- Professional learning is collaborative, involving reflection and feedback (not just individual inquiry).
- Professional learning is evidence based and data driven (not anecdotal) to guide improvement and to measure impact.
- Professional learning is ongoing, supported and fully integrated into the culture and operations of the system (not episodic and fragmented).
- Professional learning is an individual and collective responsibility at all levels of the system (not just the school level) and it is not optional. (pp. 14–16)

Other examples of guiding principles for professional learning may be found at content-specific professional organization websites.

According to Archibald, Coggshall, Croft, and Goe (2011), there are five characteristics of high-quality professional development that are supported by research:

1. alignment with school goals, state and district assessments, and other professional learning activities including formative teacher evaluation;

2. focus on core content and modeling of teaching strategies for the content;

3. inclusion of active strategies for learning new teaching strategies;

4. provision of opportunities for collaboration among teachers; and

5. inclusion of embedded follow-up and continuous feedback. (p. 16)

Last, guidelines regarding professional development (see Standard 6 from the NAGC Pre-K–Grade 12 Gifted Programming Standards) and teacher preparation (specifically see the NAGC-CEC Teacher Preparation Standards in Gifted and Talented Education) can provide planners of professional development with additional resources that are aligned with best practices in the field of gifted education.

In addition to using the principles and research-based characteristics of professional development and the recommendations from the gifted education field, the following probing questions in eight key areas may assist planners in their efforts to offer high-quality professional learning for teachers.

Allgnment

- To what extent do the professional learning experiences align with the district mission statement and the professional development for general education?
- To what extent does the professional development align with the Knowledge and Skill Standards in Gifted Education for All Teachers (NAGC, 2014)?
- To what extent does the professional development address the learning needs of the teachers and administrators who work with gifted students in your school or district?
- To what extent are the professional development sessions purposefully aligned and sequenced with each other to deepen professional learning?
- To what extent are professional learning experiences linked with professional responsibility?

Content

- To what extent are the desired learning outcomes based on a sound diagnosis of participants' prior knowledge and experience (Learning Forward, 2011)?
- To what extent does the content reflect current research or best practice?
- Is the content grounded in theory?
- Does the content have meaning and/or relevance for the participants?

Comprehensiveness

- Do professional learning opportunities span the needs of gifted education students, Pre-K–Grade 12?
- To what extent do professional learning opportunities attend not only to cognitive, but also to the social and emotional learning and counseling needs of gifted and talented students?

Nature of Professional Learning Opportunities

- To what extent do the professional learning experiences provide practitioners with opportunities to construct meaning about their new learning (e.g., focused conversations, small-group conversations for reflection or summarizing, guided practice)?
- Is the professional development differentiated to attend to critical differences among practitioners?
- To what extent are different formats used to deliver the professional development activities and attend to critical differences among the learners (see Figure 12.1)?

Figure 12.1   Formats for Professional Development

Professional development planners need to consider a variety of formats when designing staff development options for educators. The following models are offered as possible ideas and should be shared with teachers so as to allow choice and buy-in to the improvement efforts that are the focus of school and district. Planners may wish to survey staff members to determine their preferences for particular formats and use the data to build or refine their professional development efforts.

___ Whole-Group Workshop	___ Conference Presentation
___ Conference Attendance	___ Online Courses
___ Staff Share Sessions	___ Professional Learning Communities
___ Retreats	___ Technology
___ Brown-Bag Lunch	___ Community Expert
___ Classroom Demonstrations	___ Critical Friends Groups
___ Peer Review	___ Cross-Grade Cadres
___ Resource Team	___ Friday Forums
___ Multiyear Model	___ Grade-Level Leaders
___ Coaching	___ Action Research
___ Independent Study	___ Analyze Student Work
___ Graduate Coursework	___ School or Classroom Visits
___ Study Groups	___ Institutes or Academies

- To what extent do teachers have a choice in the ways in which they acquire new information, deepen understanding, and practice new skills in supportive environments?
- To what degree is there an alignment of individual educator's professional development goals with the program goals?

Follow-Up Opportunities

- To what extent are there structured opportunities for reflection?
- What is the nature and extent of follow-up learning (e.g., critical friends groups, planning time for collaborative lesson planning, analyses of student work samples)?
- To what degree do opportunities exist for coaching and scaffolding teachers' practice?
- Are there procedures to refine skills, share successes, address concerns, and problem solve new issues?
- Are there opportunities for educators to share their expertise either as presenters, coaches, critical friends, and so forth?

Resources

- To what extent are resources made available to support the professional development?

- Are multiple ways of learning incorporated into the professional development plan (e.g., multimedia, print articles, supplementary readings, videos)?

Scheduling

- Are learning opportunities scheduled in such a way throughout the year so that they maximize professional learning?
- To what extent are teachers released during the school day to attend professional development activities?

Evaluation

- Are evaluations conducted about the quality of professional learning experiences?
- To what extent are the data from these evaluations used to inform subsequent professional development practices?

EXAMPLE IN NEED OF REVISION

The following e-mail was sent during the summer to all faculty and staff of Ellen B. Smith School:

To: All Ellen B. Smith School Faculty/Staff
From: G. R. Dunn, Principal
Subject: Upcoming In-Service Date: August 8, 2016

I hope that you are having a pleasant summer. To meet state and district requirements, our school's annual in-service for gifted and talented education will be held on August 8 from 1:00–3:30 p.m. This will be in combination with two other workshops that we will hold on this first day back in our buildings. For you to get credit for attending this training, you must sign in when you arrive after lunch. All faculty and support staff are required to attend. The in-service presenter will be our enrichment specialist, Mr. Baker.

Sincerely,

G. R. Dunn
Ellen B. Smith School

"Learning Is Something We Do"

During the in-service, Mr. Baker presented a PowerPoint that was prepared by the district office. Mr. Baker reviewed the state requirements for gifted identification and the schedule of gifted classes for the school year. In addition, he explained the Individualized Education Plan process that each special education team follows in the state. The teachers and staff who attended were given a copy of the PowerPoint notes at the end of the training.

MAKEOVER EXAMPLE

Quality professional development is not achieved in one-shot in-service sessions on random topics. These kinds of professional learning opportunities would certainly not be sufficient to address the needs of gifted and talented students. Professional learning

- is sustained over time,
- involves groups of teachers from the same school,
- provides opportunities for active learning,
- is coherent with other reforms and teachers' activities, and
- is focused on specific content and teaching strategies.

After reviewing the example above, it is clear that there may be a few components of the professional development plan that are either off the mark or completely missing. For instance, there is no indication that these professional learning opportunities will be sustained over time or differentiated for the varying needs of the faculty. All faculty and staff are required to attend, but there isn't a clear reason provided for why it is important for everyone to attend. Without clear goals, it would be hard for faculty and staff to see how their learning will be tied to student learning.

How we communicate about professional development sets the stage for transformational learning. The administrator in the example in need of revision clarified how faculty and staff would receive credit for attending the workshop (sign-in sheets at the meeting), but little information was shared about the content or purpose of the workshop itself.

Finally, the workshop was structured to disseminate information in a PowerPoint presentation, including content that was loosely connected to classroom practice and was unlikely to provide support for all teachers working to meet the needs of gifted students. There was no mention of any next steps in the training, and it was unclear if teachers were actively engaged in the learning. In addition, with the increase in utilizing technology to extend professional development beyond the four walls of the in-service session, it would benefit the district to think of other ways to connect with teachers. Without framing the needs of gifted and talented learners within the greater context of all students, many teachers may walk away from the presentation not realizing how the information shared in the workshop connects to the students in their classrooms.

The makeover example of the professional development plan for the Ellen B. Smith School has been revised to address these concerns and incorporate the characteristics of high-quality professional development plans described previously.

The following e-mail was sent during the summer to all faculty and staff of Ellen B. Smith School:

To: All Ellen B. Smith School Faculty/Staff

From: I. M. Thotful, Principal

Subject: Upcoming In-Service

Date: August 8, 2016

This year we will continue our professional learning about techniques for improving student learning and achievement. To respond to the feedback received from teachers about their preferred professional development topics, we will focus on the diversity of students in our classrooms. Our professional work will include careful examination of the characteristics of not only those learners who are experiencing difficulty in our classrooms, but also those who have advanced learning needs. The goals for our professional learning this year include:

- identifying the characteristics and needs of our student population,
- implementing strategies and techniques to respond to the needs of our students,
- collaborating with colleagues to grow in differentiation and documenting that growth, and
- fostering reflection in our practice to help us grow in teacher expertise.

We have created a series of carefully planned professional development experiences that are based on the most recent and research-based instructional practices. Many sessions will be based on the book you received in May, *The Differentiated Classroom: Responding to the Needs of All Learners* by Dr. Carol Ann Tomlinson, who is an expert in differentiated instruction. We have in-house and district specialists who can assist us with planning and delivering ideas. Each month we will have a presentation for the entire faculty that focuses on one type of learner. After the presentation for the entire staff, each grade-level team or department meeting will include time to share teachers' successes and struggles related to meeting these students' needs. By doing so, we hope that practitioners will benefit from each other's practices.

As always, your comments and reflections are important. We will be conducting evaluations, or Exit Cards, at the end of each session and seeking your input regarding how we can increase our overall effectiveness. All presentation videos, materials, and website links will be available through our school's Google Connect network. We will also put all materials in our school's shared folder online. We look forward to a rich online discussion.

The following schedule is proposed for this semester's monthly in-service meetings. As in the past, these sessions are scheduled during the school day and substitutes will be provided:

August: Advanced learners

September: Students with learning disabilities

October: English language learners and twice-exceptional learners

(Continued)

(Continued)

November: Student work samples reviewed

December: Planning our next steps for follow-up

As each monthly session approaches, you will receive a packet of information about each topic. The selections, which may be print, electronic, or video, have been carefully selected as noteworthy resources.

You will be receiving a link to the materials for the August 8 session in the next week. We look forward to our growth together as professionals this year.

Sincerely,

I. M. Thotful
Ellen B. Smith School

"Committed to Lifelong Learning"

It is important to note that the professional development in the make-over example is really targeting the needs of all learners in the district and is incorporated thoughtfully into the broader school mission and plan. When developing a professional development plan for the needs of gifted and talented learners, planners need to take into account where their goals fit within the school or districts' overall goals and capitalize on this opportunity. As in the revised example above, the gifted and talented teacher is contributing to the following learning goal: identifying the needs and characteristics of our student population. Given that goal, the content provided needs to be focused on what classroom teachers and other leaders in the building need to know about advanced learners. This is only a small part of what might be the professional development plan for the district. Inherent in this plan is the need for gifted education practitioners to receive the professional development they need to learn and grow in their career. The next section will focus on advice for getting started on a professional development plan that encompasses the needs of classroom teachers and gifted education practitioners.

ADVICE FOR GETTING STARTED

How can one improve on a professional development plan? Compare your district professional development opportunities to each of the markers of exemplary professional learning contained in the section on Guiding Principles and Attributes That Define High Quality (page 171). For example, to what extent is your professional development based on current research and best practices? Or to what extent does your plan provide for multiple ways of learning, such as through print, videotapes, and/or tools of technology? On one hand, if your assessment reveals that your professional development rates highly on each of the markers, you need to maintain the quality of your professional development for gifted education. On the other hand, if you find that your professional development does not measure up on one or more of the quality markers, identify all areas in need of improvement and then prioritize where you should concentrate your efforts. Work systematically to increase the quality of each of the elements until you are satisfied that you have an effective professional development program for gifted education teachers and administrators. Finding colleagues from around your state or within a professional organization like NAGC can be a good source of information and help. There are also numerous well-respected resources available online to help you identify key content as well as delivery strategies for professional learning opportunities. Additional resources follow.

Example of a Professional Development Plan

This strategic plan is based on the assumption that no professional development plan exists for gifted education practitioners. Readers in districts that already have a plan in place are invited to pinpoint, within the following plan, where they need to address their efforts. This takes into account that professional development occurs in a cycle that typically follows these phases: (a) assessment, (b) planning, and (c) implementation (see Figure 12.2). The following plan provides examples of each phase.

- **Objective:** To develop a plan for professional development for gifted education practitioners.
- **Evidence:** A comprehensive plan for professional development that is aligned with the mission statement of the school, the professional development plan for general education, and the learning needs of the gifted education teachers and administrators. It will address the competencies expected of all educators of the gifted and talented.
- **Tasks:** Tasks are included on the following pages.

Figure 12.2 The Professional Development Cycle

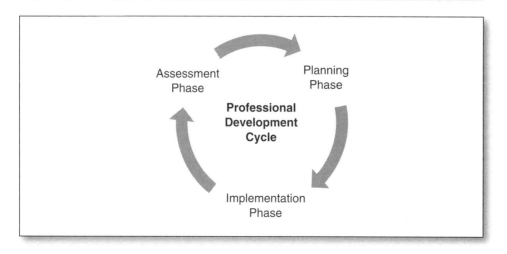

December (Planning Phase)

Convene a committee that is charged with designing, implementing, and evaluating an effective professional development plan for gifted education practitioners. Invited members should include (a) classroom teachers from general education, (b) gifted education teachers, (c) a building administrator, and (d) central office personnel.

January–February

Meet with the committee members over time to review the following:

- the existing school mission statement,
- the existing plan for professional development for general education,
- the gifted education position statement, and
- the goals for the gifted education program.

March

Develop, administer, and analyze a simple needs assessment to evaluate the competencies. A list of competencies is shown in Figure 12.3.

April

Keeping the results, gifted program goals, mission statement, and schoolwide professional development plan in mind, generate one to two long-range goals for professional development (e.g., practitioners will be able to provide standards-based curriculum differentiation options for high-ability students both in the regular and the gifted program).

May

For each long-term goal, generate two to three short measurable objectives (e.g., gifted education teachers will be able to develop differentiated lessons in social studies in Grades 4–8 that attend to students' learning needs, gifted education teachers will be able to develop differentiated lessons in mathematics in Grades K–3 to attend to students' unique learning needs).

June–August

Create an ongoing series of learning opportunities that will support the acquisition of the target knowledge and methodologies. Identify who will provide the training, when and where it will be held, and the duration of the training. Ensure a variety of learning formats and differentiated learning options, based on the prior knowledge of the practitioners involved. (See Figure 12.1.)

Secure any resources that will be needed to support the training (e.g., books, articles, audiovisual materials).

Figure 12.3 Competencies for Gifted Education Specialists

What follows is a basic list of competencies for gifted education specialists. It is not intended to be comprehensive, nor does it attend to the variations that exist among states' certification and endorsement regulations. It can be used, however, to help educational leaders who are charged with developing professional development plans for gifted education practitioners (NAGC, 2010; NAGC-CEC, 2013). See also Appendix B, page 261.

Identification

1. Understand the most commonly used assessment instruments for the identification of gifted students, including those instruments that are likely to identify underserved populations. Common assessments for all populations of students include: disaggregated state assessment data, IQ assessments, ability tests (verbal and nonverbal), norm-referenced assessments, achievement tests, primary grade assessments, teacher recommendations, behavior rating scales, portfolios, and peer nominations.
2. Select those assessments most appropriate for the demographics of the community.
3. Create and implement the procedures for the identification of gifted and talented students, Pre-K–12.
4. Understand and communicate to any constituency the state policies that regulate the identification and service of gifted education students.
5. Explain the alignment between the state definition and the district-level definition, should there be a variation.
6. Based on the identification process, develop a general learning profile of the students who have been identified that includes a composite picture of students' interests, academic strengths and weaknesses, learning style preferences, expression style preferences, and social and emotional needs.

Program Planning

7. Understand broadly the district-level curriculum in all content areas: language arts, science, social studies, mathematics, foreign languages, and the visual and performing arts.
8. Identify the most appropriate theoretical and administrative model(s) for service delivery.
9. Create program goals and objectives that take into consideration gifted education students' learning needs and that are aligned with the district-level curriculum.
10. Create, implement, and assess an aligned and comprehensive set of curriculum units for gifted education students who are served in a pull-out administrative model.
11. Create and implement a continuum of acceleration and enrichment options that is aligned with the learning needs of gifted education students, Pre-K–12, and the district curriculum.
12. If one is required, prepare an Individual Education Program (IEP) in concert with parents.
13. Prepare and maintain a program budget.
14. Identify and purchase high-quality resources.
15. Plan and implement ongoing activities for students related to college planning.

Program Evaluation

16. Plan and implement a program evaluation, and disseminate the results of the evaluation to all stakeholders.

Advocacy

17. Manage an ongoing communication initiative.
18. Develop and sustain advocacy at the local and state level that is aligned with the district plan.

Professional Development

19. Design and implement a professional development plan for gifted education teachers that is aligned with the district professional development plan.
20. Develop and implement a professional development plan for regular classroom teachers about the learning needs of gifted education students.
21. Work collaboratively with regular classroom teachers to support curriculum differentiation for students.

Develop and implement an assessment of the professional learning opportunities that is tied to the teachers' work resulting from the professional learning: (a) checklists of various types (e.g., the number of requests of differentiated lesson plans from regular classroom teachers), (b) teacher reflections, (c) student work, (d) teacher lesson plans, and (e) sample assignments.

September–May (Implementation Phase)

Implement and coordinate the professional development activities.

June (Assessment Phase)

Analyze, compile, and share the assessment data with all stakeholders. Make recommendations and adjust the professional development plan as required.

This professional development plan is just an example of a plan that models the cycle of professional development. At the end of this plan, all involved will evaluate where they are with the original goals and return to the planning phase again for a new cycle. In a district, there are many opportunities to share resources and get the support needed when developing a plan for professional development. If a gifted education practitioner is on his or her own, it can be challenging, but not impossible. The following section highlights suggestions for sole practitioners.

ADVICE FOR THE SOLE PRACTITIONER

Designing a quality professional development program should be the responsibility of several individuals within a school system, and a person who has sole responsibility for a program will find collaborating with others a benefit. Seek out other employees who may be of assistance in designing and implementing professional development opportunities, as well as individuals in your school or district who have demonstrated an interest in better meeting the needs of gifted students. This collaboration can also increase the likelihood that such efforts will match goals that are part of a total school focus and perhaps solicit help in carrying out the work. If it is not possible to find someone within your district to help plan professional learning, working with others in neighboring districts, professional organizations, state departments of education, and/or service centers can enhance your efforts in developing a district plan and also maximize limited resources. There may be additional individuals not highlighted here who would be helpful in this endeavor, but regardless of with whom or where you find others to collaborate, your plan is likely to be more comprehensive and complete if you can share the responsibility with other interested educators. An added benefit to working with other professionals is that the work can be more enjoyable and ultimately more effective to benefit all teachers and students.

SUGGESTED RESOURCES

Department of Education and Training. (2005). *Professional learning in effective schools: The seven principles of highly effective professional learning.* Abbotsford, Victoria, Australia: McLaren Press.

This publication offers a quick review of best practices when planning professional development highlighting each of the principles noted in this chapter and offering ideas in the Appendices on how to use the principles in practice.

Learning Forward. (2011). *Standards for professional learning.* Oxford, OH: Author.

This publication reviews each of the seven professional learning standards, offering more detailed information about each and how they might be implemented in different settings.

National Association for Gifted Children, & Council for Exceptional Children. (2013). *NAGC-CEC Teacher Preparation Standards in Gifted and Talented Education.* Washington, DC: Author.

This publication outlines seven standards that should guide the preparation of professionals in gifted education. Each of the seven standards represents important emphases within a program of study in gifted education for preservice or in-service educators seeking their initial preparation in this field. Each set of underlying emphases is described by knowledge and skills essentials to the work of personnel preparation and provides additional text elaborating on the intent and scope of the standard.

REFERENCES

Archibald, S., Cogshall, J. G., Croft, A., & Goe, L. (2011). *High quality professional development for all teachers: Effectively allocating resources* (Research and Policy Brief). Washington, DC: The National Comprehensive Center for Teacher Quality.

Department of Education and Training. (2005). *Professional learning in effective schools: The seven principles of highly effective professional learning.* Abbotsford, Victoria, Australia: McLaren Press.

Garet, M., Porter, A. C., Desimone, L., Birman, B. F., & Yoon, K. S. (2001). What makes professional development effective? Results from a national sample of teachers. *American Education Research Association Journal, 38,* 115–145.

Guskey, T. R. (2014). Planning professional learning. *Educational Leadership, 71*(8), 10–16.

Learning Forward. (2011). *Standards for professional learning.* Oxford, OH: Author.

Massachusetts Department of Education. (2012). *The Massachusetts standards for professional development.* Retrieved from www.doe.mass.edu/pd/standards.docx

Mizell, H. (2010). *Why professional development matters.* Oxford, OH: Learning Forward. Retrieved from www.learningforward.org/advancing/whypdmatters.cfm

National Association for Gifted Children. (2010). *NAGC Pre-K–Grade 12 Gifted Programming Standards: A blueprint for quality gifted education programs.* Washington, DC: Author.

National Association for Gifted Children. (2014). *Knowledge and skill standards in gifted education for all teachers.* Washington, DC: Author.

National Association for Gifted Children, & Council for Exceptional Children. (2013). *NAGC-CEC Teacher Preparation Standards in Gifted and Talented Education.* Washington, DC: Author.

National Association for Gifted Children, & Council of State Directors of Programs for the Gifted. (2015). *State of the states: Gifted and talented education report, 2014–2015.* Washington, DC: National Association for Gifted Children.

Chapter 13

Collaborating With Families to Support Gifted Students

Mallory M. Bagwell, PhD,
and Michele Femc-Bagwell, PhD

DEFINITION

The two most common definitions for *collaborate* are: (a) work jointly on an activity, especially to produce or create something; and (b) cooperate traitorously with an enemy (Collaborate, n.d.). Both interpretations are important and useful, if not mutually inclusive, especially for those individuals charged with developing or expanding programs and services for gifted students. Moreover, the timing of collaboration is essential; *timely collaboration* with families in support of gifted children suggests a dynamic urgency to the task at hand. As in many areas of education, health, and human development, time is a common benchmark for identification, placement, progress, and definition. With respect to the second definition and program planning, keep time as an ally in your program structure, not an enemy.

Current efforts in school reform have seen the emergence, discussion, and research of parent engagement as a factor for student success and school accountability (Epstein, 2010; Hornby & Lafaele, 2011; Jeynes, 2012). The term *parent engagement* broadly refers to parent involvement, volunteering, partnering, parent advocacy, communication strategies, home learning practices, shared decision making, and various community-school relationships (Dearing, Kreider, Simpkins, & Weiss, 2006; Henderson & Mapp, 2002; Porter, 2008). Gifted practitioners can use this expanding definitional landscape in a comprehensive way that acknowledges various stakeholders' agendas, including parents and caregivers of gifted children. Maintaining a broad sense of parent engagement can greatly enhance the objectives of gifted education programs. In addition, effective collaboration with families can build awareness of the "similarities and differences with respect to the development and characteristics of advanced and typical learners and support students with gifts and talents' needs" as described in the National Association for Gifted Children's (NAGC, 2010, p. 8) Pre-K–Grade 12 Gifted Programming Standards. Ultimately, strategic planning and programming that value and foster collaboration with family and communities can become a powerful source for simultaneous renewal and creative innovation to better meet the needs of gifted and talented students. Within the context of gifted programs and services, successful collaboration with parents is: child- and family-centric (as opposed to only program-centric), equitable in decision/vision making, results oriented, and timely from the moment a child starts formal schooling, if not sooner.

Hoover-Dempsey and Sandler (1997) identified three major factors of parental involvement in the education of children: (a) parents' beliefs about what is important, necessary, and permissible for them to do with and on behalf of their children; (b) the extent to which parents believe that they can have a positive influence on their children's education; and (c) parents' perceptions that their children and school want them to be involved. In essence, family collaboration revolves around the need for priorities and permission, empowerment and advocacy, and acceptance and access to be granted to and developed with parents.

RATIONALE

Research overwhelmingly suggests that academic performance, as well as positive cognitive and affective growth, are bolstered when families are engaged[1] and involved in student learning (Dearing et al., 2006; Epstein, 2010; Hornby & Lafaele, 2011; Jeynes, 2012). Meaningful collaboration with families of gifted students is especially important as educators work toward the standards of developing self-understanding and building an awareness of needs. Moreover, active student participation in gifted programs is more likely to reflect the cultural and socioeconomic diversity of the wider community when family members are informed and engaged in innovative and respectful ways (Ford, 2006; Lawrence, 2009; Olszewski-Kubilius & Clarenbach, 2012).

During the past few decades, perceptions and roles in the home-school communication process have evolved from a top-down, directive style toward one with mutual contribution from parents and educators (Hammitte & Nelson, 2001; Porter, 2002). For all students, parent-teacher

---

[1]A comprehensive literature review on parent engagement can be found in Henderson and Mapp (2002) and Epstein (2010).

partnerships and home-school communications have been encouraged. Collaborative partnerships between parents and teachers value the different skills, experiences, and knowledge that parents and teachers bring to educational decisions on the needs of individual students (Epstein, 2010). This orientation toward mutual contributions can enhance many of the programmatic decisions in gifted education including those concerning identification, acceleration, curriculum, instructional strategies, professional development, and resource allocation.

Porter (2008) provided an overview of the different roles of parents and teachers in her "continuum of parent-teacher relationship styles" (p. 4). Porter portrayed the preferred home-school communication style as falling between the family-allied and family-centered orientations. (These preferred styles have been highlighted in Table 13.1.)

Porter (2008) offered a collaborative structure that embraces the research and serves as a start for considering the means and methods of delivering program services. Ideally, school and family should be striving toward communication and interactions described in the column labeled Family Centered. Nevertheless, a profile of engagement can draw from multiple columns simultaneously and is not expected to be static. It is not unusual for first-time parents of a gifted child to initially follow the lead of the specialist on many points. As they better understand the field and their child's abilities, communication and collaboration styles tend to shift to the right of the chart with more requests, self-direction, and generated solutions. Ultimately, the focus is on continued development for all involved. The shaded columns of Table 13.1 depict a realistic and workable fit, because the combination allows school and family to give and take of their expertise without putting the burden of programming wholly on one or the other.

GUIDING PRINCIPLES AND ATTRIBUTES THAT DEFINE HIGH-QUALITY COLLABORATION

Effective collaboration for the gifted education professional strives to:

- **be understood, aligned, and utilized by all educational professionals.** In a nationwide survey of 900 teachers in Grades 3–12, more than half the respondents indicated little to no emphasis in their preservice training on meeting the needs of academically advanced students (Farkas & Duffett, 2008). Administrators and general education teachers are often the first contact for families seeking answers to their questions about giftedness and educational opportunities within the district. Without training and support, teachers may struggle in understanding parents' unique perspectives and answering questions about available identification and services. Therefore, establishing understanding and open communication across *all* members of a school community is the first priority in successful collaboration with parents and families.

Table 13.1   Continuum of Parent-Teacher Relationship Styles

	Professional Driven	Family Allied	Family Centered	Family Driven
View of Parents	Sources of their child's concerns	Facilitators of the program's objectives	Equal participants with complementary skills and expertise	Family as leader Teacher as guide/resource
Parents' Role	Comply with practitioner advice Defer to professionals	Carry out assigned tasks to support their child's learning at home and school	Egalitarian approach to planning and enacting programs	Parents direct their child's education and style of participation
Assessment	Practitioners locate deficits within the child or family	Practitioners assess children's needs	Practitioners assess children's needs and family's strengths	Solution focused: Identify solutions that are already in place
Source of Goals or Priorities	Professionals dictate goals and interventions	Parents consent to a program designed by practitioners	Joint goal setting and shared decision making to meet family needs	Parents and students articulate their own goals or aspirations
Purpose of Interactions with Parents	To advise parents of their child's needs and program	To engage parents in helping practitioners teach their child	To empower parents to meet their child's and family's needs	To listen to parents so that practitioners can provide a service to meet their goals
Communication Style	Top-down flow of information and parents receive training	Communication is task focused and parents are educated	Communication builds relationships and empowers parent participation	Communication maintains a responsive and collaborative relationship that supports parents' interests in their child's education

Source: Adapted from Porter (2008, p. 4).

- **support a family-centered and family-allied perspective.** Families arrive in your program with various degrees of awareness, needs, and visions. They will not remain in your sphere of influence forever, so educate them, enable them, empower them, design programs for them, and rely on them. Provide parents with strategies and tools for communicating effectively with school personnel and collaborating with teachers to define meaningful academic and social goals for their child. Informed parents become identifiers of talent, deliverers of services, and advocates; they represent more "hands on deck" for the work you are trying to do. There must be times, places, and materials for this exchange of information to occur.

- **be proactive in getting to know and valuing all parents by tapping into the collective resource of the families in the entire school community.** Effective collaboration is as much about relationship building as it is about information sharing. Create opportunities that will allow you to get to know the families in your community, build relationships, and identify parental talents in your school or district. Casting a wide net by way of assessing the interests, talents, skills, and relationships of parents is one way to do this. Parents, like their children, possess a tremendous amount of skills, talents, resources, and social capital that can be brought to bear on gifted education programs via enrichment programming, mentorships, career exposure, and specialized knowledge.

- **be known to all the parents in the school from Year 1 of their arrival.** Whether parents will have children directly in your program or not, it is minimally imperative to have name recognition and be recognizable (not so much by title) as someone to whom all parents view as a potential resource for their children regardless of whether or not their child receives direct services from your program.

- **differentiate communication methods and develop a consistent personal—yet instructional—style of speaking, writing, and acting.** Communication has various forms (e.g., text, call, e-mail, letter, flyer, meeting, visit, website) and styles (e.g., authoritative, supportive, assistive, family-centric, proactive, reactive) that need to be used with a heightened consciousness of placement and purpose. Don't confuse the means of communication (the "taxi") with the purposes of communication (the agreed upon "destination"). Moreover, communication must be proactive and maintain a consistent pattern of timely contact with individual families.

  There is a multitude of options for transmitting information between school and home. Be cognizant of what works best and when for each family. One method does not fit all situations and definitely does not fit everyone's preferences for communication—especially families of English language learners (ELLs) or those with limited Internet access, shared custody, or childcare constraints, for example.

- **use print and web-based resources for description, reference, and documentation.** A comprehensive and orderly online presence is essential. A mission statement, rationale, objectives, and procedures regarding your gifted program should all be readily available for any interested community member, including families. In addition, informational articles and links to trusted gifted education websites can also be helpful. A blog can be part of the site for archival reference but should not be relied on as the primary means of disseminating information or contacting parents.

- **develop intake, orientation, and follow-up procedures that ensure parents understand the uniqueness of their child's abilities with a sense of seriousness and are prepared to nurture them in the most appropriate ways possible.** Be sensitive and responsive to family history (language, culture, concerns, strengths, visions) and keep the information in mind when programming. Know the families in your community by using timely, informative, and authentic communication—and provide families with pathways for connecting and sharing with one another. Assist parents in accumulating a toolbox of experiences, techniques, and understanding. Share and explain professional language and methodologies. Let the parents lead, you guide.

EXAMPLE IN NEED OF REVISION

The program at Little Elementary School is a stand-alone gifted and talented program, seemingly self-contained and self-supporting. The surrounding community is glad to have this component of the educational spectrum in place to meet the needs of its high-ability students. The program has some visibility and looks administratively compliant but can still be difficult to comprehend and access. Parent contact is minimal to nonexistent until identification of students in the program is made, usually at the end of second grade. The program is a one-size-fits-all pull-out program with 10% of the school population in Grades 3–5 having contact with the school gifted specialist. There is not a broad understanding by the majority of parents or community members about what the program does, can do, for whom, or why. There is a palpable distance between it and other programs because it does not serve as many students (or families) as other programs, and at times it may be viewed as academically tangential.

The gifted program's objectives, description, and procedures are described in a Board of Education booklet that suggests useful websites and contains checklists of "Dos" and "Don'ts" about parenting bright kids. The program is administered in a top-down fashion with goals recommended by the school's gifted specialist with a focus on core academics and performance on annual standardized tests.

Each year, parents are invited to attend a short, pro forma meeting to discuss their child's Individualized Education Plan (IEP) with the gifted education specialist. However, print seems to be the dominant method of information transmittal with flyers, handouts, packets, permission slips, agendas, and notices all arriving with a consistent look and regularity. Family members have no in-school access to books, articles, or resources. Record-keeping is immaculate, but no records are kept of the students after they exit the program and the school. There is a year-end forced choice survey ("Like" or "Dislike") for feedback. People are grateful, and the program survives.

Not all staff members are aware of the research and pedagogy in gifted education. As a result, program integration with the rest of the school is tentative and unintentionally reclusive. The gifted specialist is not part of kindergarten orientation, nor does she collaborate with music, art, or physical education teachers who observe their own examples of extreme talent in the school and do their own thing with concerts and exhibitions. School assembly programs are sporadic with some recognizable alignment to the curriculum. Parents are seen at biannual parent conferences (Thanksgiving and late April). Portfolios are nonexistent.

The Little Elementary Parent Teacher Organization (PTO) meetings have a good turnout (32 parents) with at least one teacher representative attending. The gifted specialist attends occasionally for purposes of informing or specific requests.

MAKEOVER EXAMPLE

Arguably, the gifted program at Little Elementary School could be deemed successful. It has a gifted education professional, funding, structure, and clarity. It identifies and provides services for academically advanced students and strives to keep those students' families informed about activities and student progress. It wrestles with issues most school programs have regarding resource allocation, public awareness, and effective outreach. It's tidy, so the inclination might be to tweak rather than overhaul it. What's the problem? Relationships have value. Every colleague, parent, family member, and community member can exert influence on your program, *if* you know where they are, what they can do, and build a system in which collaboration can flourish.

Let's start with the overarching guiding principle, "reduce distance," and rework the example in need of revision. An effective first step would be the creation of a small advisory team, comprised of parents, teachers, and community members who will act as extra sets of eyes and in critiquing and guiding the structuring and revision process. Members of this team can also promote transparency of the change process through communication to their respective constituencies. (See Appendix A, page 256, for additional guidance on assembling and implementing an advisory team.)

To improve the program at Little Elementary School, members of the advisory team worked together to identify and outline three key changes to foster a more family-centered program:

1. greater understanding by and synchrony with the staff;

2. earlier, broader, and more frequent information sharing for and from parents; and

3. a transition from a hierarchical administrative style to a more lateral and interpersonal style for providing and supporting families with information.

Greater Understanding By and Synchrony With the Staff

The first thing that the advisory team recognized was the need throughout the community for an increased awareness of the needs of gifted students as well as services and programs available in the school to foster students' gifts and talents. The gifted specialist and a parent from the advisory team worked with the school principal to identify an efficient way to engage the entire faculty in this important conversation. They decided to poll the teachers about their comfort with talking to parents on various topics of gifted education and existing services and programming. This information allowed the specialist to prioritize what she will share in a new, 7-minute Gifted Education FAQ segment at monthly faculty meetings.

In addition, the gifted specialist at Little Elementary decided to promote synchrony with the general education staff by collaborating within the kindergarten registration, screening, and orientation processes. This strategy has the added benefit in that it provides direct contact with all families and students as they enter into the school and recognizes the role of families in promoting and identifying emergent potential. To extend further opportunities for collaboration and support, the parent advisory team also hopes to define a contributing role within parent conferences and music, art, and physical education programs and events.

Earlier, Greater, and Frequent Information Sharing for and From Parents in the Gifted Education Program

To accomplish this goal, the advisory team set a priority of meeting with *all* families of identified gifted students prior to entry into the program to discuss questions, concerns, goals, needs, and skill and information sets. Ideally, these initial meetings will be face-to-face. The plan is to find ways to identify best times, places, and methods (including preferred language) for information to be exchanged.

The advisory team also generated a list of strategies for regular and ongoing communication to promote parent empowerment and access:

- back-to-school letters;
- personalized notes home;
- parent support group;
- after school/before school drop-in;
- specific informational material (web-based and hard copy);

- regular columns in school newsletters;
- monthly phone calls, texts, and e-mail; and
- monthly book club.

To continue to build their knowledge base and constituency, members of the advisory team also constructed a calendar to highlight and encourage participation of interested family members at:

- PTO meetings;
- classroom, grade-level, and schoolwide events;
- small-group, evening forums for updates and feedback;
- individual conferences; and
- opportunities to participate in conferences or workshops sponsored by local, state, and national organizations (e.g., NAGC, Supporting Emotional Needs of the Gifted [SENG]).

Finally, as the level of expertise and awareness grows within the community, the responsibility for some of these communication tasks (e.g., website maintenance, newsletters) can be shared with interested individuals in the community. This shared responsibility implies and helps initiate the transition from a hierarchical administrative style to a more lateral and interpersonal style.

A Transition From a Hierarchical Administrative Style to a More Lateral and Interpersonal Style for Informing and Supporting With Information

Defining how best to work toward this change was perhaps the most daunting for the Little Elementary advisory team; however, once everyone acknowledged that this was a long-term goal that would continue to evolve over time, they were able to map out some important first steps. Initially, a small group of parents met to collect and review all the materials and gifted program information available for distribution to family members. These print- and web-based documents were edited to ensure a supportive and inclusive style that strives to elicit as well as inform, and new resources were created where holes were identified. Several volunteers also translated the documents into Portuguese and Spanish to better connect with non-English-speaking families in the district.

Excited about the prospect of reaching out and connecting with more families—and thinking about the untapped expertise in the community— the gifted specialist proposed a strategy to shift the personal dynamic even further. She found the ASPIRE Survey and other free resources online for inventorying the collective resource pool of a school community (Bagwell & Femc-Bagwell, 2012). Working with the school's family liaison, the gifted specialist was able to begin collecting information and community expertise to broaden and support the opportunities for students both in and outside the gifted program. The fifth-grade teachers were shocked when she was able to bring in an off-season NBA player to talk to students in math class about percentages and probabilities, but she suspects it will be much easier to convince teachers and families of the many benefits of collecting this information moving forward.

Finally, the advisory team members also agreed that increased transparency in the redesign process would promote more family-centered interactions. Therefore, they made it a priority to set the agenda, share the process, use common terminology, and build consensus for objectives and desired outcomes in their continued work together.

ADVICE FOR GETTING STARTED

- **Start with your digital presence.** Creating a well-designed web page (preferably one that links from the main school page) will require the gifted educator to assemble mission and vision statements, school and program policies, procedures, and program objectives, most of which should be readily available. The process demands that an organization and its employee(s) know what they believe in, why they believe it, and how they will make these beliefs manifest. Completed, it should clearly define the program and hold up to professional, public, and political scrutiny. The language should be as inclusive and inviting to the broadest group of parents as possible.

  The need for a web page is a good opportunity to create synchrony with other staff, especially those specifically responsible for technology. Eventually you will find a parent who loves this stuff and will make you look like a rock star (e.g., web code that automatically e-mails birthday greetings to all the other staff—or students or parents—or invites them to touch base once a month, or uploads a gifted education cartoon on Monday mornings). These are simple innocuous things that work in the background with no effort on your part but contain style and will shape your image and relationships in small but significant ways.

- **Become an integral part of the orientation process.** Meet all the parents and explain what your program does and share the various capacities in which they may engage with you during their time at the school. Be inclusive, not exclusive. Those capacities can include traditional direct services to their child, but explain the enrichment experiences available to all children be they in, or after, school, weekends, summer, or customized (e.g., student-designed playgrounds). Provide the website address at orientation meetings and consider sharing a simple handout with contact information to provide an overview and allow for questions. (A clever refrigerator calendar would work longer and be memorable. Perhaps one of your parents is a professional graphic designer and can help you.) Cast yourself front and center as a cultivator of existing and new talent, as a resource for all families, and a facilitator for their particular family situation when it comes to interests, abilities, and exceptionalities. Explain the difference between program-centric and family-centric approaches and the attendant responsibilities of the latter. Summarize with a thumbnail summary of the Hoover-Dempsey and Sandler (1997) study: priorities, permission, empowerment, advocacy, acceptance, and access. This is your desired process for, and outcome of, collaboration. There is nothing ignoble in creating advocacy by all parents for their children in line with the goals of your program. Get the succinct articulated message about your program out to everyone—in person if possible—and definitely from the day they set foot into your school.

- **Bridge the distance by going to where your constituency is: Meet parents on their turf.** Meet parents—all the school's parents—face-to-face, if possible. Be visible at assemblies, orientations, parent conferences, and board meetings; during student pick-up/drop-off; on bus routes (once); and at special events, not just at formally scheduled one-on-one meetings or conferences. Not all parents have cars, Internet, work schedules, or financial resources to accommodate school-based meetings, and so accommodating connections in nonschool settings and times is a serious consideration.

  Phone calls and face-to-face conversations are quite often the most effective forms of communication (and most time intensive) because they embrace simultaneous give and take, require being in the same place and/or time, and have a narrower audience and focus. Familiarize yourself with preferred times for calls. Letter writing is a close second. A hand-written thank you to parents who have helped you is essential and will be remembered for a lifetime. It is very powerful and tightly completes the circle of effective collaboration.

- **Provide opportunities for parents to come to you.** Look at your program from a content perspective. All children receive instruction in art, music, and physical education, yet are not necessarily in exhibits, concerts, or competitions. Not all children will fit the criteria for receiving the services your program provides and others will cycle in and out. Create an afterschool interest-based enrichment program that is available to all students and parents (as facilitators). All families can contribute to a unique and advantageous talent pool that is beneficial to the school community in general and gifted education programming in particular.

- **Collaborate to create a vision.** High-quality collaboration with families in support of gifted education programming will embody a set of traits that are logical extensions of the guiding principles described earlier in the chapter and grounded in the work of Hoover-Dempsey and Sandler (1997). Table 13.2 includes guiding questions that can be used to assess the presence of these traits in the development or redesign of a gifted program as well as suggestions for addressing needed improvements.

Table 13.2   The Actionable Intersections of Defining and Supporting Factors for Gifted Parent Engagement

Questions within the shaded boxes are overarching ones used for generating more specific ones within each cell.

	Definition Components	Centricity "Where is the primary focus?"	Equality "How and by whom are processes and services decided?"	Programmatic "Is the program product-oriented or process-oriented?"
What Aspects of Research Are Present?	Research Factors	**Child or Family or Program Centeredness**	**Vision and/or Decision Making**	**Results Timely Oriented**
	Priorities "What do I think is important to do on behalf of my child?"	Do I know my child's concerns, interests, and strengths, and is the school aware of them? Have opportunities been provided to share family history and concerns?	Are concerns heard, expanded on, or redirected? Is a plan of action explained, given, or solicited?	How and when will I be informed of my child's progress in his or her work and in the program?
	Permissions "What will the gifted program allow me to do on behalf of my child?"	Can I volunteer my own interests and skills to enrich the program or is my involvement limited by parameters defined narrowly by the school?	Will I be invited to be a part of the vision and decision-making processes? How might I contribute to the development of gifted program goals?	Will I have input to my child's educational plan based on my knowledge of his or her interests and learning styles? What policies exist to support access to advanced learning opportunities (e.g., acceleration, grouping, assessment)?
	Empowerment "What kinds of resources are available from and through the gifted program?"	Will I be able to share resources and programs of interest (that my child has experienced) in addition to those identified by the school? Will the school support specific requests?	How might I help plan and support a network for sharing available resources? Can I nominate my child for services?	How can my child participate in gifted programming and/or access available services?

	Definition Components	Centricity "Where is the primary focus?"	Equality "How and by whom are processes and services decided?"	Programmatic "Is the program product-oriented or process-oriented?"
	Research Factors	**Child or Family or Program Centeredness**	**Vision and/or Decision Making**	**Results Timely Oriented**
What Aspects of Research Are Present?	**Advocacy** "How strongly do I believe I can shape positive outcomes?"	Will parent learning opportunities be provided to help me better understand giftedness and how to advocate for my child and the program?	How will I promote the gifted program and available services to other parents and stakeholders?	Will my program improvement ideas be heard and considered? Will I be invited to be a part of the ongoing assessment/evaluation of the program's impact on my child's learning?
	Acceptance "Do I believe the school wants me to be involved?"	How will I know that my involvement is important to the gifted program as well as the broader school community?	How can relationships of trust and collaboration be developed between school and home?	How are students and their family members introduced to giftedness and services provided by gifted program staff? What role can I play in welcoming new members to this community?
	Access "What is necessary for my child and my child's family?"	Are there identified expectations for my child and our family for supporting his or her success?	To whom can I turn with questions, comments, or concerns about my child's talents or participation in the gifted program?	How will I learn of appropriately challenging educational opportunities for my child? How will I be informed of my child's performance in a timely way?

ADVICE FOR SOLE PRACTITIONER

Olympic curling is interesting, not so much for the sport as for its analogy to nature and nurture. Curlers (parents) show up at one end of the ice (school) and slide their stone (child) down to other curlers (teachers) with brooms (didactic materials) who sweep like crazy (pedagogy) in an attempt to shape (nurture) the trajectory (nature) of the stone they cannot touch. All want to get the stone to the best possible place (school performance) to win the gold medal (accountability). The broom sweeping is the best part. It can seem silly, useless, and frustrating all at the same time.

So go easy on yourself. You still have influence. You are not alone; not the only broom on the ice. There is more than one stone to come.

SUGGESTED RESOURCES

ASPIRE Survey (http://www.aspiresurvey.com)

The ASPIRE Survey is an easily administered web-based asset mapping instrument that assesses six aspects (Assets, Skills, Professions, Interests, Relationships, and Environment) of all people associated with a school. Its primary purpose is to create higher valuations of, and returns on, parent-participant contributions to their involvement within the school program at large and goal-oriented projects in particular; specifically curricular objectives and funding strategies. Download the free manuals on the homepage.

Center on School, Family, and Community Partnerships (http://www.csos.jhu .edu/p2000/center.htm)

Established at Johns Hopkins University in 1996, National Network of Partnership Schools (NNPS) invites schools, districts, states, and organizations to join together and use research-based approaches to organize and sustain excellent programs of family and community involvement that will increase student success in school. Based on more than three decades of research on parental involvement, family engagement, and community partnerships, NNPS's tools, guidelines, and action team approach may be used by all elementary, middle, and high schools to increase involvement and improve student learning and development.

Davidson Institute for Talent Development (http://www.davidsongifted.org)

This website provides resources for and about gifted students. It features easy search capabilities for articles, resources, and state policy pages to help students, parents, and educators pinpoint gifted information.

REFERENCES

Bagwell, M., & Femc-Bagwell, M. (2012). *The ASPIRE Survey: Six points of engagement for school communities.* Storrs, CT: Kavonia LLC.

Collaborate. (n.d.). In *Oxford online dictionary.* Retrieved June 30, 2015, from http://www.oxforddictionaries.com/us/definition/american_english/collaborate

Dearing, E., Kreider, H., Simpkins, S., & Weiss, H. B. (2006). Family involvement in school and low-income children's literacy: Longitudinal associations between and within families. *Journal of Educational Psychology, 98,* 653–644. doi:10.1037/0022-0663.98.4.653

Epstein, J. (2010). *School, family, and community partnerships: Preparing educators and improving schools* (2nd ed.). Boulder, CO: Westview Press.

Farkas, S., & Duffett, A. (2008). *High-achieving students in the era of NCLB: Results from a national teacher survey.* Washington, DC: Fordham Institute.

Ford, D. Y. (2006). Creating culturally responsive classrooms for gifted students. *Understanding Our Gifted, 19*(1), 10–14.

Hammitte, D. J., & Nelson, B. M. (2001). Community professionals' roles with families. In D. O'Shea, L. O'Shea, R. Algozzine, & D. Hammitte (Eds.), *Families and teachers of individuals with disabilities: Collaborative orientations and responsive practices* (pp. 250–270). Boston, MA: Allyn & Bacon.

Henderson, A., & Mapp, K. L. (2002). *Annual synthesis 2002: A new wave of evidence— The impact of school, family, and community connections on student achievement.* Austin, TX: SEDL National Center for Family and Community Connections With Schools.

Hoover-Dempsey, K. V., & Sandler, H. (1997). Why do parents become involved in their children's education? *Review of Educational Research, 67,* 3–42.

Hornby, G., & Lafaele, R. (2011). Barriers to parental involvement in education: An explanatory model. *Educational Review, 63,* 37–52. doi:10.1080/00131911.2010 .488049

Jeynes, W. (2012). A meta-analysis of the efficacy of different types of parent involvement programs for urban students. *Urban Education, 47,* 706–742. doi:10.1177/0042085912445643

Lawrence, B. K. (2009). Rural gifted education: A comprehensive literature review. *Journal for the Education of the Gifted, 32,* 461–494.

National Association for Gifted Children. (2010). *NAGC Pre-K–Grade 12 Gifted Programming Standards: A blueprint for quality gifted education programs.* Washington, DC: Author.

Olszewski-Kubilius, P., & Clarenbach, J. (2012). *Unlocking emergent talent: Supporting high achievement of low-income, high-ability students.* Washington, DC: National Association for Gifted Children.

Porter, L. (2002). *Educating young children with special needs.* Crows Nest, Australia: Allen & Unwin.

Porter, L. (2008). *Parent collaboration: Early childhood to adolescence.* Camberwell: Australian Council for Education Research.

Chapter 14

Planning
for Advocacy

Julia Link Roberts, EdD

DEFINITION

Advocacy is "the act of pleading or arguing in favor of something—an idea, cause, or policy" (National Association for Gifted Children, n.d.). This discussion of advocacy focuses on connecting with decision makers at the school, district, state, and national levels to provide the information and insight that will enable them to support strategies, services, and policies to initiate, implement, and support gifted education. Advocacy may be a onetime event; however, advocacy is most effective when it is an ongoing process. Both individuals and groups may find this discussion of advocacy useful.

RATIONALE

Why advocate? Informed and well-organized advocates can raise the level of awareness about the needs of children with gifts and talents at the school, district, state, and national levels. They can show that there is a positive impact on schools and communities when all children and young people, including those who are gifted and talented, are provided opportunities to make continuous progress and reach their potential. Advocates can influence the change of practices, policies, and laws that impact the education of gifted children (Roberts, 2014; Robinson & Moon, 2003). Without individuals and groups advocating on behalf of children who are gifted and talented, it is unlikely that decisions will be made to advance educational opportunities for gifted and talented young people.

One of the most important reasons to develop advocacy skills and strategies is the potential for positive changes that can benefit gifted students, their families, and the community. One example of effective advocacy took place in a medium-size city without gifted education programs or services. A parent of a young gifted child knew that as a newcomer in town, she would need to establish credibility before asking for accommodations for her daughter and other children who are gifted and talented. She spent the first year focused on schoolwide issues, including providing leadership for building a new playground. She also joined a small group of advocates for gifted education, and together they began to educate school and district administrators of the need to provide appropriate programming for gifted children. The next year, the advocacy continued with a focus on educating members of the district school board. The goal was to have a gifted resource teacher at each school, and the advocates were successful in reaching their goal. One person could not have done it alone. People without credibility or correct information could not have reached this goal. Well-informed advocates were able to achieve their goal because they had an agreed upon message (their goal) and worked together to educate the decision makers who could make the goal a reality.

Another example of effective advocacy occurred at the national level in the late 1980s. The vote was going to be close to get legislation through the Appropriations and Revenue Committee in the U.S. House of Representatives. The legislative chair of the National Association for Gifted Children (NAGC) called a longtime supporter of gifted children whom she knew was a friend of the chair of the committee, a gentleman whose vote would likely make the difference on this issue. In turn, the friend called the committee chair to talk about the issue. The result was a vote of support for the legislation by the Congressman. The rest is history. The Jacob K. Javits Gifted and Talented Students Education Act was passed. Knowing who in the organization has a long-term relationship with members of key committees is critical information. Having individuals follow up with decision makers is essential. Working together, advocates can make a difference for gifted children.

GUIDING PRINCIPLES AND ATTRIBUTES OF A HIGH-QUALITY ADVOCACY PLAN

A well-developed, strategic plan is required to provide the blueprint for an effective advocacy campaign. Moreover, a clear, focused message that is known and shared by advocates must be the centerpiece of this high-quality plan. Advocates not only should have a clear understanding of the message, but must also be well informed on gifted and general education issues and know where to locate answers they don't have.

Individuals developing a high-quality advocacy plan must also consider how interpersonal factors can affect the outcomes of their efforts. Advocacy is more likely to be successful when personal relationships are established with decision makers and communication is ongoing and responsive. Although the larger the number of advocates, the more likely decision makers will respond positively to the advocates' message, personalized communications—including hand-written letters—are often more effective and preferred to mass, computer-generated letters or e-mail. Finally, advocates must understand that perseverance is a key to effective advocacy and that gifted children need individuals who will be lifetime spokespersons on their behalf.

A plan for speedy communication with advocates (e.g., Listservs) is an important component of effective advocacy, so there is a way to get quick action when needed.

A high-quality plan for advocacy is characterized by four key attributes: clarity, information, specificity, and inclusiveness.

Clarity

The advocacy plan has a clear message.

- What are the key points or ideas of your message? If your advocacy resulted in a sound bite, what would it be?
- Does the message relate directly to the goal of the advocacy plan?
- Is the message carefully crafted to capture the interest of the audience?
- Is the message clear for a general audience as well as the targeted audience?
- Does your group have members or connections with public relations experience that could help craft the message?

Support Information

The advocacy plan includes support information.

- What critical information do key individuals and groups need to know to provide support or justify decisions?
- What is the impact of this advocacy plan on children who are gifted and talented?
- What is the impact of the advocacy plan on other children?
- What policies at the school, district, state, and federal levels support (or negate) the point of advocacy?
- What research is available that will strengthen your message?

Specificity

The advocacy plan provides specifics for implementation.

- Who will carry out the plan? When? With whom?
- Who are the key individuals who will make the decisions or who will influence the persons who will make the decisions?

- Who will communicate with the key decision makers and with individuals who may influence decision makers?
- Who will coordinate the plan, and how will advocates report back? (This person or small group of individuals will be able to provide feedback based on responses from key decision makers. This coordinating individual or group will allow the advocacy plan to be responsive rather than fixed.)
- How will the efforts be funded? What resources will be needed and/or used?
- If the decision makers have constituencies, who are the constituents (specific names), and who will communicate with them? (Elected officials prefer to hear from those who vote in their districts.)
- If the advocacy plan includes action by a policy-making body (e.g., school board, state legislature), who are the leaders in the body (e.g., Speaker of the House, President of the Senate, Board President)? Who are the leaders of key committees (e.g., Education, Appropriations and Revenue, Curriculum and Instruction)? These people will be especially important in the process.
- Who will assess progress and evaluate the implementation of the plan? When and how will progress be assessed and the plan be evaluated? What can be learned to be increasingly effective with the next advocacy plan?

Inclusiveness

The advocacy plan involves interested parties.

- Who might have reason to care about this message and/or advocacy effort?
- Which individuals and groups have similar goals?
- What groups share an interest in excellence and would join the advocacy effort? Consider the following possibilities:

  o parents (parents of current students and of those who have graduated);
  o students (current and former students);
  o educators (active and retired);
  o representatives of business and industry;
  o The Chamber of Commerce;
  o university and college faculty;
  o professional and education organizations at the local, state, and national levels;
  o family members or close personal/professional friends of policy makers or other individuals of influence who can be very effective advocates; and
  o other potentially interested individuals or parties who share a belief in excellence and the development of potential talent.

PLANNING FOR AN ADVOCACY INITIATIVE

To ensure effectiveness, advocacy must be both strategic and responsive. Individuals and/or organizations that are launching an advocacy plan must agree on its goal and a well-crafted message. As a cornerstone of the initiative, a clear, focused message is key. Therefore, soliciting feedback from others will help determine if the message will be clearly communicated to the individual(s) who will make the decision(s) concerning whether the advocacy initiative moves forward or is stopped.

The individual(s) who have the authority to make the desired decisions must be identified so communication can be targeted to them and to individuals who influence them. Then the plan must specify who will communicate with each decision maker, how, what (the message), and when. The timeline may be established by the group or dictated by scheduled meetings of the decision-making body (legislature, school board, or school council).

Review Table 14.1 for key questions that will help you develop your own effective advocacy plan. Once you've answered the questions, you are ready to assign specific tasks—who will do what, and who will communicate with whom—and to establish a series of individual deadlines to implement your advocacy initiative.

Table 14.1 Planning for an Advocacy Initiative

What is the goal?	
Who is the target audience?	
What is the specific message?	
Who will make the decision?	
When will the decision be made?	
Who are key individuals in and out of your organization to influence decision makers?	

EXAMPLES OF ADVOCACY IN NEED OF PLANS

Example 1

Two mothers are very interested in having teachers at the neighborhood middle school provide services for their children who are advanced in mathematics. These parents approach their children's teachers with concerns that the children are bored in class. One teacher was sympathetic and started providing different, more challenging work; but the other teacher reacted as though he were offended, saying that the child did not do well with the work that she was originally given.

Comments: This first example illustrates how people frequently act alone without the benefit of others and without a specific plan that contains a clear message. In the revised example that follows, not only do the mothers align themselves with others seeking the same services for their children, but they also collaborate to research viable options and craft a message.

Example 2

A half-dozen boys and girls at a summer camp for academically talented high school students are comparing opportunities for Advanced Placement (AP) classes that are offered at their high schools. One student has several AP classes that are offered regularly. Two young people have no AP classes in their schools. Others have AP classes in their school's list of courses; however, they are seldom taught due to low enrollment. After talking, the students realize that opportunities for taking college-level classes are not equal for students across the state.

Comments: In this second example, the students were not aware of the information indicating a lack of equity in their respective school offerings— and most likely decision makers were lacking in this information as well. As a result, the students lacked the wherewithal to act on their own behalf. In the revised example below, students organized and developed a targeted message to share with interested parties across the state. Finally, they capitalized on personal connections to enhance the likelihood that their state-level advocacy plan would succeed.

MAKEOVER EXAMPLES

Example 1

The goal of the two parents is to have their children receive instruction in mathematics that allows them to make continuous progress. The problem with only approaching each teacher individually as need arises is that the situation may be repeated each year with different teachers.

The two mothers identified other parents and educators at the school who shared their concerns for making math more challenging for students who demonstrate mastery on pre-assessments. The mothers were able to find several people who were very interested, including a group of professional engineers.

The newly organized group met and articulated the message in a recommendation: "Every learner who is advanced in math will become a mathematician, mastering challenging content to make continuous progress." Then the group developed a plan for presenting their recommendation. They gathered research, policies, and reports that supported their recommendation. They also included statements and articles from professional groups supporting the need for a rigorous curriculum for advanced middle school students.

The group scheduled a time to present its recommendation to the school council. The group members discussed who would make the recommendation. They arranged for a group of parents and educators to attend the meeting to show support. When members of the school council had questions, the spokesperson(s) provided additional information. The result was a schoolwide emphasis on continuous progress in mathematics.

Example 2

The students at the summer camp asked the director if they could have an evening meeting of all campers who were interested in creating more AP opportunities for high school students in the state. They held a meeting, and approximately half the campers attended, representing 35 school districts in the state. They sketched out a rough advocacy plan and gathered names and e-mail addresses to continue to communicate after the camp ended.

After returning home, several of the students set up meetings with their state representatives and senators. One of the students was from the governor's hometown, and she arranged a time to visit with the governor on the unevenness of the opportunity to take AP or other college-level classes across the state. The joint education committee of the State House of Representatives and Senate initiated a study of the situation. Three of the campers who had taken AP classes were asked to come to a joint House and Senate Education Committee meeting to talk about the advantages they had or didn't have with choices of AP classes in their high schools.

The e-mail addresses and social media tools were essential in maintaining efficient communication and coordinating the campers' advocacy efforts as the issue moved through the legislative process. The campers were encouraged to make personal contacts with decision makers and to talk with family members, educators, and friends in the community to get others who shared their concern to make personal contacts with the legislators as well. Active involvement led to legislation requiring each high school to have a minimum of four AP classes, one in each of the core content areas.

SOURCES OF MESSAGES AND INFORMATION

Where do you get the ideas for crafting the message and providing information to convince decision makers to support your advocacy initiative?

- Mission and vision statements of your local school, schools in the district, and the school district.
- Reports in the media (e.g., stories on issues related to gifted education in news outlets like National Public Radio, CNN, the *Wall Street Journal*, or the *Washington Post*).
- Results of research studies provided by credible sources in print or online (e.g., peer-reviewed journals, universities, government agencies, and nonprofit organizations like NAGC).
- Policies on gifted education that a local school board or the state has adopted. Policies are often printed in gifted education handbooks and are available on websites.
- Position statements from state and national educational and professional organizations.
- State and national reports as well as reports released by foundations that discuss issues that impact the education of children who are gifted and talented. Examples include *A Nation Deceived: How Schools Hold Back America's Brightest Students* (Colangelo, Assouline, & Gross, 2004) and *A Nation Empowered: Evidence Trumps the Excuses That Hold Back America's Brightest Students* (Assouline, Colangelo, VanTassel-Baska, & Lupkowski-Shoplik, 2015).
- Local, state, and national associations that advocate for gifted children (e.g., visit the NAGC website at www.nagc.org and The Association for the Gifted's website at www.cectag.org).
- Economic statistics for your community or state (e.g., visit www.neweconomy.index.org to see how your state ranks in the numbers of scientists and engineers and other indicators of potential success in the 21st century economy).
- *State of the States* reports issued biennially by NAGC provide current snapshots of state policies and statistics related to gifted education nationwide and in individual states.

ADDITIONAL POINTS FOR BUILDING EFFECTIVE ADVOCACY NETWORKS

- Assumptions are dangerous. Mythology in gifted education is believed by educators, parents, and the public, so advocates for gifted children need to be prepared to inform and educate.

- Effective advocates plan to be "in the room" when decisions are made.
- A central person or organization coordinates the advocacy initiatives so people will know whom to contact with current information and how to respond strategically to developments on an issue.
- Personalized communications are the most effective. Spoken communication is important and needs to be followed up with the same message in writing.
- Ongoing communication is very important. Being known as an advocate for excellence in education and appropriate opportunities for all children, including children who are gifted and talented, can add credibility to advocacy initiatives.
- Providing accurate information is critical to establishing and maintaining credibility. If the advocate doesn't know the answer, then he or she should find the information and get back with the answer.
- Be recognized. Wear name badges or identification tags so that others become familiar with you and your organization.

ADVOCATING ON AN ONGOING BASIS

Keeping the academic needs of children and young people who are gifted and talented in the conversation as decisions are considered is very important. Two key questions can raise awareness of their needs:

- How will this [decision] affect our brightest students?
- How will this [decision] help other students begin to achieve at higher levels? (Plucker, Burroughs, & Song, 2010, p. 30)

These questions allow for extending consideration of advanced learners on an ongoing basis and making continuous progress for all students a priority in a school or school system.

ADVICE FOR THE SOLE PRACTITIONER

Advocacy is seldom conducted successfully by a single concerned individual. At a minimum, advocacy requires a small number of people to plan effectively and deliver messages to key stakeholders. Therefore, identifying sources of collaboration and support is a necessary first step for the sole practitioner.

Although advocacy collaborators may not yet be apparent in your school or local community, seeking out individuals with similar interests and concerns can be an excellent way to identify key information and potential avenues for advocacy. Investigate whether there is anyone at the state department of education charged with overseeing programs for the gifted and talented. Many states have at least part-time personnel charged with overseeing gifted education programming. If such personnel are available at the state department of education, they may be able to put the sole practitioner in touch with other advocate groups in the state, as well as put him or her on an electronic distribution list that provides updates on important issues related to gifted education and advocacy initiatives. Even if there are no organizations or groups within a manageable travel distance, online communities or resources may provide alternate means of connecting and advocating for gifted learners.

In all likelihood, a single practitioner will collaborate with others in a learning community to support gifted students, and ideally there is an advisory group within your school or district. Although the purpose of the advisory group is to assist the gifted practitioner with all aspects of programming and service delivery, the environment of the group meetings will afford an opportunity to pinpoint key individuals who might be interested and available to move the advocacy initiative forward. A few conversations with prospective individuals will start the ball rolling.

Another helpful step that the single practitioner can take is to keep an ongoing list of local family members and other adults who have an interest in gifted education. This list can be provided to those who step forward to help with advocacy. With a small set of names in hand, the advocacy group can grow the list and develop a network of people who can be connected through efficient means. E-mail, texting, and social media tools prove invaluable during advocacy campaigns when it is crucial to get the word out about developing issues and events, some of which have tight timelines for when decisions will be made.

Please remember that numbers matter in advocacy, so join with others to maximize your opportunity to reach your advocacy goals.

Collaboration Counts

1 parent   = A fruitcake

2 parents = Fruitcake and friend

3 parents = Troublemakers

5 parents = "Let's have a meeting"

10 parents = "We'd better listen"

25 parents = "Our dear friends"

50 parents = A powerful organization

Source: Henderson, Jacob, Kernan-Schloss, and Raimondo (2004, p. 40).

SUGGESTED RESOURCES

Lord, E. W., & Clarenbach, J. (2012). Off the page and into practice: Advocating for implementation of the gifted programming standards. In S. K. Johnsen (Ed.), *NAGC Pre-K–Grade 12 Gifted Education Programming Standards: A guide to planning and implementing high-quality services* (pp. 255–268). Waco, TX: Prufrock Press.

This chapter ties advocacy to the gifted programming standards. The authors highlight the important steps that are key to successfully implementing standards that will positively impact the education of children with gifts and talents.

Matthews, M. S., Georgiades, S. D., & Smith, L. F. (2011). How we formed a parent advocacy group and what we've learned in the process. *Gifted Child Today, 34*(4), 28–34.

This article shares the experiences of three advocates as they worked to establish a successful parent advocacy organization in one large school district in Florida. The authors offer practical strategies and guidance with a focus on a collaborative and proactive approach that is inclusive of educators and community members.

Roberts, J. L. (2010). A case study for advocating for a specialized school of mathematics and science. *Roeper Review, 32,* 42–47.

This article describes 10 years of advocacy targeted at establishing a statewide residential school of mathematics and science, and lessons learned from this advocacy journey. Roberts highlights 11 lessons learned from this experience with the goal that they can be used to guide planning to build advocacy efforts on behalf of advanced students.

Roberts, J. L. (2014). Advocacy. In J. A. Plucker & C. M. Callahan (Eds.), *Critical issues in gifted education* (2nd ed., pp. 65–76). Waco, TX: Prufrock Press.

This chapter examines research relating to advocacy as well as best practice leading to successful advocacy. The author provides a summary of advocacy as it relates to policy and practice related to the education of children and young people with gifts and talents.

Roberts, J. L., & Siegle, D. (2012). Teachers as advocates: If not you—who? *Gifted Child Today, 35,* 58–61.

This article focuses on the essential role teachers can play in supporting effective advocacy efforts for gifted education. Practical advocacy strategies are described, including those for advocating with colleagues at the school, community, state, and national levels.

REFERENCES

Assouline, S. G., Colangelo, N., VanTassel-Baska, J., & Lupkowski-Shoplik, A. (Eds.). (2015). *A nation empowered: Evidence trumps the excuses holding back America's brightest students* (Vols. 1–2). Iowa City: The University of Iowa, The Connie Belin & Jacqueline N. Blank International Center for Gifted Education and Talent Development.

Colangelo, N., Assouline, S. G., & Gross, M. U. M. (2004). *A nation deceived: How schools hold back America's brightest students* (Vol. 1). Iowa City: The University of Iowa, The Connie Belin & Jacqueline N. Blank International Center for Gifted Education and Talent Development.

Henderson, A., Jacob, B., Kernan-Schloss, A., & Raimondo, B. (2004). *The case for parent leadership.* Retrieved from https://www.pepartnership.org/media/69213/Case%20for%20Parent%20Leadership.pdf

National Association for Gifted Children. (n.d.). *Advocate for high-ability learners.* Retrieved from http://www.nagc.org/get-involved/advocate-high-ability-learners

Plucker, J. A., Burroughs, N., & Song, R. (2010). *Mind the (other) gap! The growing excellence gap in K–12 education.* Bloomington, IN: Center for Evaluation & Education Policy.

Roberts, J. L. (2014). Advocacy. In J. A. Plucker & C. M. Callahan (Eds.), *Critical issues in gifted education* (2nd ed., pp. 65–76). Waco, TX: Prufrock Press.

Robinson, A., & Moon, S. (2003). A national study of local and state advocacy in gifted education. *Gifted Child Quarterly, 47,* 8–25.

Chapter 15

Developing Local Policies to Guide and Support Gifted Programs and Services

Jay McIntire

DEFINITION

In the United States, the federal government has allocated the responsibility for creating policies and regulations about educating gifted students to state governments. Although many states have gifted and talented requirements for Local Education Agencies (LEAs), great variability exists regarding the detail provided in legislative and administrative code, the flexibility for local decisions in how identification and services are provided, and in accountability (National Association for Gifted Children [NAGC] & Council of State Directors of Programs for the Gifted, 2015). Scholars in the field of gifted education have noted that state policies tend to focus almost exclusively on identification practices; however, there is a pressing need for further articulation and guidance on the numerous decisions that affect all gifted students, including policies focused on curriculum and instruction, grouping arrangements, and counseling and guidance services (Brown, Avery, VanTassel-Baska, Worley, & Stambaugh, 2006; Swanson & Lord, 2013).

At a bare minimum, school districts must be in compliance with state code and policies where those exist. However, where state gifted education laws are absent or ambiguous, local school boards generally approve gifted curriculum, set guidelines for grade placement, approve programs for gifted students, and budget for accommodations for high-ability students (Swanson, 2007). In these instances, the requirements placed on teachers and the latitude afforded them to provide for gifted students is driven largely by decisions made locally by principals, superintendents, and local school boards. Among these decision makers, the school board is primary because its policies and selected type of involvement determine resource availability and how much discretion the superintendent, principal, and teachers will have in providing for gifted students.

To develop policies impacting gifted students and to advocate for the implementation of those policies at the local level, one must have a good understanding of school governance and of school boards, their policies, and how to influence them. The National School Boards Association (2014) noted:

> School boards derive their power and authority from the state. In compliance with state and federal laws, school boards establish policies and regulations by which their local schools are governed.
>
> • Your school board is responsible for:
> • employing the superintendent;
> • developing and adopting policies, curriculum, and the budget;
> • overseeing facilities issues; and
> • adopting collective bargaining agreements. (para. 2–3)

Although those are the most concrete responsibilities of boards, they are ultimately responsible for everything that happens in a school district, from school climate and student learning, to bookkeeping, to compliance with all manner of federal, state, and local laws, rules, and legal precedents.

RATIONALE

Over the last 25 years, there have been many widely read reports that have presented the case for dramatic changes in how the nation educates our most highly able students (see, for example, The Association for the Gifted, 2009; NAGC, n.d.; Plucker, 2015; Plucker, Giancola, Healey, Arndt, & Wang, 2015; Plucker, Hardesty, & Burroughs, 2014; Ross, 1993; Wyner, Bridgeland, & DiIulio, 2007; Xiang, Dahlin, & Durant, 2011). In effect, these have called on families, teachers, researchers, and others concerned about high-ability students to lobby for improvements. Although these have attracted much interest from those in the field of gifted education, the impact thus far at the local level has been minimal.

Although states vary widely in delegating decision making to districts, most gifted education across the country is driven by local policies. There are numerous benefits to developing and enacting local policies, which articulate options for meeting the needs of gifted students (Long, Barnett,

& Rogers, 2015; Swanson & Lord, 2013). Local policies made at the district level can help coordinate resources, provide horizontal articulation between buildings that house the same grade levels, and offer vertical articulation for continuous growth K–12. Moreover, policies approved by the school board are crucial to the development of a reliable commitment to a long-standing program and/or service delivery model. Research suggests that principals are more likely to provide professional development and resources to support gifted education in schools where policies exist (Long et al., 2015). With approved policies in place, shifts in administrative personnel, budgets, and instructional pedagogy will be far less likely to negatively influence gifted education opportunities within a school district. The program will remain until the local board officially removes it.

GUIDING PRINCIPLES AND ATTRIBUTES THAT DEFINE HIGH SUCCESS

It's one thing to get a policy passed that is supportive of gifted students; it's another thing to have it implemented and for quality programming to become institutionalized. The current national trend is for superintendents to have short tenures, so having strong superintendent support does not guarantee long-term success of a gifted program. However, school board policy support is a must. Even boards change membership too quickly to sustain some quality efforts.

For long-term success, good policies need to be embedded in an overall culture that institutionalizes the pursuit of excellence at the student level. One example is the Carrollton-Farmers Branch Independent School District (CFB ISD) in Texas and its commitment to quality programming for its gifted students. This commitment has become an intrinsic part of the district. It certainly helps that Texas sets higher gifted education standards at the state level than do many others, but even in times of waffling at the state level, CFB ISD marches on. It does so because its culture has developed over decades. The challenge for those seeking to develop policies is to find ways to use policy as a lever to change culture.

Many school board members are not trained educators. They may not be well versed in the field of education, and may lack even basic knowledge about gifted education. School boards often have members who turn over each year, so although there may be some very seasoned members, other school leaders are still learning the role and are neophytes when it comes to the district's policy tome.

Many superintendents serve districts with multiple boards and therefore multiple policy manuals. The terminology of the Policy Governance Model (PGM; Carver & Carver, 2009) is very helpful in understanding how boards and their policy manuals provide the foundation for schools. A coherent approach to governance such as PGM can lead to both policy and cultural change. The guiding questions and conceptual framework provided in the PGM framework can be useful in developing policies and changing culture even in school districts that have not considered this model.

The PGM (Carver & Carver, 2009) calls for policies serving four specific functions, including:

1. how the board will operate (governance process policies),

2. what outcomes the school district will pursue (ends policies),

3. how the board and superintendent will interact (board-staff linkage policies), and

4. with what guidelines must the school district comply (executive limitations policies).

Even if your local board uses a buckshot approach to policy (as many do), advocates for gifted students who think of policies serving these functions and who advocate for packages of policies of these types that are aligned will be more likely to be effective in educating board members and in getting support for systematic efforts to foster student advancement.

Ends policies establish the effects to be produced, as well as for whom, and establish their priority (Carver & Carver, 2009). Many ends policies are based on a school board's values, and all are measures of effectiveness.

The most direct way for advocates for gifted students to impact a school system is to have the school board adopt ends policies that require advanced opportunities for students. It's not the board's job to *produce* the ends, only to define them. Once they are defined, however, their achievement becomes the responsibility of all district employees: the superintendent, building administrators, and teachers. Although the term *ends policies* has specific meaning in a PGM district, all boards establish something related through their strategic plan, annual goals, or superintendent's job description. These are the key targets for changing district priorities. Ends policies answer the question, "What effect is sought, for whom, and at what cost?"

One example of a district that uses ends policies is Milford (CT) School District. It uses the Policy Governance Model and has three ends policies:

1. Foundational Skills and Competencies;

2. Understanding and Applications: Discipline-Based and Interdisciplinary Skills; and

3. Aspects of Character (Milford Public Schools, n.d.).

They express the school's intended impact and are written to set expectations for all students in in the district. For example, Milford's writing expectation 1.1.2 in Ends Policy 1 reads, "Students will use the conventions of standard English to communicate clearly" (Milford Public Schools, 2008, p. 1). Milford's ends policies are written to apply to all students, but they can be written to pertain to few or even one student, such as, "Any student, regardless of age or grade level, who has scored at a level 4 or 5 on an AP exam and who is not yet eligible to graduate shall be provided opportunities to enroll in appropriate college or university course in the same content area for dual credit, at local expense." The "effect" sought is college participation.

The "for whom" is students who have demonstrated readiness as measured by AP success. The "cost" is not specified, but is defined as being at district expense. There could be cost limitations built into administrative procedures for implementing the policy.

Ends can be concrete (e.g., "By the graduating class of 2018, at least 60% of high school graduates will have completed at least one AP course and achieved a score of 3 or higher with at least 30% achieving a 4 or higher") or relative (e.g., "Effective immediately, investments in new programs or services designed to remediate weaknesses in student performances should be matched by investments in programs designed to enhance opportunities for superior performance").

Key concepts to advocate for in ends policies include any that require (a) opportunities to learn be matched to instructional level, (b) students to advance toward realizing their highest potential, or (c) students to advance at their own pace.

Means policies in PGM are any of the three types that do not proscribe ends. Although they are less often the target for gifted advocacy, they can be instrumental in establishing processes and internal requirements. Means policies are of three types: governance process, board-staff linkage, and executive limitations. All these exist functionally in all types of districts, but Carver's (1997) structure distinguishes among them and provides clarity that serves both a school district and those hoping to influence it.

1. **Governance process policies** are those that determine the board's processes. How is a quorum defined? How will public input be heard at meetings? Governance process policies that have implications for gifted advocates include those that create pertinent board subcommittees (not recommended in the pure PGM), establish processes for public input to the board, and establish how the board or its members will become informed about education matters, including gifted education. As part of a governance process policy establishing the content of board meetings, a school board could require that the administration regularly provides information about extraordinary student accomplishments. Although indirect, such routine reports could make the outer reaches of student capability better known to the board and the public.

2. **Board-staff linkage policies** establish the relationship between the board and the superintendent. In the Policy Governance Model, the superintendent is the board's only employee, so the board would never establish policies that assign responsibilities to other school system employees. Board-staff linkage policies seem the least likely to be targets of gifted advocates. These policies address topics such as superintendent evaluation, the authority of the superintendent when there are no limiting policies, and the role of the superintendent at board meetings.

3. **Executive limitations policies** constrain the head of the school district to acting ethically within the boundaries of the law. Thus the

superintendent (or the school district CEO) must run a system that complies with all federal, state, and local laws, rules, and ordinances. States vary widely in what local policies and programs are required to address gifted learners, if any.

Most boards have dozens of additional policies that narrow the playing field for the superintendent. This is a fertile area for gifted advocacy. For example, executive limitation policies could

- prohibit the superintendent from refusing early entrance to kindergarten for children for whom there is evidence of academic and social and emotional readiness;
- require placement of new students based on their academic and emotional readiness;
- exempt students from high school prerequisites if they can provide evidence of proficiency in content knowledge;
- require district-administered achievement tests to be normed such that students are tested at their achievement level, not chronological age or grade level (i.e., out-of-level testing); or
- require that any student, regardless of age or grade level, who has scored at the mastery level on a high school course pretest shall be exempt from taking the course as a prerequisite.

Some policy proposals can take many forms and be argued in a variety of ways, so the effective advocate shapes his or her argument to align with the interest of the decision maker. For example, consider the following executive limitations policy: "The Oceanside School Department will determine eligibility for kindergarten on a variety of readiness factors, of which age shall only be one." This is an executive limitation policy because it ties the hands of the superintendent—somewhat loosely in this case—but in a way that could open the door for many students to start school when they are ready instead of when the calendar dictates.

Another board might consider this an appropriate ends policy as part of the essential purpose of the school district. Such a policy would likely be written a bit more broadly:

The Oceanside School Committee believes that students should be grouped according to their instructional level, so long as doing so is not harmful to them socially or emotionally. To that end, enrollees will be placed based on their academic, social, and emotional readiness, not solely chronological age.

EXAMPLE IN NEED OF REVISION

Policies can, and should, drive decision making, so they should be crafted with care and foresight. They also have both intended and unintended consequences. A policy from one Maine district is not unlike those in other districts. One recent educational decision certainly would not be supported by many advocates for gifted students. The policy, which is not required by law, is titled "Basic Instructional Program."

> Rangeley Lakes Regional School will offer a basic instructional program designed to support the Guiding Principles of Maine's system of Learning Results and provide all kindergarten through grade 12 students with equitable opportunities to access and demonstrate achievement of the content standards of Maine's system of Learning Results.
>
> The school will provide programs and instructional approaches that support the variety of learning styles of its students. Through the basic instructional program, the school will strive to provide for a wide range of individual differences in student abilities and interests. Students who have difficulty meeting the standards will be provided opportunities to obtain additional support or instruction.
>
> The Board believes that through the basic instructional program, students should develop a body of basic knowledge, skills, and attitudes that will lead to a successful adult life and informed participation in our democratic society. The educational program should provide students with the opportunity to develop the intellectual curiosity, critical thinking, problem-solving abilities, and appreciation for the arts that are important to lifelong learning, and the social and citizenship skills that are needed for work and community life.
>
> The instructional program shall be developed with the objective of maintaining a balanced, integrated, and sequentially articulated curriculum. Priority should be given to learning that serves as a foundation for further educational development in language arts, mathematics, science, social studies, the arts, foreign language, health and physical education, and career education.
>
> The basic instructional program shall meet requirements established by Maine law and Department of Education regulations. The instructional program shall be implemented through a written curriculum aligned with the system of Learning Results and designed to provide uniformity of content within and across grade levels. (Rangeley School Department, 2006, p. 1)

This policy acknowledges the importance of critical thinking, intellectual curiosity, and problem solving, and requires that the district "strive to provide for a wide range of individual differences in student abilities and interests" (Rangeley School Department, 2006, p. 1). Nevertheless, these expectations are overshadowed by the emphasis on minimum proficiency. The term *basic* is used five times. It explicitly prioritizes foundational learning. It even calls for "uniformity of content within and across grade levels" (Rangeley School Department, 2006, p. 1).

There is no expectation set that the basic education is to include elements that are advanced, accelerated, or enriched. It also sets no expectation that the program be comprehensive.

Most board policies establish the priorities for the superintendent and guide the board's decision making. You may not be surprised to learn that only a few months after this policy was adopted, the board opted to eliminate having a certified teacher provide services to identified gifted and talented students. Instead, a paraprofessional position requiring no formal training in gifted education was created to serve these students. This move was certainly influenced by budgetary concerns, but this policy's emphasis on minimum standards may also have played a key role.

The Rangeley Lakes Regional School Board has recently begun to grapple with its ends goals. It is engaging the community in conversations about what it wants from its high school. The district is seeking to transform the school system from one that offers a solid general education to all to one that is creative and nimble in adjusting to the learning needs, styles, capacities, and interests of its students. Once the board has determined how it will work, what it will delegate, and what ends it wants, it will revise policies to support decision making that serves the district's students.

Consider as a contrast Carrollton-Farmers Branch ISD's (2013) policy, which has exactly the same title, "Basic Instructional Program." It has aspects of an ends policy and aspects of an executive limitation policy. Texas's law and CFB ISD's policy are far more detailed. Whereas Rangeley's (2006) policy is a brief one page, CFB ISD's (2013) seven-page policy goes into specific details on areas such as student/teacher ratios, steroids, and content of human sexuality instruction. For our purposes, though, the contrast is between the emphasis in the Rangeley policy on basic foundations and uniformity with CFB ISD's extensive requirements for enrichment and for opportunities matched to students' instructional levels.

CFB ISD's (2013) policy defines that "basic" education

- includes both a foundation curriculum and an enrichment curriculum (p. 1),
- ensures that all children participate in curriculum "designed to meet individual instructional needs" (p. 1), and
- encourages the district to "exceed minimum requirements of law and of State Board rule" (p. 2).

ADVICE FOR GETTING STARTED

The types of policies supportive of gifted students are well known. They put pressure on schools to provide, among other things

- differentiated instruction based on interest, ability, and instructional level;
- differentiated instruction that includes both acceleration and enrichment options;
- grouping and regrouping of students to promote academic achievement and/or affective growth;

- support for the social and emotional stressors experienced by gifted students and their families; and
- breadth and depth of learning opportunities.

It is unlikely that a policy as traditional and basics-oriented as Rangeley's (2006) will change to one as supportive of higher-level learning as CFB's overnight. So how does one proceed? Unless you are a board member, a superintendent, or someone else who has significant influence over the entire district, policy development and policy improvement are usually incremental. Three simple—not easy—steps are suggested.

1. Get to know the chosen ends policies of your school district. Whether these are called ends, mission, priorities, or goals, find out what results your school system is attempting to achieve. Linkages to these goals will serve as your rationale for advocated changes.

2. Before deciding to whom you should propose policy improvements, you need to know who controls that which you seek to change. If your concern is about administrative decisions on available placements, you might want to make the case to the school board that having a variety of placement options should be required as an executive limitation.

3. Consider whether there are existing policies that either are not being implemented or need improvement. In either case, advocating for increased pressure on the policy assurance ladder (see Figure 15.1) can be helpful. What is less well known is how to increase the effectiveness of a policy by increasing its intensity. This scale of intensity is referred to as the *policy assurance ladder*. The policy assurance ladder's steps determine how much force is placed on the school to conform to the policy. Conformance can mean either taking or avoiding a specific action. The highest levels of the ladder attempt to force what *will* occur, and the lowest attempts to force what *won't* occur. In between is where incremental language changes can have huge results for students.

Looking back to the two examples provided, there are opportunities in both. In Rangeley Lakes Regional School District's (2006) instructional policy, the school is charged with striving "to provide for a wide range of individual differences in student abilities and interests" (p. 1). This implies programming for students with gifts and talents, but this is left ambiguous given the policy's focus on basic skills. This policy could be improved by establishing that the district will strive

- to provide for a wide range of individual differences in student abilities and interests, which may include students identified as gifted and talented; or
- to provide for remediation, enrichment, and acceleration options necessitated by the wide range of individual differences in student abilities, interests, and instructional levels; or
- to provide the resources and fully trained staff necessary to provide for students identified as gifted and talented.

Figure 15.1 Policy Assurance Ladder

WILL

Mandated

- Must be accomplished, with funding either provided or required to be raised. Criminal or civil penalties or subsidy loss or other legal implications apply if the policy is not followed. Formal mandates are established by federal or state laws or rules, not by local policies.

Required

- Expected, with evidence provided to the entity of compliance.

Supported

- Specified as an optional, with funding (which may be the same year as expense or reimbursed).

Permitted

- Used as an example of an allowable option, but not fully funded.

Implied Acceptance

- The action seems logical given related policy, but is not specified.

Tolerated

- Not mentioned at all, presumably left to local discretion. Decision makers, such as grant managers or state department of education personnel, are aware that some apply the practice, and they do not prohibit it.

Ignored

- The action is not listed either among prohibited acts or among allowed ones.

Discouraged

- Taking the action can lead to closer scrutiny and possible sanction.

Prohibited

- Taking the action can lead to withholding of subsidy.

Illegal

- Taking the action can lead to jail or fines.

WON'T

Force placed on the school to conform.

The first of these options would increase the policy from the *implied acceptance* to the *permitted* level. The second bullet moves it to a *supported* level, and the third moves this policy to a *required* level.

Even the CFB ISD (2013) policy, which is much higher on the ladder, has room for strengthening. One section of it, taken from Chapter 19 of the Texas Education Code, states "instruction may be provided in a variety of arrangements and settings, including mixed-age programs" (CFB ISD, 2013, p. 1). This state code is at the *supported* level. Either the state or CFB ISD's board could put more teeth in this by revising it to the *required* level, such as noting "the district will provide a variety of arrangements and settings, including mixed-age programs."

Although influence for the creation and passage of these policies may ultimately rest within the school board and superintendent's offices, it is important to acknowledge and foster a shared responsibility for meeting the diverse educational needs of gifted students through effective policy implementation (see Figure 15.2).

The creation and passage of solid policies, grounded in research and aligned with the school mission, are the first important step in strengthening and maintaining the programs and services afforded to gifted students. Building administrators, as instructional leaders, must demonstrate knowledge of and support for the strategic use of student data, gifted education pedagogy, and policy implementation to maximize student performance and promote a positive learning environment for

Figure 15.2   Shared Responsibility for Differentiation for Gifted Learners

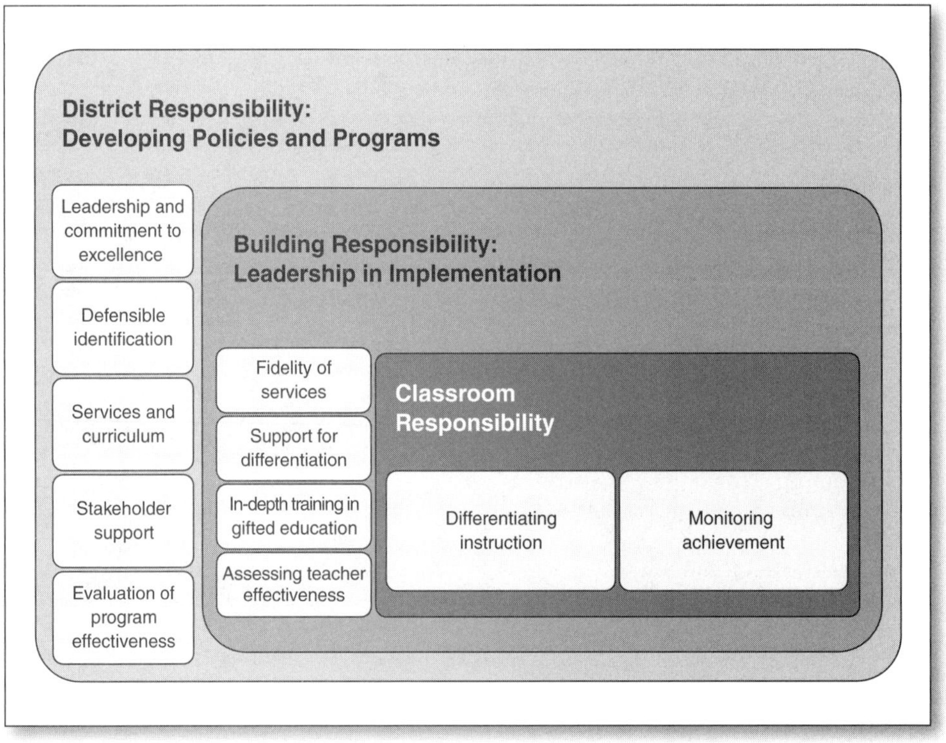

Source: Speirs Neumeister and Burney (2011, p. 77). Copyright 2011 by Prufrock Press. Reprinted with permission.

all students—including those who are identified as gifted. Ultimately, classroom teachers are responsible for working within this structure to create challenging and supportive learning opportunities for gifted students and to track their continued growth and development in school.

ADVICE FOR THE SOLE PRACTITIONER

Change is a complex process—and successfully navigating this process to create policies supportive of gifted education is even more so. Progress is often incremental and requires a long-term commitment, which can be particularly daunting for an individual working alone.

One way in which to increase the likelihood of success for such an investment of time and energy is to do your homework before advocating for a policy change. Investigate the policy language and implementation used by other districts to support gifted programming and review advice and examples provided by professional organizations such as NAGC and the National School Boards Association. Consider what options and ideas best align with your school district's mission and concerns. You may find it helpful at the outset to narrow your focus on one policy change to address a specific concern rather than trying to advocate with your school board for a comprehensive overhaul.

Another way in which to increase the likelihood of your success is to invest in relationships. Connecting with stakeholders from relevant constituencies can be a great foundation for a sole practitioner and may eventually lead to the establishment of a cohort to whom you can turn for support and guidance. This could take many forms, from a broad-based policy-planning committee within your school or district, to an online group of like-minded individuals. Fortunately, there is no one, right way to connect with others—but there are many benefits in doing so.

SUGGESTED RESOURCES

Peters, S. J., Matthews, M. S., McBee, M. T., & McCoach D. B. (2013). *Beyond gifted education: Designing and implementing advanced academic programs.* Waco, TX: Prufrock Press.

This book reviews the current range of gifted education practices and policies and provides research-based suggestions for designing or recreating programs to meet the needs of gifted students in today's schools. Examples of issues commonly encountered in K–12 settings are provided including discussions of cluster grouping, acceleration, identification, and increasing diversity.

Plucker, J. A., & Callahan, C. M. (Eds.). (2014). *Critical issues and practices in gifted education: What the research says* (2nd ed.). Waco, TX: Prufrock Press.

Grounded in current research, this comprehensive reference book presents more than 50 summaries of essential topics in the field of gifted education. Leading scholars in the field review the available research on each topic and provide guidance about how the research applies in the lives of gifted children. Discussions of important topics such as gifted programming standards, the Common Core State Standards, assessment, administrative leadership, and legal issues are included.

REFERENCES

The Association for the Gifted. (2009). *Diversity and developing gifts and talents: A national call to action.* Arlington, VA: Council for Exceptional Children.

Brown, E., Avery, L. D., VanTassel-Baska, J. L., Worley, B. B., II, & Stambaugh, T. (2006). Legislation and policies: Effects on the gifted. *Roeper Review, 29,* 11–23. doi:10.1080/02783190609554379

Carrollton-Farmers Branch ISD. (2013). *Basic instructional program.* Retrieved from http://pol.tasb.org/Policy/Download/359?filename=EHAA%28LEGAL%29.pdf

Carver, J. (1997). *Boards that make a difference: A new design for leadership in nonprofit and public organizations* (2nd ed.). San Francisco, CA: Jossey-Bass.

Carver, J., & Carver, M. (2009). *Ends and the ownership.* San Francisco, CA: Jossey-Bass.

Long, L. C., Barnett, K., & Rogers, K. B. (2015). Exploring the relationship between principal, policy, and gifted program scope and quality. *Journal for the Education of the Gifted, 38,* 118–140. doi:10.1177/0162353215578279

Milford Public Schools. (n.d.). *BOE ends policies.* Retrieved from http://www.milforded.org/page.cfm?p=2643

Milford Public Schools. (2008). *Ends (E-1) foundational skills and competencies.* Retrieved from http://www.milforded.org/page.cfm?p=2643

National Association for Gifted Children. (n.d.). *Advocacy toolkit.* Retrieved from http://www.nagc.org/get-involved/advocate-high-ability-learners/advocacy-toolkit

National Association for Gifted Children, & Council of State Directors of Programs for the Gifted. (2015). *2014–2015 state of the states in gifted education: Policy and practice data.* Washington, DC: Author.

National School Boards Association. (2014). *Frequently asked questions about school boards and public education.* Retrieved from https://www.nsba.org/about-us/frequently-asked-questions

Plucker, J. (2015). *Common Core and America's high-achieving students.* Washington, DC: Fordham Institute.

Plucker, J., Giancola, J., Healey, G, Arndt, D., & Wang, C. (2015). *Equal talents, unequal opportunities: A report card on state support for academically talented low-income students.* Lansdowne, VA: Jack Kent Cooke Foundation.

Plucker, J., Hardesty, J., & Burroughs, N. (2014). *Talent on the sidelines: Excellence gaps and the persistence of America's permanent talent underclass.* Storrs: University of Connecticut, Neag School of Education.

Rangeley School Department. (2006). *Basic instructional program.* Retrieved from http://www.rangeleyschool.org/wp-content/uploads/2011/12/IHA-Basic-Instructional-Program.pdf

Ross, P. (1993). *National excellence: A case for developing America's talent.* Washington. DC: U.S. Department of Education.

Speirs Neumeister, K. L., & Burney, V. H. (2011). *An introduction to gifted education: The complete kit for facilitators, coordinators and in-service training professionals.* Waco, TX: Prufrock Press.

Swanson, J. D. (2007). Policy and practice: A case study of gifted education policy implementation. *Journal for the Education of the Gifted, 31,* 131–164.

Swanson, J. D., & Lord, E. W. (2013). Harnessing and guiding the power of policy: Examples from one state's experiences. *Journal for the Education of the Gifted, 36,* 198–219.

Wyner, J. S., Bridgeland, J. M, & DiIulio, J. J., Jr. (2007). *Achievement trap: How America is failing millions of high-achieving students from lower-income families.* Lansdowne, VA: Jack Kent Cooke Foundation.

Xiang, Y., Dahlin, J., & Durant, S. (2011). *Do high flyers maintain their altitude? Performance trends of top students.* Washington, DC: Thomas Fordham Institute.

Chapter 16

Developing a Plan for Evaluating Services Provided to Gifted Students

Carolyn M. Callahan, PhD

DEFINITION

High-quality evaluation of services provided to gifted and talented students should be a systematic process of collecting data from multiple sources to help decision makers at all levels make informed judgments about the effectiveness of the various components of those services. Hence, effective evaluation involves collecting data that will be useful to and will be used by decision makers. If evaluation is done well, decision makers will not only have information on programmatic strengths and weaknesses, but they will also have guidance in making changes that will enhance the services offered to gifted students.[1]

A comprehensive evaluation will be designed to collect both formative and summative data. *Formative evaluation* is the process of gathering data about a program during their evolution and as part of an effort to make services better as they develop. Formative evaluation guides

---

[1]The term *services* is used here to signify a belief that gifted students are a heterogeneous group and that more than one option should be available to respond to the distinct learning characteristics they present. From this point forward, the terms *program* and *program evaluation* will be used to denote the collection of those services.

various stakeholders in understanding the strengths and weaknesses of a program, in recognizing factors that contribute to overall program effectiveness, and in identifying factors that may hinder the achievement of the program goals. In formative evaluation, the evaluator may discover that the teachers have not been trained to use appropriate instructional strategies with gifted students and therefore, it is unlikely the students will achieve the expected educational outcomes. At that point, it would be appropriate for the evaluator to suggest specific staff development or coaching interventions. *Summative evaluation* is designed as a process of collecting data that will serve as a decision maker to judge the merit or worth of the program or specific components of a program based on outcome measures. These data may be used to determine whether the program and/or specific components of the program should be maintained as is, modified, or eliminated. In the summative evaluation stage of evaluation, data are presented to inform stakeholders about the success of the program in achieving its goals and possibly about other unanticipated effects of the program. For example, summative data may document that the expected goal of increased numbers of students enrolling in and achieving a score of 3 on Advanced Placement (AP) tests had not been achieved.

RATIONALE FOR PROGRAM EVALUATION

Evaluation is critical to the success of gifted education programs (Reineke, 1991; Tomlinson, Bland, & Moon, 1993; Tomlinson, Bland, Moon, & Callahan, 1994; VanTassel-Baska, 2006; Yarborough, Shulha, Hopson, & Caruthers, 2011). Equally important, gifted education programs, like all educational programs, are accountable to their constituencies to document that resources committed to the program are effectively and efficiently expended. Funding agents have the right and responsibility to ensure that the resources are well used, parents have the expectation that the educational program offered to their children is of high quality, teachers and administrators should be eager to know that their efforts are in line with best practices in the field, and gifted students have the right to expect us to provide a challenging and engaging program of studies addressing their educational and social and emotional needs.

An effective evaluation plan and its implementation:

- Should *be specifically and purposefully planned.*
- Must be supported with an *adequate budget.*
- Should *involve key stakeholders* from the very beginning of the process through the stage of planning for implementation of the recommendations. (See Appendix A, page 256.)
- Are both *formative and summative* in design and implementation.
- Must *match data collection strategies to the evaluation questions* asked.
- Use *multiple data collection methods and sources.*

- Must use *reliable and valid assessment tools*.
- Present findings in oral and written forms that are directed toward *the specific interests and needs of the stakeholders* in program.
- Take into account the *unique issues* involved in programming for gifted students.
- Are an *open, public, and interactive* process.

GUIDING PRINCIPLES OR ASSUMPTIONS THAT DEFINE HIGH QUALITY

Evaluation of a gifted program is an integral part of the program development cycle. There are many groups of people who have a vested interest in the services offered to gifted students in any school division (e.g., students, classroom teachers, counselors and psychologists, building administrators, central office personnel, members of the board of education, parents of gifted education students, citizens, state department of education personnel). Because these stakeholders are critical sources of guidance in the formulation of a quality evaluation plan, they should be represented on a steering committee that is consulted in the formulation of the plan and in its subsequent implementation. The steering committee should be guided by these axioms:

- The evaluation of a gifted program can be a very threatening activity, especially if stakeholders are not given the opportunity to participate in the planning of the evaluation.
- Traditional indicators of success in educational programs such as standardized achievement tests are not likely to be valid or reliable in measuring the goals and objectives of gifted programs.
- Effective evaluations cannot rely on only process or survey data; outcomes or goals must be carefully and operationally defined and assessed.
- Although outcomes must be assessed, a quality evaluation will also provide data to help understand the reasons why outcomes are achieved or why those goals have not been achieved.
- Effective evaluations are sensitive and respectful of the persons involved in delivering services to gifted students.
- Effective evaluations communicate findings in meaningful, relevant, clear, and precise summaries that reflect local context and take into account state and local policies and regulations.
- Effective evaluations are conducted by persons who are knowledgeable about both the field of gifted education and the field of evaluation.
- Effective evaluators communicate their findings in a timely fashion.

The basic attributes that define a high-quality program evaluation have been categorized by the Joint Committee on Standards for Educational

Evaluation as utility, feasibility, propriety, accuracy, fairness and impartiality, respect for all, adequate funding, and timeliness and relevance.[2]

Utility/Responsiveness/Accountability

- The evaluation is conducted by qualified people who know both the gifted education field and the field of program evaluation.
- The evaluation takes into consideration and is responsive to the concerns of those individuals who have a stake in the implementation and outcomes of the services offered to gifted students.
- The evaluation plan identifies and takes into consideration individual and cultural values unpinning the purpose of the evaluation, the processes to be used, and the judgments that are to be made.
- The evaluation design addresses important evaluation questions, not just those easy to answer.
- The evaluation gives appropriate attention to defining and taking into account the goals, objectives, and intended outcomes of the program.
- The evaluation is designed to give equal voice to all constituencies and examine all issues, no matter how sensitive, with appropriate weight to all voices, not just those with power and influence.

Feasibility

- The evaluation process should be practical, apply effective project management strategies, recognize and balance the cultural and political interests of all groups and individuals, and use resources effectively and efficiently.

Propriety

- The evaluation is designed and conducted to protect human and legal rights and maintain the dignity of participants and other stakeholders.
- The evaluation provides complete descriptions of findings, limitations, and conclusions to all stakeholders, unless doing so would violate legal and propriety obligations.
- Evaluations should openly and honestly identify and address real or perceived conflicts of interests that may compromise the evaluation.

Accuracy, Fairness, and Impartiality

- Assessment tools are selected or created with careful attention to reliability and validity in measuring the component under consideration.

---

[2]These statements are derived from an application of the *Program Evaluation Standards* (Yarborough et al., 2011) of the Joint Committee on Standards for Educational Evaluation and the research on evaluation utility reported in Tomlinson et al. (1993).

- Evaluation conclusions and decisions are explicitly justified in the cultures and contexts where they have consequences.
- Evaluations should employ technically adequate designs and analyses that are appropriate for the evaluation purposes.
- Evaluation reasoning leading from information and analyses to findings, interpretations, conclusions, and judgments should be clearly and completely documented.
- Data collection strategies are multifaceted and care is taken to triangulate findings across data sources and data collection strategies.

Respect for All Involved

- Care has been taken to design an evaluation that is considerate of the context and the situational factors impacting schools and the personnel in those schools.
- All instruments and data-gathering procedures have been examined to ensure they will not offend constituencies involved.
- Data yield information that can actually be used for decision making. Care has been taken not to waste students', teachers', or other stakeholders' time in evaluation activity that does not contribute to good decision making.

Adequate Funding

- Sufficient funding has been allocated to complete the evaluation as designed.

Timeliness and Relevance

- Data are collected, analyzed, and reported in time for consideration in the decision-making process.
- Results and recommendations are presented to relevant audiences in formats that make the information clearly understood.

EXAMPLE IN NEED OF REVISION

When asked to provide an evaluation of the gifted program, the program administrator called together the gifted program staff members and asked them to generate questions for a questionnaire to be sent out to parents. The coordinator and the staff generated a survey that addressed parent satisfaction with the identification process, the curriculum, and communication. In addition, the questionnaire addressed parent perceptions of the students' satisfaction with instruction they were provided. No one other than the program staff was involved in determining the process, in gathering the data, or in processing or interpreting the data.

MAKEOVER EXAMPLE

The flaws in the example above cut across several of the criteria for a quality evaluation. Only the most egregious will be listed here.

- First, consider the personnel involved in deciding what the focus would be of the evaluation. The approach described fails to be responsive by limiting the stakeholders involved in the process of planning the evaluation to only program staff. This approach not only limits the range of input around the kinds of questions that will yield useful data for decision makers, but it also likely limits the opportunity for input around the cultural contexts of the critical components of the program. For example: Is the identification process structured in ways that might inhibit the demonstration of talent by students of particular ethnicities or socioeconomic groups?
- Second, although parent perceptions of satisfaction with the program is an important evaluation question, that question is extremely limited relative to the scope of evaluation questions that *should* be asked. For example, the design fails to address the important question of impact of the program on student learning and development—focusing on the easy questions rather than the full range of important questions.
- Third, the exclusive use of surveys means that the data collection strategies are not multifaceted, and thus, there will be no opportunity to corroborate findings across data sources and data collection strategies.
- Fourth, the survey asks parents to report on student perceptions. Whenever possible, data should be collected directly from the informant (in this case, the students in the program).

The following example provides guidance for creating a planning process that addresses the key criteria of utility, responsiveness, accountability.

Task 1: Identification of Key Stakeholder Groups

First, a committee of representative groups from the school community is formed. This committee is carefully structured to include expertise in gifted education and program evaluation or is led by an individual from outside who has evaluation expertise. The committee first familiarizes itself with the NAGC Pre-K–Grade 12 Gifted Programming Standards (National Association for Gifted Children [NAGC], 2010) to have a broad sense of the important components of gifted services and to frame thinking about excellence in programming.

The members of the committee then identify all those groups that have a vested interest in the way gifted services are delivered, the quality of administration of the program, the curriculum and its effectiveness, and the like. The persons on the committee are asked to be as broad as possible in identifying these groups. The stakeholder groups they might identify include

- parents of gifted students,
- gifted students,
- superintendent and other central office administrators,
- school board members,
- gifted facilitators,
- classroom teachers,
- the coordinator of the program,
- building principals,
- parents of students not identified as gifted and talented, and
- counselors.

Task 2: Development of Strategies for Gathering Information on Areas of Concern From Each of the Stakeholder Groups

Once the stakeholder groups are identified, the committee identifies a small group of key persons (five to six) in each group who are likely to be able to articulate the areas that should be considered in creating an evaluation plan. A survey is constructed based on the NAGC Pre-K–Grade 12 Gifted Programming Standards. The select group of stakeholders then puts in rank order a series of statements derived from the standards according to how important they think these areas are to the program and, therefore, how important they are for focus in the evaluation. An open-ended question is added that gives the respondents the opportunity to identify any other areas of concern they might have and to write down any questions they might ask if they were conducting the evaluation. The survey is mailed to the designated parents, students, classroom teachers, building principals, counselors, and the parents of students not identified as gifted.[3] Interviews are scheduled and held with the chair of the school board, the superintendent, and the assistant superintendent of curriculum seeking the same information.

Task 3: Review of Data

The members of the committee review all the data resulting from Task 2 and create a comprehensive list of evaluation concerns emanating from the priorities identified by the stakeholder groups in their rankings and in their responses to the open-ended questions. They then put this list in rank order based on the frequency of mention, the level of intensity, and their judgment of the importance of the concern to gathering data that would improve the services to gifted students.

---

[3]An alternative strategy could be to hold focus groups in which the standards are examined, discussed, and then ranked by members of the stakeholder groups.

Task 4: Identifying Evaluation Questions and Deciding on Data Collection Procedures

A prioritized list of evaluation questions is created and a comprehensive plan to gather data from multiple sources using multiple data collection strategies is developed.

ADVICE FOR GETTING STARTED

In the section that follows, the steps for revising the inadequate evaluation plan are enumerated. However, the sequential nature of these steps also provides a good guideline for program administrators who are in the process of developing a strategic plan for evaluation. For each step, accompanying question(s) are provided to guide the actions one would take in this process.

Step 1: Preparing for the Evaluation

Action	Questions to Ask
a. Identify or develop a clearly articulated list of goals and objectives for all components of the services for gifted students.	What are the projected outcomes of the identification process? The curriculum development process? The staff development for teachers? For administrators? What is the projected outcome of the instruction given to gifted students? How do the NAGC Pre-K–Grade 12 Gifted Programming Standards (NAGC, 2010) inform us about which components of our program we should evaluate and what standards we should apply?
b. Assure commitment to meaningful evaluation.	Have adequate time, resources, and money been provided to carry out and disseminate the results of the evaluation?
c. Identify varied internal and external interest groups or stakeholders to serve as an active evaluation steering committee.	Have all stakeholders been invited? Do they represent the array of stakeholders with an interest in the operation and outcomes of services to gifted students? Do they represent the varied perspectives and points of view? Can they work effectively as a guiding force to ensure the evaluation will be used?
d. Gather evaluation concerns from identified stakeholder groups.	Has sufficient input been gathered from all groups that have a vested interest in the quality of services for gifted students? Are the strategies used to collect the data sensitive to cultural differences in responding to queries from the school?
e. Develop a written evaluation plan based on priorities of concern.	Does the plan reflect the most important concerns raised by stakeholders? Does it have clearly delineated steps and procedures for implementing the evaluation? Are there appropriate guidelines for data gathering, analysis, and dissemination?

Action	Questions to Ask
f. Select individuals to conduct the evaluation who are knowledgeable about evaluation and gifted education.	Is there someone from the school system who has the appropriate level of expertise to conduct an evaluation or is there a need for an outside consultant? Who might provide the expertise or suggest names of reputable evaluators?
h. Establish provisions for confidentiality and sensitivity in handling data and evaluation results.	Has permission to conduct a program evaluation been granted from the school's governing body? How will information be kept confidential? What steps have been taken to ensure all respondents are treated respectfully and with attention to cultural differences?
g. Consider the political implications of evaluation.	Have persons been identified who are key decision makers? Has someone contacted them? Have they been involved in creating the evaluation plan? Have we considered political implications both inside and outside the program and inside and outside the school district?

Step 2: Designing Data Collection

Action	Questions to Ask
a. Develop clearly stated evaluation questions.	Do the evaluation questions address program goals and expected outcomes (cognitive and affective), structures, functions, and activities? Can they be answered? If they are answered, will the answers affect decisions? Are findings likely to yield information that will be useful in improving services to gifted students?
b. Develop plans to use multiple data sources.	Does the plan include collecting data from parents of students identified as gifted, parents whose children have not been identified, teachers, students identified as gifted, administrators, and so forth so that various perspectives will be considered?
c. Plan to employ varied data collection strategies.	Are there plans to include such strategies as face-to-face interviews, focus groups, surveys, telephone interviews, classroom observations, objective and subjective measures of student outcomes, and the like? Have we tailored our data collection and data instruments to *our* evaluation questions?
d. Collect process data.	Are there ways to collect process data that can show whether the program is functioning as desired? Have we considered, for example, attendance records, documents from staff development sessions, newsletters or other communications to parents or classroom teachers, observation data from classrooms where gifted students are served, teacher or student journals, lesson plans or other curriculum documents, identification procedures and documents, and/or values data (e.g., interviews, surveys)?

(Continued)

(Continued)

Action	Questions to Ask
e. Collect outcome data.	Are there ways to collect outcome data that can show whether growth in student cognitive and affective growth has occurred as a result of program participation (comparison of varied achievement measure outcomes of eligible participants and eligible nonparticipants, use of out-of-level assessments, use of comparison groups, portfolio/product ratings, use of valid and reliable self-concept or self-efficacy measures)?
f. Select valid and reliable measures.	Which sources of information on test quality have been consulted, such as the *Mental Measurements Yearbook*?
g. Specify ways data will be analyzed and reported.	What techniques will be used to analyze quantitative and qualitative data? What is the best way to communicate what was learned about gifted education programming? Who needs to know what we learn, and what is the best communication vehicle for sharing that information?

Step 3: Conducting the Evaluation

Action	Questions to Ask
a. Involve multiple stakeholders consistently and in meaningful ways.	Do representatives of all stakeholders have the opportunity to review data collection and analysis plans?
b. Ensure that understanding of process by all sources of information.	Are there multiple opportunities and multiple vehicles for explaining how and why data are being collected?
c. Monitor and review evaluation process to ensure that samples are representative and not biased.	Have all data collection plans been reviewed to ensure that everyone has had an opportunity to have a voice in the process? For example, is there an open forum time when those who might not have been preselected for interview can share their perspectives?
d. Ensure timely data analysis and feedback.	Does the data management plan include clear timelines and contingencies for ensuring data are collected and analyzed in time for the decision-making deadlines (e.g., budget development, hiring, teaching assignments)?
e. Develop a plan for use of the findings—aimed at turning findings into action.	Is there a plan that identifies the roles that evaluators, program personnel, and stakeholders play in using the evaluation findings?

Step 4: Reporting Findings and Follow-Up

Action	Questions to Ask
a. Interpret evaluation findings.	Have representatives of stakeholder groups been involved in the interpretation of the findings?
b. Prepare reports according to interests and needs of stakeholders.	Has jargon been avoided in the reports? Have reports been tailored to the needs of decision makers? Are relevant and accurate executive summaries prepared for relevant groups of decision makers? Have we read all reports to ensure that confidentiality has been preserved as promised?
c. Include specific recommendations in the report that guide decision makers to follow through.	Can decision makers see the context in which recommendations are made? Do recommendations take into account the philosophy, the politics, and the financial circumstances of the school district?
d. Present the report in a timely fashion.	When are key decisions made?

Finally, Figure 16.1 shows a checklist that is a tool that can be used to assess the quality of a design for and implementation of evaluation procedures. Consider each statement and rate how successfully this step or component of your evaluation plan has been addressed: 1 indicates that the characteristic has not been addressed at all; 2 indicates that some attention has been given to this factor, but it still needs development; and 3 indicates that the characteristic has been fully addressed and is clearly a part of the evaluation process in the school district.

Figure 16.1 Checklist for Assessing Strengths

Characteristic	1	2	3
1. We have clearly defined the goals and objectives of our services for gifted students. Those goals and objectives include learning and development goals for gifted students.			
2. We have involved key stakeholders in creating our evaluation plan. They have been involved in ensuring we have identified the critical issues and concerns in the evaluation process, in identifying the kinds of data that will be considered in decision making, and in reviewing who will provide data.			
3. Key stakeholder groups are kept informed of the implementation steps throughout the evaluation process.			
4. We have adequate funds for the evaluation.			

(Continued)

Figure 16.1 (Continued)

Characteristic	1	2	3
5. We have a written plan for evaluation approved by the key stakeholder groups.			
6. We have the expertise to conduct the evaluation or have sought outside expertise.			
7. A variety of effective communication vehicles is used with each constituent group.			
8. We have identified important evaluation questions that include assessment of the effects of services on gifted students.			
9. All process and product goals of our program are evaluated.			
10. We have considered gathering data through a variety of means to answer each evaluation question and have chosen the most direct means of gathering data.			
11. We have selected reliable and valid instruments for our data collection.			
12. We have gathered data from a variety of sources.			
13. We have gathered data in ways that allow us to attribute outcomes to services to gifted students, rather than to other programs, the students' natural development, or other factors.			
14. We have made sure to adequately sample our sources to reduce potential bias in data.			
15. We have selected appropriate procedures for analyzing quantitative and qualitative data.			
16. We have a clear plan to communicate and distribute the results of the evaluation to decision makers.			

The higher the total score, the more likely it is that your district has a high-quality evaluation initiative. Low scores (1 or 2) on any item draw attention to aspects of the plan that are in need of revision.

ADVICE FOR THE SOLE PRACTITIONER

A program evaluation is a complex and demanding undertaking for even a team of well-trained evaluators. It is considerably more daunting for the sole practitioner. The most important advice to offer is to focus on the most important issues and let the other things go until later. For example, four criteria can guide the choice of evaluation foci:

1. This area of concern is critical or central to program success. For example: If the curriculum is not appropriate for identified gifted students, all other activities are probably for naught.

2. This area of concern impacts subsequent events. Lack of appropriate identification processes results in not serving all qualified gifted students from all ethnic, racial, and socioeconomic groups.

3. This area of concern has been identified by some relevant audience. Does the school board want to know the impact of the financial investment in the program?

4. Experience suggests that the area of concern is likely to be a problem. In a differentiation in the regular classroom service delivery model, some teachers may be unwilling or unable to differentiate instruction. Is this true in the district? If so, can they be identified? Can the evaluation provide strategies for changing that concern?

The single practitioner can consider the following suggestions to assist in the program evaluation process.

- First, consider resources within the school system. What other programs have recently been evaluated? How was that process structured? What resources can be borrowed from the prior evaluations—particularly focus on developed staff expertise?
- Reach out to colleagues in neighboring districts. Colleagues can work collaboratively to assist each other in many of the tasks related to program evaluation.
- Sole practitioners who do not have the expertise, either by themselves or collectively as a regional duo or team, can consider an alternative option. Collectively they can hire an outside expert either to conduct the respective program evaluations or to act as an advisor as program coordinators undertake the program evaluation tasks.
- A final option is to contact the state consultant on the gifted and talented. On occasion, these individuals are available to assist in the evaluation process. If they are unable to assist in conducting the evaluation themselves, they will surely have available a list of well-qualified, locally accessible consultants.

SUGGESTED RESOURCES

Callahan, C. M. (Vol. Ed.). (2004). Program evaluation in gifted education (Vol. 11). In S. M. Reis (Series Ed.), *Essential readings in gifted education*. Thousand Oaks, CA: Corwin.

This volume pulls together the important articles published in *Gifted Child Quarterly* over the past several decades. The articles provide guidance on asking the right evaluation questions, collecting formative evaluation data, anchoring assessment data, and other important topics.

Callahan, C. M., & Caldwell, M. S. (1995). *A practitioner's guide to evaluating programs for the gifted*. Washington, DC: National Association for Gifted Children.

As a practitioner's guide, this work provides step-by-step instructions for planning and executing an evaluation plan based on decision making using formative and summative evaluation.

National Association for Gifted Children. (2010). *NAGC Pre-K–Grade 12 Gifted Programming Standards: A blueprint for quality gifted education programs*. Washington, DC: Author.

The standards provide evaluators with criteria for judging quality in the process dimensions of gifted programs across every aspect of gifted services based on current research, theory, and practice. (See Appendix B, page 261.)

Renzulli, J. S. (1975). *A guidebook for evaluating programs for the gifted and talented*. Ventura, CA: Office of the Ventura County Superintendent of Schools.

This classic on gifted program evaluation provides readers with a strategy based on the key features of gifted programs ranging from philosophy of gifted programs to identification, curriculum, and funding.

Speirs Neumeister, K., & Burney, V. H. (2012). *Gifted program evaluation: A handbook for administrators and coordinators*. Waco, TX: Prufrock Press.

This handbook provides examples of specific surveys and approaches to data gathering for program evaluation.

REFERENCES

National Association for Gifted Children. (2010). *NAGC Pre-K–Grade 12 Gifted Programming Standards: A blueprint for quality gifted education programs*. Washington, DC: Author.

Reineke, R. A. (1991). Stakeholder involvement in evaluation: Suggestions for practice. *Evaluation Practice, 12*, 39–44.

Tomlinson, C. A., Bland, L., & Moon, T. R. (1993). Evaluation utilization: A review of the literature with implications for gifted education. *Journal for the Education of the Gifted, 16*, 171–189.

Tomlinson, C. A., Bland, L., Moon, T. R., & Callahan, C. M. (1994). Case studies of evaluation utilization in gifted education. *Evaluation Practice, 15*, 153–168.

VanTassel-Baska, J. (2006). A content analysis of evaluation findings across 20 gifted programs: A clarion call for enhanced gifted program development. *Gifted Child Quarterly, 50*, 191–215. doi:10.1177/001698620605000302

Yarborough, D. B., Shulha, L. M., Hopson, R. K., & Caruthers, F. A. (2011). *The program evaluation standards: A guide for evaluators and users* (3rd ed.). Thousand Oaks, CA: Sage.

Chapter 17

Using Scientifically Based Research to Make Decisions About Gifted Education Programs, Services, and Resources

Tonya R. Moon, PhD

DEFINITION

In 2008, the American Educational Research Association (AERA, n.d.) defined *scientifically based research* (SBR) as the application of rigorous, systematic, and objective methodologies to obtain reliable and valid knowledge about educational programs and services. SBR requires specific components:

- the development of a logical, evidence-based chain of reasoning;
- methods appropriate to the questions posed;
- observational or experimental designs and instruments that provide reliable and generalizable findings;
- data and analysis adequate to support the findings;

- explication of procedures and results clearly and in detail, including specification of the population to which the findings can be generalized;
- adherence to professional norms of peer review;
- dissemination of findings to contribute to scientific knowledge; and
- access to data for re-analysis, replication, and the opportunity to build on findings. (AERA, n.d., para. 1)

Furthermore, AERA (n.d.) stated that "the examination of causal questions requires experimental designs using random assignment or quasi-experimental or other designs that substantially reduce plausible competing explanations for the obtained results" (para. 2). It is important to distinguish the term *scientifically based research* or *research-based* from *evidence-based*. Although educators regularly consult data and seek out reliable evidence as part of their reflective practice, not all evidence is equal or should be given equal weight in decision making—particularly when considering programmatic or policy decisions. According to Whitehurst (2002) from the U.S. Department of Education, Figure 17.1 outlines the distinctions between evidence-based practices and SBR.

It is important to note that SBR is one component of evidence-based research and that for an educational practice to be evidence based it must be evaluated using scientifically based research and have the accumulation of professional wisdom. Unfortunately, research that meets SBR standards for evaluating the effectiveness of educational programs and services is limited, particularly in the field of gifted education. In these cases, decision makers, including those responsible for gifted education services, need to rely on the best empirical evidence available and their professional judgment until such time that SBR evidence is available. The

Figure 17.1 Scientifically Based Research Versus Evidence-Based Practices

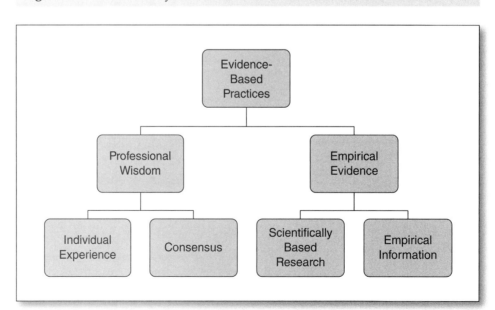

higher the level of research evidence (Whitehurst, 2002) related to a model or service, the greater the likelihood that the model or service in question will deliver the intended impact. As the availability of SBR increases, stronger conclusions about the effects of strategies and services and the learning of students in gifted programs can be drawn.

RATIONALE

There are many reasons why decision making about gifted education services must be based on the strongest evidence possible. The first reason concerns professional responsibility. Specifically, the primary responsibility of professionals in charge of administering and coordinating gifted programs is to create a unified and comprehensive set of services and practices that promote student learning, emotional well-being, and the development of individual potential. To make the very best professional decisions about identification models, identification processes and instruments, curriculum, instructional resources, teaching and learning strategies, assessments, and related guidance services, gifted education administrators and specialists need sound evidence on which to base their judgments.

A second reason for careful, evidence-based decision making concerns the vast number of resources available to decision makers. Since the mid-1970s, the number of books and articles that have been written about how to meet the needs of gifted students and how to manage gifted education programs has expanded exponentially. Journal articles, publishers' catalogs, and texts written for gifted education personnel proclaim the benefits and advantages of various identification models and instruments, student services, programming models, instructional strategies, and learning materials. Although this bounty of publications is welcomed, the sheer number has also resulted in a plethora of perspectives, techniques, tools, claims, and advertisements that must be independently peer reviewed, critically analyzed, and evaluated to determine their credibility and worth. On many occasions, practitioners indicate that this storehouse of materials also causes confusion, bewilderment, and, in the case of harried educators with scant support services and technical assistance, an all-too-frequent hasty rush to judgment and implementation.

The third reason for evidence-based decision making is related to accountability. Like our expectations for general education, gifted education programs and services are expected to increase student learning and should be accountable for costs, quality, and equity of opportunity for all students. The National Association for Gifted Children (NAGC, 2010) has identified six broad standard statements to provide guidance for Pre-K through Grade 12 that help inform and provide clarity about gifted programming. (For additional details, see Appendix B, page 261.) As decision makers for gifted education services, we must be able to explain to all stakeholders how our sound and evidence-based, decision-making process has led to the continuous improvement in all aspects of our programming.

Quite simply, the most respected educational groups have provided us with criteria by which to make evidence-based decisions. These expectations are comparable to what we insist on from the medical, legal, and engineering professions. As clients of these professionals, we require our doctors, lawyers, and contractors to base their recommendations and practices on defensible evidence that demonstrates results; gifted education students should be treated no differently.

The Every Student Succeeds Act (ESSA, 2015)[1] is the reauthorization of the Elementary and Secondary Education Act, and it is the fourth reason for using evidence-based decision making. ESSA requires knowledge and application of SBR in several areas: the strategies and interventions used to improve student learning, instruction, and schools; improving and supporting parental and family engagement; and professional development activities for educators. With the newly signed ESSA legislation, there exists language specifically relating to evidence-based activities that "improves the capability of schools to plan, conduct, and improve programs to identify and serve gifted and talented students" (Section 4644).

GUIDING PRINCIPLES AND ATTRIBUTES THAT DEFINE HIGH-QUALITY EVIDENCE

The following principles apply to the evidence provided about particular gifted education programs or services. These principles, used to make decisions regarding the education of gifted students, should occur not only at the macro level (i.e., district and school) but also in conversations and interactions with colleagues in the daily work of educating gifted students (e.g., data team meetings, professional learning communities).

- **Principle 1:** The program, identification process, resources, and service components of a gifted education program should be based on a specified and sound theoretical foundation.
- **Principle 2:** A sound theoretical foundation should lead to the development, field-testing, and investigation of related and promising services, instructional strategies, resources, and programming practices for gifted education.
- **Principle 3:** Significant questions should be asked and systematically investigated to study the effectiveness and appropriateness of specific program or service components and promising practices. Such questions should focus on the evidence that supports, refutes, or stipulates when, with whom, and under what conditions a promising practice promotes student learning.
- **Principle 4:** The data collected to assess a promising practice should be appropriate to address the question(s) identified in Principle 3.

---

[1]Signed into law by President Obama on December 10, 2015, with bipartisan support.

- **Principle 5:** Evidence that supports a promising practice claim or hypothesis should be collected systematically and empirically.
- **Principle 6:** The data collected as evidence to evaluate the effectiveness of a promising practice should be subjected to appropriate data analysis.
- **Principle 7:** The methods used to assess the program and service components should allow for the direct investigation of the questions posed in Principle 3.
- **Principle 8:** Evaluation and investigation procedures should be replicated at different times, in different places, and in different contexts to substantiate or modify the original evaluation conclusions and inferences.
- **Principle 9:** Once an evidence-based program, service component or instructional practice is adopted and implemented, periodic evaluations of the related program or service components should be conducted to ensure that the component is still achieving its original goals and desired impact.

QUESTIONS TO CONSIDER REGARDING HIGH-QUALITY RESEARCH

To gain an understanding of the potential usefulness of a particular program or service component(s), decision makers are advised to act as cautious consumers and test pilots who carefully examine the evidence about particular programs or services from three perspectives:

1. **The theoretical base of the program or service.** Does the program or service documentation contain a list of specific goals and clear and logical explanations about how and why each practice or service is expected to be effective with clearly identified target populations?

2. **Information about the implementation and transferability of the program or service.** Does accompanying documentation identify and describe the situations, conditions, student characteristics, and time frame under which the program or service has been effectively implemented?

3. **The available evidence about the effects of identified and relevant student outcomes.** Does the program or service have high-quality research studies that investigate and describe outcomes and effects?

Particular questions that should be asked to address these three areas are listed below.

Theoretical Base

- Is there a theoretical foundation for the program or service?
- What ideas and assumptions form the foundation for the program or service?

- Is there an operational definition of the term *gifted* that is tied to the stated philosophy and identified goals of the program or service and that is aligned with the district's particular definition of gifted?
- Are there clear descriptions for each of the central aspects of the program (e.g., identification, curriculum) or service?
- Are the key features of the program well aligned with the district's stated philosophy, goals, and gifted definition?

Application and Transferability

- In what settings has the program or service component been implemented? With whom? And are these settings and individuals similar to the district considering the program or service component?
- How many other schools or districts have implemented the program or service component?
- Is there clear and detailed evidence that the program or service has been successfully implemented at a local level, a state level, and/or nationally?

Evidence of Effectiveness

- Is there evidence that the program or service has a positive effect on identified outcomes (e.g., student achievement, increased number of underrepresented populations in gifted education programs, improved teacher capacity to meeting the needs of gifted and talented students)?
- Are there research studies investigating the effects on identified outcomes of the program or service? Are those studies carried out using the processes and procedures of scientifically based research?
- Are those studies of reasonable quality (i.e., systematic, empirical, and use of appropriate data analysis with reliable and valid data)?
- Who conducted the research? Does the individual(s) or organization have the necessary qualifications and resources to conduct research on the topic?
- What is being investigated? Is the topic focused appropriately so that reliable and valid data could/can be gathered?
- When was the research conducted? In some instances, seminal research has as much validity as recent research. However, the timing of the results is important and should influence how one uses the results. If the research is recent, does it acknowledge the previous research and findings? How does it build on the seminal (earlier) work?
- Where was the research conducted? Is the number of individuals involved in the study sufficient for the conclusions that are being made about the topic? Are the school and student demographics similar to the district considering the practices?

- Are the methods employed to carry out the research sound? That is, are there clearly identified research questions? Were the data gathered in a systematic way? Do the data-gathering techniques align to the research questions being asked?
- Are the findings connected to the research questions and the research methods employed?

MAKEOVER EXAMPLE

The coordinator of Rolling Hills School District's gifted program is in charge of support services for students (e.g., guidance counseling) and afterschool programs. He has to appear before the district's school board to deliver the annual report about the gifted program and, in particular, information on the identification procedures, the populations being served in the program, and the services that are implemented to address the populations' needs.

For the last several years, the school board has attempted to increase the representation of minority students in the gifted program. To address the board's priority, the coordinator has attended numerous national and regional conferences and participated in regional gifted meetings with other coordinators. He has gathered information about the practices in other districts and the types of instruments and procedures they use to identify minority students. As a result of his attendance at these meetings, the coordinator and an appointed committee changed the identification process twice during the last 3 years.

Each year the coordinator is asked to explain the identification decisions and the effects the decisions have on the underrepresentation of particular student populations in the gifted program. Each year he shares the successes other school districts have experienced with similar strategies. He also shares the results that test developers shared with him about the test the gifted program is using to identify more minority students.

Because of recent funding issues and the implementation of a new teacher evaluation system, the school district is facing increased expectations for accountability and transparency. The teachers who are responsible for implementing the multiple changes to the identification process have also voiced concerns, as have numerous parents. For this reason, the gifted education program coordinator is apprehensive about the upcoming school board meeting and the response he may receive to his report.

CONCERNS AND ISSUES IN THE EXAMPLE

Many gifted education coordinators face a situation that is similar to the one presented in the preceding example. Making decisions based on what others are doing or what appears to be the latest trend means operating from a low-evidence standpoint. The two specific concerns illuminated in this example are explained below.

The coordinator made significant program decisions without data related to his or her local program. In this case, he changed an identification process without considering the following items:

- program philosophy,
- program goals, and
- the operational definition of gifted and talented used in the school district.

The coordinator did not participate in organized data collection efforts—either within the program or as part of a larger school initiative or data team—and a significant question or objective was not established with the change to the new identification process. Moreover, the coordinator did not have access to or did not use longitudinal databases and data analysis software to review information (e.g., test scores, participation in special programs, grades, feeder schools, student demographic data) about students who did and did not receive gifted education services. To evaluate the effectiveness of an experimental identification procedure, the gifted education coordinator and/or strategic planning committee must be able to retrieve relevant data about students before and after the new procedures went into effect or data based on a matched comparison group of students who did not participate in the program. In this case, without the longitudinal student database, decisions were made based on gut feelings rather than on systematic and empirically collected data about the effectiveness and impact of the new identification processes. With such data, the coordinator might have been able to evaluate the degree to which the process aligned with the needs and strengths of underrepresented students and the district's program definition of giftedness.

MAKEOVER EXAMPLE

Revising the example requires that we follow eight steps, which are explained next. As you read through these steps, think back to a time when you made a weighty decision related to your gifted education program's model or services. Try to identify the steps you incorporated into your decision-making process. Which steps did you incorporate? Which ones might you have overlooked inadvertently?

Step 1: Identify Area of Concern and Any Data Related to the Identified Area

The first task that must be accomplished is to identify a focus for your subsequent data collection and review. To guide your work, it may be helpful to articulate your concern or issue in the form of an open-ended research question.

Step 2: Review Existing Program Data

The second task to resolve the problem illuminated in this example involves the development of a committee that represents the various stakeholders in the school district community who are vested in this question and problem. The committee should collect sufficient data to describe the context in which the gifted program operates. This information might include but is not limited to (a) demographic data about student participants and nonparticipants (e.g., socioeconomic levels of students, needs, strengths, available services to address these needs, students' academic proficiency levels, numbers of students having dual or multiple classifications); (b) community and district-wide perceptions of student needs, strengths, and services; (c) funds available for the program's operation (e.g., salaries, resources, professional development opportunities) demographic data about student participants and nonparticipants (e.g., socioeconomic levels of students, needs, strengths, available services to address these needs, students' academic proficiency levels, numbers of students having dual or multiple classifications); and (d) professional development needs of the teachers responsible for the delivery of student services.

Step 3: Analyze the Data and Prioritize Needs

The third item for this committee involves reviewing and analyzing of the information gathered in Steps 1 and 2 and the establishing of priorities. In the earlier example, the committee might examine the district's philosophy, goals, and operational definition of gifted and talented to ensure alignment. Assuming that the alignment exists, the committee can prioritize the need to establish a defensible identification process within the context of the existing or revised program parameters. If there is no alignment of the philosophy, goals, and definition, the committee needs to address the necessary alignment before taking the next step—deciding on the service delivery model, services, and identification procedures and processes.

Step 4: Identify a Research Base

Once the committee is confident about the alignment of the program's philosophy, goals, and definition, the next task is to gather relevant research about identification strategies for gifted and talented learners and related strategies to identify underrepresented gifted and talented minority students.

Step 5: Discriminate Between Applicable and Nonapplicable Research and Information

After the latest research has been gathered, the next step is to discriminate potential and valuable sources of information from irrelevant sources.

A review of each piece of information is critical to ensure that the research has a strong theoretical basis, to ensure that there is evidence of its potential usefulness for the district regarding its identified priorities and context, and to determine if there is any evidence about the effects of particular identification procedures.

Step 6: Critically Review Applicable Information Sources

If Step 5 suggests that some studies are applicable, the committee should review each relevant study. Specifically, the committee should verify that the evidence collected was done in a systematic way, that the evidence collected was reliable and valid for the purpose of the study, that the data were subjected to appropriate and rigorous data analysis, and that the study was replicated in different settings with different student populations or has the potential for replication.

Step 7: Implementing Changes Based on Sound Evidence

With the information obtained from Step 6, the committee can begin to establish a revised identification process that can be implemented in the district. The committee can also work with district personnel to establish a local database to maintain longitudinal information for use when making decisions. All information concerning students nominated, screened, and receiving services should be kept for 5 to 7 years to ensure that the identification process is identifying the appropriate population of students for the services that are being delivered. This database is even more important when there are no research studies to use as a basis for decision making. With the use of a well-managed database, the coordinator can begin to collect and provide evidence about the impact of the decisions concerning the identification of students for services (Step 8).

Step 8: Evaluating Implemented Changes

With the ongoing collection of data from Step 7, the committee can begin to internally evaluate the effectiveness of the implementation of the changes, although an external evaluation is always recommended every 3 to 5 years. Findings from internal evaluations tend to be more positively received, even if issues are identified, than are the findings from an external evaluation. Furthermore, conducting an internal evaluation can increase introspection on why program impacts are or are not occurring. However, it is always advisable that at some point (e.g., every 3–5 years) an external evaluation be carried out by an individual with expertise in gifted programming and evaluation.

ADVICE FOR GETTING STARTED IN SELECTING AND EVALUATING PROGRAMS AND SERVICES BASED ON EVIDENCE

Table 17.1 shows steps that can be used to analyze claims made or evidence cited by a researcher, publisher, or developer related to a gifted education service, strategy, or practice. The same steps may also prove useful when developing a program or district plan to gather and analyze local evidence about the effectiveness of program services and strategies, or in larger

Table 17.1   Steps for Analyzing Claims for Evidence

Step 1: Identify area of focus and any data related to the area	Articulate your concerns or areas of interest. It may be helpful to create open-ended research questions to guide your work in subsequent steps.
Step 2: Data collection	Collect data or information that gives an overall and accurate picture of the current context and situation in which the proposed program and/or services will be implemented.
Step 3: Data analysis and prioritization	Analyze data or information to determine and prioritize the needs of the students or clients.
Step 4: Identifying the research base	Gather literature to identify the research base for the potential programs or services being considered. (See the Suggested Resources section of this chapter for potential sources for research.)
Step 5: Discriminating relevant from nonrelevant	Use obtained results to determine (a) if there is a theoretical basis for a program or service, (b) if there are identified issues with the implementation of the program or service, (c) if there is evidence provided about the transferability of the program or service across different contexts, and (d) if there is evidence of the effects of the program or service on identified student outcomes. It is important to note that not all research will address all four areas, but more than one may be addressed in any given research study.
Step 6: Critical review of relevant studies	If the results indicate that the study is relevant to the identified needs in Step 2, each study should be further examined. Use the characteristics of high-quality research, outlined earlier in this chapter, to determine if the relevant research is of high quality, transferable to other contexts, and relevant to identified goals and needs. The examined research should meet the criteria for SBR. In some cases, there will be no, or little, high-quality evidence that the program or service will obtain the identified student outcomes. Refer to the Guiding Questions section when reviewing relevant studies.
Step 7: Making changes	Using the evidence provided in Step 5, defensible changes are made to the particular program/service under consideration.
Step 8: Ongoing evaluation	Continue to collect pertinent student data and research literature to support program decision making.

school or district strategic planning conversations. There is no single time-table or context for conducting these activities. Instead, they can be used when needed.

AN EVIDENCE-BASED HIERARCHY THAT CAN BE USED TO ASSESS THE TRUSTWORTHINESS OF EDUCATION PROGRAMS, MODELS, AND SERVICES

Educators make hundreds of decisions every year. When they make decisions that impact student learning and/or influence the implementation of ser-vices, models, practices, strategies, products, or tools, they must be mindful of students' learning needs. Specifically, children are best served when deci-sions regarding their educational program are based on solid evidence. In the context of ESSA, many call this process *evidence-based decision making*: the integration of professional wisdom with the best available empirical evidence in making decisions about how to deliver instruction (Whitehurst, 2002).

The quality of this evidence can be rated according to its reliability and trustworthiness. When we apply the guiding principles from educa-tional research, we can rate—from low to high—the validity of most gifted education services, models, practices, strategies, or tools.

Table 17.2 has been designed to help practitioners assess the evidence base for gifted education services, models, practices, strategies, and tools. It is divided into three columns. The left-hand column contains the Evidence Rating. Examples of models, program components, and products that are rated at the low end of the hierarchy have less evidence that can be used to support their effectiveness. Models, program components, and products rated at the upper end of this continuum hold great promise for delivering their intended impacts. The middle column, Evidence Sources, contains an increasingly rigorous set of research-related factors or condi-tions. The greater the number of research conditions that are met by a particular model, program component, or product, the more likely it is to be a trustworthy and reliable choice for decision makers. The right-hand column contains an example that may be associated with the rating and can be used to illustrate the Evidence Rating.

As you use this hierarchy, think of models, programs, program compo-nents, and products you have used or have operating within your district's gifted program. Try to determine each element's standing by locating it in the hierarchy and noting its Evidence Rating.

GUIDING QUESTIONS FOR THE ANALYSIS OF RESEARCH REPORTS

Gifted education specialists, general education teachers, and school admin-istrators usually rely on colleagues, regional service centers, their state department of education, local universities, conferences, journal articles,

Table 17.2   An Evidence-Based Hierarchy

Evidence Rating (Low to High)	Evidence Sources	Examples of Related Education Services or Strategies
1 (No Evidence)	A colleague's idea for curriculum, a service, identification, or grouping practice.	Your colleague's curriculum unit that he or she recommended to you last year. It has no empirical evidence to support it. (No design; no empirical data have been gathered)
2 (Emerging Practices)	Expert-developed services, models, practices, strategies, products, or tools that are accompanied by convenient sampling and teachers' subjective observations about effectiveness.	An identification practice or strategy for providing professional development that has come from a credible source. (Professionally developed materials; subjective reflections)
3 (Promising Practice)	Theory-based, expert-developed services, models, practices, strategies, products, or tools accompanied by nonrandom sampling and student work that provides evidence of practical effectiveness.	A curriculum unit that has been field-tested by a teacher. It includes the teacher's systematic observations about the effectiveness of the unit and samples of student work. (Convenience sampling + student work)
4 (Promising Practice)	Theory-based, expert-developed services, models, practices, strategies, products, or tools accompanied by nonrandom sampling—treatment group only—and pre- and post-assessment data that provide evidence of statistical effectiveness.	The conventional action research project conducted by a classroom teacher who used his or her own students in the study. (Convenience sampling + pre- and post-assessment)
5 (Promising Practice)	Theory-based, expert-developed services, models, practices, strategies, products, or tools accompanied by nonrandom assignment to groups and treatment and control group data that provide evidence of statistical effectiveness.	A research study conducted within one district. Nonrandom treatment and comparison groups used to determine the effectiveness of an intervention. (Convenience sampling + treatment and comparison group design)
6 (Evidence-Based Practice)	Theory-based, expert developed services, models, practices, strategies, products, or tools accompanied by nonrandom matched assignment and treatment and comparison group data that provide evidence of statistical effectiveness.	A study that explores the effectiveness of an instructional strategy or practice using a treatment and control design. The effectiveness of the instructional strategy is examined across subgroups of students, such as males and females, cultural groups, and/or income levels. (Nonrandom, matched assignment + treatment and comparison group design)

(Continued)

Table 17.2 (Continued)

Evidence Rating (Low to High)	Evidence Sources	Examples of Related Education Services or Strategies
7 (Evidence-Based Practice)	Theory-based, expert developed services, models, practices, strategies, products, or tools accompanied by random sampling and treatment and comparison group data that provide evidence of statistical effectiveness in one or more settings.	A study that explores the effectiveness of a strategy or process (e.g., early kindergarten entrance, grade skipping) using a treatment and control design. The effectiveness of the instructional strategy or process is examined across subgroups of students, such as males and females, cultural groups, and/or income levels. (Random assignment + treatment and comparison group design + more than one setting)
8 (Evidence-Based Practice)	Theory-based, expert developed, services, models, practices, strategies, products, or tools that were implemented in multiple settings, accompanied by random assignment to treatment groups and treatment and comparison group data that were subjected to a meta-analysis that provides evidence of statistical and practical effectiveness.	A study pulls together all the rigorous research (i.e., multiple studies conducted with various groups in different locations) on the effectiveness of a strategy or process (e.g., early kindergarten entrance, grade skipping) using a treatment and control design. (Random assignment + treatment and comparison group design + multiple settings + meta-analysis)

Note: Ratings go from "none to low evidence" (1) to "strong evidence (SBR + Professional Wisdom)" (8).

and websites as their primary sources of information about an educational practice, recommendation, or innovation. To assess the quality of the proposals, explanations, and recommendations provided by these sources, practitioners can use the criteria listed in Table 17.2. To evaluate the extent to which the description, evidence, claim, or recommendation meets the definition of SBR, practitioners should consider using the following questions as guidelines:

- Is the study systematic and empirical? High-quality research is conducted through the use of a discipline-based inquiry process. This means that the developer, researcher, and/or evaluator are able to provide evidence of careful planning and attention to details that is grounded in evidence drawn from observation or experimentation. Any findings from the research should be based on measurable evidence, and not on opinions or speculation.
- Does the research have a theoretical foundation?

- Were data collected using observation and/or experiment?
- Were data collected from appropriate groups? From multiple participants (e.g., students, teachers)?
- Are the findings supported by measurable evidence?
- Did the procedure allow for the collection of reliable and valid data? Reliable and valid data with appropriate data analysis produce credible findings. Reliable data provides assurance that the results could be replicated if the same individuals were tested again under similar circumstances. Valid data allow one to support particular types of inferences that are drawn.
- Was data collection consistent across all groups (e.g., training of data collectors, standardization of test administration)?
- Were the data collected appropriate for the research questions being investigated?
- Were appropriate data analysis procedures used to analyze the data? Appropriate data analysis is critical, with failure to use such methods resulting in inaccurate or misleading findings.
- Does the research address the identified research question?
- Do the findings justify the conclusions that are drawn?
- Are sample sizes and methods of analysis (statistical procedures, qualitative techniques) fully described?
- Does the type of analysis employed address the research question?
- Are all procedures described in the research presented with sufficient detail to allow others to replicate the study?
- Are findings clearly described and reported?
- Are the findings presented objectively?
- Is the description of the methodology such that replicating the study is possible?
- Are limitations and/or issues concerning the research reported? Were explanations provided that contradicted the researcher's expectations?
- A high-quality study should be subjected to peer review. These peer reviewers provide quality control in the form of outside, objective, blind reviews of the research.
- Has the research been accepted and published by a scholarly journal or was it only reported in the media (newspapers, magazines, etc.)?
- If the research has not been published, is there evidence that it was reviewed by outside, objective reviewers? Is there evidence that the reviewers approved the study?

ADVICE FOR THE SOLE PRACTITIONER

Being the only gifted education personnel in a district can be a lonely job, and it always helps to have critical friends. Critical friends can help you evaluate the practices in your gifted education program and identify the evidence or research base that underlies each component. They can work cooperatively with you to help you decide which components may need to be examined, and possibly redefined, because no compelling evidence supports the efficacy of its practices.

Critical friends, however, do not always have to work with you in real time or space. Conducting a search of *Gifted Child Quarterly*—or other outlets identified in Suggested Resources—for research articles and studies that identify program components and characteristics that have a research or evidence base is one good way to start your hunt. Skimming texts (like this one) sponsored as a service publication or endorsed by a reputable organization like NAGC or CEC-TAG provides another source for a meeting of the minds. Additionally, many universities with a research focus on gifted education maintain websites that provide information on several research-based practices and professional development opportunities.

However you find your evidence-based practices—through colleagues, research articles, or websites—please remember that it is up to you, the practitioner in a local school or district, to determine if these practices are relevant to your setting. Consider the demographics of your site, relevant programming variables (e.g., costs, personnel required), and the needs of students and setting before deciding to implement a promising practice.

SUGGESTED RESOURCES

Buros Center for Testing (http://buros.org)

Buros is the publisher of the *Mental Measurement and Tests in Print* series, which provides critical reviews to support the informed selection of commercial tests.

The National Center for Research on Gifted Education (NCRGE; http://ncrge.uconn.edu)

The work of the NCRGE is to examine gifted programming currently being implemented in three specific states that have strong commitments to serving underrepresented populations and that show promise for improving student outcomes. This work is funded by the Jacob K. Javits Gifted and Talented Students Education Act and represents collaborative efforts from the University of Connecticut, University of Virginia, Florida State University, and University of California, Berkeley.

Scholarly journals in the field of gifted education

These journals have a peer-review process for their published materials. Journals that specialize in the field of gifted education include *Gifted Child Quarterly, Journal for the Education of the Gifted, Roeper Review*, and *Journal of Advanced Academics*. *Gifted Child Today* is another resource that is more practical than the research-based journals listed earlier.

What Works Clearinghouse (http://ies.ed.gov/ncee/wwc)

This website, sponsored by the U.S. Department of Education, helps educators make choices based on SBR. It is important to note that the site is continually updated.

Vogt, W. P., & Johnsen, R. B. (2015). *The SAGE dictionary of statistics and methodology: A nontechnical guide for the social sciences*. Thousand Oaks, CA: Sage.

This practical reference provides a range of explanations and examples that will assist practitioners in reading and understanding research reports. Definitions for frequently used terms, concepts, and theories are provided, as well as concepts from both qualitative and quantitative research methods.

REFERENCES

American Educational Research Association. (n.d.). *Definition of scientifically based research*. Retrieved from http://www.aera.net/ResearchPolicyAdvocacy/ResearchPolicyAdvocacyNews/DefinitionofScientifically-basedResearch/tabid/10277/Default.aspx

Every Student Succeeds Act. Pub. L. No. 114–95 (2015).

National Association for Gifted Children. (2010). *NAGC Pre-K–Grade 12 Gifted Programming Standards: A blueprint for quality gifted education programs*. Washington, DC: Author.

Whitehurst, G. J. (2002). *Evidence-based education* (slide presentation). Retrieved from http://www.ed.gov/nclb/methods/whatworks/eb/edlite-slide020.html

Appendix A

Establishing Gifted Education Advisory Committees

Jann H. Leppien, PhD,
and Karen L. Westberg, PhD

THE PURPOSE OF A GIFTED EDUCATION ADVISORY COMMITTEE

Members of a gifted education advisory committee play an important and necessary role in the development of successful gifted education services. This group of stakeholders offers perspective, expertise, time, and commitment to the implementation of comprehensive gifted program services. By establishing a gifted education advisory committee, school districts create program ownership, increase the likelihood that services for capable students will be of high quality, and ensure program longevity.

A gifted education advisory committee is composed of volunteers who meet regularly on a long-term basis to provide advice and support to those responsible for the implementation of gifted education services. Advisory committees serve important functions, such as establishing an initial gifted education program, revising or expanding services, developing new identification guidelines, reviewing the extent to which a school district has implemented gifted education services, lobbying for appropriate funding, establishing public relations, disseminating information, or advocating for comprehensive gifted education services. Typically, a gifted education coordinator takes responsibility to staff the advisory committee. However, in the absence of a full-time coordinator, a central office administrator or principal should assume this role.

When establishing an advisory committee, a school district needs to consider the roles represented by the committee members and the processes and procedures that will guide their work. An advisory committee is more likely to be effective when the school district's administration genuinely desires the committee's input; therefore, decisions regarding the roles and responsibilities of this committee must be determined prior to its establishment. The committee members should be knowledgeable, committed individuals who are interested in volunteering their time to support the district's gifted education services. Procedures for governance should provide a sense of engagement, ownership, and access to information about the program. Committee members must understand that they have no administrative policy-making or legislative authority and that these meetings are a time to discuss and review the overall program, not individual students or personal concerns.

FUNCTIONS OF A GIFTED EDUCATION ADVISORY COMMITTEE

The scope of the advisory committee's work will vary depending on the size of the school district, the stage of program development, and the provisions within states' legislative gifted education mandates. Contextual factors influence the activities in which advisory committees engage, but the activities will likely include the following:

- Review features of the program plan, including mission statement, philosophy, goals, identification procedures, a continuum of services, and curriculum for advanced learners.
- Evaluate and improve the current gifted education services based on best practices in the field of gifted education.
- Determine annual goals and priorities, commit to ongoing program evaluation, and assist in interpreting data for improvement of gifted educational services.
- Communicate and advise the superintendent and the school board on the educational needs of highly capable students and appropriate services for enhancing their growth.
- Focus attention on issues relative to improving services for students who have been traditionally underserved by gifted programs including twice-exceptional learners, and those from culturally, linguistically, and economically diverse backgrounds.
- Support professional development training for parents, faculty, school administrators, and counselors.
- Promote community awareness about the goals and objectives of gifted education programming.
- Build positive relationships among schools, teachers, administrators, counselors, gifted education staff, parents, and the community to support current gifted education services and to advocate for future programming needs.
- Champion efforts to solicit additional funding for student scholarships, awards, and competitions.
- Support local, state, and national efforts regarding gifted education by attending legislative meetings, writing letters, and promoting gifted education programs.

THE MEMBERSHIP OF THE ADVISORY COMMITTEE

The size and composition of the advisory committee will vary depending on the number of elementary, middle, and high schools represented, as well as any state or local regulations that govern its existence. The members might include parents of students in the gifted program, professional staff and community members from each school, business leaders, gifted education program directors or teachers, board of education members, higher education representatives, and perhaps a student appointed by the administration. A school district curriculum and instruction representative and at least one principal might also serve on the committee. Committee membership should reflect the ethnic and geographical composition of the school district. Members' terms should be determined prior to their appointment, staggered, and at least 2 to 3 years long.

STEPS FOR ESTABLISHING AND IMPLEMENTING A GIFTED EDUCATION ADVISORY COMMITTEE

- **Secure approval:** Explain the function of an advisory committee to administrators. Point out the local need for, and advantages of, the advisory committee. Provide examples of schools where advisory committees are operating successfully. Explain how an advisory committee will be an asset to administrators, the school, gifted education personnel, and ultimately students. If necessary, get approval from the school board for the establishment of a gifted education advisory committee.
- **Establish the mission for the advisory committee:** Prior to the selection of the committee members, the committee chair (often a gifted education coordinator) should consult with district administration to establish the mission for the advisory committee, determine the role of committee membership, create guidelines or bylaws to govern its operations, and determine how often the committee will meet.
- **Select and contact committee members:** Develop a list of people from whom committee members will be selected or solicit applications from various groups to serve on the advisory committee. Contact selected members to explain the role of the committee and determine their interest in serving.
- **Call the first meeting:** Avoid time conflicts as much as possible and stress the importance of attendance. Remind committee members by e-mail or telephone of the meeting date and time shortly before the first meeting. Establish an agenda for the meeting.

EXAMPLE OF AN AGENDA
FOR THE FIRST MEETING

1. Welcome and opening remarks by school personnel

2. Introduction of committee members

3. Discussion of the role of the advisory committee

4. Brief overview about the school district, its mission, and its goals for all students

5. History and overview of the gifted education services in the district

6. Review of the state's standards for gifted education, if any

7. Organization of the committee (e.g., selection of chairperson and secretary, selection of dates and times for future meetings)

8. Discussion about future agenda items

HELPFUL REMINDERS WHEN WORKING WITH
EXISTING OR NEW ADVISORY COMMITTEES

- Provide biographical information about the chairperson and other members of the committee.
- Explain what is expected of committee members regarding advice, assistance, cooperation, and time, and discuss with them the potential activities in which the committee may be engaged.
- Communicate the gifted program's purpose and goals so committee members can provide appropriate advice and guidance. Familiarize committee members with the overall plan for the gifted program services.
- Provide committee members with continuous information about educational developments in the field of gifted education at the local, state, and national levels.
- Invite committee members to attend school functions, board of education meetings, or special events sponsored by the gifted and talented program.
- Demonstrate enthusiasm for, and commitment to, the committee's role in improving gifted education services.
- Provide opportunities for representatives to meet with students throughout the school year.
- Establish subcommittees of three to four members to address specific issues and accomplish specific tasks when needed.
- Schedule meetings at a convenient time.
- Notify committee members at least 2 weeks in advance of meetings.
- Before each meeting, provide members with an agenda containing a brief background statement of the issues to be discussed and adhere to the announced meeting time.

- Recognize committee members' service in newspaper articles, pre-sentations, and the gifted and talented program's annual report.
- Always provide refreshments!

Advisory committees can have a direct, positive impact on the types and quality of services that a school district provides for its gifted learners and to the overall improvement of gifted program services. By sharing their expertise and knowledge, committee members support the quality and longevity of gifted education services.

Appendix B

NAGC Pre-K–Grade 12
Gifted Programming Standards

Gifted Education Programming Standard 1: Learning and Development

For teachers and other educators in Pre-K–12 settings to be effective in working with learners with gifts and talents, they must understand the characteristics and needs of the population for whom they are planning curriculum, instruction, assessment, programs, and services. These characteristics provide the rationale for differentiation in programs, grouping, and services for this population and are translated into appropriate differentiation choices made at curricular and program levels in schools and school districts. While cognitive growth is important in such programs, affective development is also necessary. Thus many of the characteristics addressed in this standard emphasize affective development linked to self-understanding and social awareness.

Standard 1: Learning and Development

Description: Educators, recognizing the learning and developmental differences of students with gifts and talents, promote ongoing self-understanding, awareness of their needs, and cognitive and affective growth of these students in school, home, and community settings to ensure specific student outcomes.

Student Outcomes	Evidence-Based Practices
1.1. *Self-Understanding*. Students with gifts and talents demonstrate self-knowledge with respect to their interests, strengths, identities, and needs in socio-emotional development and in intellectual, academic, creative, leadership, and artistic domains.	1.1.1. Educators engage students with gifts and talents in identifying interests, strengths, and gifts.
	1.1.2. Educators assist students with gifts and talents in developing identities supportive of achievement.
1.2. *Self-Understanding*. Students with gifts and talents possess a developmentally appropriate understanding of how they learn and grow; they recognize the influences of their beliefs, traditions, and values on their learning and behavior.	1.2.1. Educators develop activities that match each student's developmental level and culture-based learning needs.
1.3. *Self-Understanding*. Students with gifts and talents demonstrate understanding of and respect for similarities and differences between themselves and their peer group and others in the general population.	1.3.1. Educators provide a variety of research-based grouping practices for students with gifts and talents that allow them to interact with individuals of various gifts, talents, abilities, and strengths.
	1.3.2. Educators model respect for individuals with diverse abilities, strengths, and goals.
1.4. *Awareness of Needs*. Students with gifts and talents access resources from the community to support cognitive and affective needs, including social interactions with others having similar interests and abilities or experiences, including same-age peers and mentors or experts.	1.4.1. Educators provide role models (e.g., through mentors, bibliotherapy) for students with gifts and talents that match their abilities and interests.
	1.4.2. Educators identify out-of-school learning opportunities that match students' abilities and interests.

Student Outcomes	Evidence-Based Practices
1.5. *Awareness of Needs*. Students' families and communities understand similarities and differences with respect to the development and characteristics of advanced and typical learners and support students with gifts and talents' needs.	1.5.1. Educators collaborate with families in accessing resources to develop their child's talents.
1.6. *Cognitive and Affective Growth*. Students with gifts and talents benefit from meaningful and challenging learning activities addressing their unique characteristics and needs.	1.6.1. Educators design interventions for students to develop cognitive and affective growth that is based on research of effective practices.
	1.6.2. Educators develop specialized intervention services for students with gifts and talents who are underachieving and are now learning and developing their talents.
1.7. *Cognitive and Affective Growth*. Students with gifts and talents recognize their preferred approaches to learning and expand their repertoire.	1.7.1. Teachers enable students to identify their preferred approaches to learning, accommodate these preferences, and expand them.
1.8. *Cognitive and Affective Growth*. Students with gifts and talents identify future career goals that match their talents and abilities and resources needed to meet those goals (e.g., higher education opportunities, mentors, financial support).	1.8.1. Educators provide students with college and career guidance that is consistent with their strengths.
	1.8.2. Teachers and counselors implement a curriculum scope and sequence that contains person/social awareness and adjustment, academic planning, and vocational and career awareness.

Gifted Education Programming Standard 2: Assessment

Knowledge about all forms of assessment is essential for educators of students with gifts and talents. It is integral to identification, assessing each student's learning progress, and evaluation of programming. Educators need to establish a challenging environment and collect multiple types of assessment information so that all students are able to demonstrate their gifts and talents. Educators' understanding of non-biased, technically adequate, and equitable approaches enables them to identify students who represent diverse backgrounds. They also differentiate their curriculum and instruction by using pre- and post-, performance-based, product-based, and out-of-level assessments. As a result of each educator's use of ongoing assessments, students with gifts and talents demonstrate advanced and complex learning. Using these student progress data, educators then evaluate services and make adjustments to one or more of the school's programming components so that student performance is improved.

Standard 2: Assessment	NAGC Standards

Description: Assessments provide information about identification, learning progress and outcomes, and evaluation of programming for students with gifts and talents in all domains.

Student Outcomes	Evidence-Based Practices
2.1. *Identification*. All students in grades Pre-K–12 have equal access to a comprehensive assessment system that allows them to demonstrate diverse characteristics and behaviors that are associated with giftedness.	2.1.1. Educators develop environments and instructional activities that encourage students to express diverse characteristics and behaviors that are associated with giftedness.
	2.1.2. Educators provide parents/guardians with information regarding diverse characteristics and behaviors that are associated with giftedness.
2.2. *Identification*. Each student reveals his or her exceptionalities or potential through assessment evidence so that appropriate instructional accommodations and modifications can be provided.	2.2.1. Educators establish comprehensive, cohesive, and ongoing procedures for identifying and serving students with gifts and talents. These provisions include informed consent, committee review, student retention, student reassessment, student exiting, and appeals procedures for both entry and exit from gifted program services.
	2.2.2. Educators select and use multiple assessments that measure diverse abilities, talents, and strengths that are based on current theories, models, and research.
	2.2.3 Assessments provide qualitative and quantitative information from a variety of sources, including off-level testing, are nonbiased and equitable, and are technically adequate for the purpose.
	2.2.4. Educators have knowledge of student exceptionalities and collect assessment data while adjusting curriculum and instruction to learn about each student's developmental level and aptitude for learning.
	2.2.5. Educators interpret multiple assessments in different domains and understand the uses and limitations of the assessments in identifying the needs of students with gifts and talents.
	2.2.6. Educators inform all parents/guardians about the identification process. Teachers obtain parental/guardian permission for assessments, use culturally sensitive checklists, and elicit evidence regarding the child's interests and potential outside of the classroom setting.

Student Outcomes	Evidence-Based Practices
2.3. *Identification*. Students with identified needs represent diverse backgrounds and reflect the total student population of the district.	2.3.1. Educators select and use non-biased and equitable approaches for identifying students with gifts and talents, which may include using locally developed norms or assessment tools in the child's native language or in nonverbal formats.
	2.3.2. Educators understand and implement district and state policies designed to foster equity in gifted programming and services.
	2.3.3. Educators provide parents/guardians with information in their native language regarding diverse behaviors and characteristics that are associated with giftedness and with information that explains the nature and purpose of gifted programming options.
2.4. *Learning Progress and Outcomes*. Students with gifts and talents demonstrate advanced and complex learning as a result of using multiple, appropriate, and ongoing assessments.	2.4.1. Educators use differentiated pre- and post-performance-based assessments to measure the progress of students with gifts and talents.
	2.4.2. Educators use differentiated product-based assessments to measure the progress of students with gifts and talents.
	2.4.3. Educators use off-level standardized assessments to measure the progress of students with gifts and talents.
	2.4.4. Educators use and interpret qualitative and quantitative assessment information to develop a profile of the strengths and weaknesses of each student with gifts and talents to plan appropriate intervention.
	2.4.5. Educators communicate and interpret assessment information to students with gifts and talents and their parents/guardians.
2.5. *Evaluation of Programming*. Students identified with gifts and talents demonstrate important learning progress as a result of programming and services.	2.5.1. Educators ensure that the assessments used in the identification and evaluation processes are reliable and valid for each instrument's purpose, allow for above-grade-level performance, and allow for diverse perspectives.
	2.5.2. Educators ensure that the assessment of the progress of students with gifts and talents uses multiple indicators that measure mastery of content, higher-level thinking skills, achievement in specific program areas, and affective growth.
	2.5.3. Educators assess the quantity, quality, and appropriateness of the programming and services provided for students with gifts and talents by disaggregating assessment data and yearly progress data and making the results public.
2.6. *Evaluation of Programming*. Students identified with gifts and talents have increased access and they show significant learning progress as a result of improving components of gifted education programming.	2.6.1. Administrators provide the necessary time and resources to implement an annual evaluation plan developed by persons with expertise in program evaluation and gifted education.
	2.6.2. The evaluation plan is purposeful and evaluates how student-level outcomes are influenced by one or more of the following components of gifted education programming: (a) identification, (b) curriculum, (c) instructional programming and services, (d) ongoing assessment of student learning, (e) counseling and guidance programs, (f) teacher qualifications and professional development, (g) parent/guardian and community involvement, (h) programming resources, and (i) programming design, management, and delivery.
	2.6.3. Educators disseminate the results of the evaluation, orally and in written form, and explain how they will use the results.

Gifted Education Programming Standard 3: Curriculum Planning and Instruction

Assessment is an integral component of the curriculum planning process. The information obtained from multiple types of assessments informs decisions about curriculum content, instructional strategies, and resources that will support the growth of students with gifts and talents. Educators develop and use a comprehensive and sequenced core curriculum that is aligned with local, state, and national standards, then differentiate and expand it. In order to meet the unique needs of students with gifts and talents, this curriculum must emphasize advanced, conceptually challenging, in-depth, distinctive, and complex content within cognitive, affective, aesthetic, social, and leadership domains. Educators must possess a repertoire of evidence-based instructional strategies in delivering the curriculum (a) to develop talent, enhance learning, and provide students with the knowledge and skills to become independent, self-aware learners, and (b) to give students the tools to contribute to a multicultural, diverse society. The curriculum, instructional strategies, and materials and resources must engage a variety of learners using culturally responsive practices.

Standard 3: Curriculum Planning and Instruction	
Description: Educators apply the theory and research-based models of curriculum and instruction related to students with gifts and talents and respond to their needs by planning, selecting, adapting, and creating culturally relevant curriculum and by using a repertoire of evidence-based instructional strategies to ensure specific student outcomes.	
Student Outcomes	**Evidence-Based Practices**
3.1. *Curriculum Planning.* Students with gifts and talents demonstrate growth commensurate with aptitude during the school year.	3.1.1. Educators use local, state, and national standards to align and expand curriculum and instructional plans.
	3.1.2. Educators design and use a comprehensive and continuous scope and sequence to develop differentiated plans for Pre-K–12 students with gifts and talents.
	3.1.3. Educators adapt, modify, or replace the core or standard curriculum to meet the needs of students with gifts and talents and those with special needs such as twice-exceptional, highly gifted, and English language learners.
	3.1.4. Educators design differentiated curricula that incorporate advanced, conceptually challenging, in-depth, distinctive, and complex content for students with gifts and talents.
	3.1.5. Educators use a balanced assessment system, including pre-assessment and formative assessment, to identify students' needs, develop differentiated education plans, and adjust plans based on continual progress monitoring.
	3.1.6. Educators use pre-assessments and pace instruction based on the learning rates of students with gifts and talents and accelerate and compact learning as appropriate.
	3.1.7. Educators use information and technologies, including assistive technologies, to individualize for students with gifts and talents, including those who are twice-exceptional.

Student Outcomes	Evidence-Based Practices
3.2. *Talent Development.* Students with gifts and talents become more competent in multiple talent areas and across dimensions of learning.	3.2.1. Educators design curricula in cognitive, affective, aesthetic, social, and leadership domains that are challenging and effective for students with gifts and talents.
	3.2.2. Educators use metacognitive models to meet the needs of students with gifts and talents.
3.3. *Talent Development.* Students with gifts and talents develop their abilities in their domain of talent and/or area of interest.	3.3.1. Educators select, adapt, and use a repertoire of instructional strategies and materials that differentiate for students with gifts and talents and that respond to diversity.
	3.3.2. Educators use school and community resources that support differentiation.
	3.3.3. Educators provide opportunities for students with gifts and talents to explore, develop, or research their areas of interest and/or talent.
3.4. *Instructional Strategies.* Students with gifts and talents become independent investigators.	3.4.1. Educators use critical-thinking strategies to meet the needs of students with gifts and talents.
	3.4.2. Educators use creative-thinking strategies to meet the needs of students with gifts and talents.
	3.4.3. Educators use problem-solving model strategies to meet the needs of students with gifts and talents.
	3.4.4. Educators use inquiry models to meet the needs of students with gifts and talents.
3.5. *Culturally Relevant Curriculum.* Students with gifts and talents develop knowledge and skills for living and being productive in a multicultural, diverse, and global society.	3.5.1. Educators develop and use challenging, culturally responsive curriculum to engage all students with gifts and talents.
	3.5.2. Educators integrate career exploration experiences into learning opportunities for students with gifts and talents, e.g., biography study or speakers.
	3.5.3. Educators use curriculum for deep explorations of cultures, languages, and social issues related to diversity.
3.6. *Resources.* Students with gifts and talents benefit from gifted education programming that provides a variety of high quality resources and materials.	3.6.1. Teachers and administrators demonstrate familiarity with sources for high quality resources and materials that are appropriate for learners with gifts and talents.

Gifted Education Programming Standard 4: Learning Environments

Effective educators of students with gifts and talents create safe learning environments that foster emotional well-being, positive social interaction, leadership for social change, and cultural understanding for success in a diverse society. Knowledge of the impact of giftedness and diversity on social-emotional development enables educators of students with gifts and talents to design environments that encourage independence, motivation, and self-efficacy of individuals from all backgrounds. They understand the role of language and communication in talent development and the ways in which culture affects communication and behavior. They use relevant strategies and technologies to enhance oral, written, and artistic communication of learners whose needs vary based on exceptionality, language proficiency, and cultural and linguistic differences. They recognize the value of multilingualism in today's global community.

Standard 4: Learning Environments

Description: Learning environments foster personal and social responsibility, multicultural competence, and interpersonal and technical communication skills for leadership in the 21st century to ensure specific student outcomes.

Student Outcomes	Evidence-Based Practices
4.1. *Personal Competence.* Students with gifts and talents demonstrate growth in personal competence and dispositions for exceptional academic and creative productivity. These include self-awareness, self-advocacy, self-efficacy, confidence, motivation, resilience, independence, curiosity, and risk taking.	4.1.1. Educators maintain high expectations for all students with gifts and talents as evidenced in meaningful and challenging activities.
	4.1.2. Educators provide opportunities for self-exploration, development and pursuit of interests, and development of identities supportive of achievement, e.g., through mentors and role models.
	4.1.3. Educators create environments that support trust among diverse learners.
	4.1.4. Educators provide feedback that focuses on effort, on evidence of potential to meet high standards, and on mistakes as learning opportunities.
	4.1.5. Educators provide examples of positive coping skills and opportunities to apply them.
4.2. *Social Competence.* Students with gifts and talents develop social competence manifested in positive peer relationships and social interactions.	4.2.1. Educators understand the needs of students with gifts and talents for both solitude and social interaction.
	4.2.2. Educators provide opportunities for interaction with intellectual and artistic/creative peers as well as with chronological-age peers.
	4.2.3. Educators assess and provide instruction on social skills needed for school, community, and the world of work.
4.3. *Leadership.* Students with gifts and talents demonstrate personal and social responsibility and leadership skills.	4.3.1 Educators establish a safe and welcoming climate for addressing social issues and developing personal responsibility.
	4.3.2. Educators provide environments for developing many forms of leadership and leadership skills.
	4.3.3. Educators promote opportunities for leadership in community settings to effect positive change.

Student Outcomes	Evidence-Based Practices
4.4. *Cultural Competence.* Students with gifts and talents value their own and others' language, heritage, and circumstance. They possess skills in communicating, teaming, and collaborating with diverse individuals and across diverse groups.[1] They use positive strategies to address social issues, including discrimination and stereotyping.	4.4.1. Educators model appreciation for and sensitivity to students' diverse backgrounds and languages.
	4.4.2. Educators censure discriminatory language and behavior and model appropriate strategies.
	4.4.3. Educators provide structured opportunities to collaborate with diverse peers on a common goal.
4.5. *Communication Competence.* Students with gifts and talents develop competence in interpersonal and technical communication skills. They demonstrate advanced oral and written skills, balanced biliteracy or multiliteracy, and creative expression. They display fluency with technologies that support effective communication.	4.5.1. Educators provide opportunities for advanced development and maintenance of first and second language(s).
	4.5.2. Educators provide resources to enhance oral, written, and artistic forms of communication, recognizing students' cultural context.
	4.5.3. Educators ensure access to advanced communication tools, including assistive technologies, and use of these tools for expressing higher-level thinking and creative productivity.

[1]Differences among groups of people and individuals based on ethnicity, race, socioeconomic status, gender, exceptionalities, language, religion, sexual orientation, and geographical area.

Gifted Education Programming Standard 5: Programming

The term programming refers to a continuum of services that address students with gifts and talents' needs in all settings. Educators develop policies and procedures to guide and sustain all components of comprehensive and aligned programming and services for Pre-K–12 students with gifts and talents. Educators use a variety of programming options such as acceleration and enrichment in varied grouping arrangements (cluster grouping, resource rooms, special classes, special schools) and within individualized learning options (independent study, mentorships, online courses, internships) to enhance students' performance in cognitive and affective areas and to assist them in identifying future career goals. They augment and integrate current technologies within these learning opportunities to increase access to high level programming such as distance learning courses and to increase connections to resources outside of the school walls. In implementing services, educators in gifted, general, special education programs, and related professional services collaborate with one another and parents/guardians and community members to ensure that students' diverse learning needs are met. Administrators demonstrate their support of these programming options by allocating sufficient resources so that all students within gifts and talents receive appropriate educational services.

Standard 5: Programming

Description: Educators are aware of empirical evidence regarding (a) the cognitive, creative, and affective development of learners with gifts and talents, and (b) programming that meets their concomitant needs. Educators use this expertise systematically and collaboratively to develop, implement, and effectively manage comprehensive services for students with a variety of gifts and talents to ensure specific student outcomes.

Student Outcomes	Evidence-Based Practices
5.1. *Variety of Programming.* Students with gifts and talents participate in a variety of evidence-based programming options that enhance performance in cognitive and affective areas.	5.1.1. Educators regularly use multiple alternative approaches to accelerate learning.
	5.1.2. Educators regularly use enrichment options to extend and deepen learning opportunities within and outside of the school setting.
	5.1.3. Educators regularly use multiple forms of grouping, including clusters, resource rooms, special classes, or special schools.
	5.1.4. Educators regularly use individualized learning options such as mentorships, internships, online courses, and independent study.
	5.1.5. Educators regularly use current technologies, including online learning options and assistive technologies to enhance access to high-level programming.
	5.1.6. Administrators demonstrate support for gifted programs through equitable allocation of resources and demonstrated willingness to ensure that learners with gifts and talents receive appropriate educational services.

Student Outcomes	Evidence-Based Practices
5.2. *Coordinated Services*. Students with gifts and talents demonstrate progress as a result of the shared commitment and coordinated services of gifted education, general education, special education, and related professional services, such as school counselors, school psychologists, and social workers.	5.2.1. Educators in gifted, general, and special education programs, as well as those in specialized areas, collaboratively plan, develop, and implement services for learners with gifts and talents.
5.3. *Collaboration*. Students with gifts and talents' learning is enhanced by regular collaboration among families, community, and the school.	5.3.1. Educators regularly engage families and community members for planning, programming, evaluating, and advocating.
5.4. *Resources*. Students with gifts and talents participate in gifted education programming that is adequately funded to meet student needs and program goals.	5.4.1. Administrators track expenditures at the school level to verify appropriate and sufficient funding for gifted programming and services.
5.5. *Comprehensiveness*. Students with gifts and talents develop their potential through comprehensive, aligned programming and services.	5.5.1. Educators develop thoughtful, multiyear program plans in relevant student talent areas, Pre-K–12.
5.6. *Policies and Procedures*. Students with gifts and talents participate in regular and gifted education programs that are guided by clear policies and procedures that provide for their advanced learning needs (e.g., early entrance, acceleration, credit in lieu of enrollment).	5.6.1. Educators create policies and procedures to guide and sustain all components of the program, including assessment, identification, acceleration practices, and grouping practices, that is built on an evidence-based foundation in gifted education.
5.7. *Career Pathways*. Students with gifts and talents identify future career goals and the talent development pathways to reach those goals.	5.7.1. Educators provide professional guidance and counseling for individual student strengths, interests, and values.
	5.7.2. Educators facilitate mentorships, internships, and vocational programming experiences that match student interests and aptitudes.

Gifted Education Programming Standard 6: Professional Development

Professional development is essential for all educators involved in the development and implementation of gifted programs and services. Professional development is the intentional development of professional expertise as outlined by the NAGC-CEC teacher preparation standards and is an ongoing part of gifted educators' professional and ethical practice. Professional development may take many forms ranging from district-sponsored workshops and courses, university courses, professional conferences, independent studies, and presentations by external consultants and should be based on systematic needs assessments and professional reflection. Students participating in gifted education programs and services are taught by teachers with developed expertise in gifted education. Gifted education program services are developed and supported by administrators, coordinators, curriculum specialists, general education, special education, and gifted education teachers who have developed expertise in gifted education. Since students with gifts and talents spend much of their time within general education classrooms, general education teachers need to receive professional development in gifted education that enables them to recognize the characteristics of giftedness in diverse populations, understand the school or district referral and identification process, and possess an array of high quality, research-based differentiation strategies that challenge students. Services for students with gifts and talents are enhanced by guidance and counseling professionals with expertise in gifted education.

Standard 6: Professional Development

Description: All educators (administrators, teachers, counselors, and other instructional support staff) build their knowledge and skills using the NAGC-CEC Teacher Preparation Standards for Gifted and Talented Education and the National Staff Development Standards. They formally assess professional development needs related to the standards, develop and monitor plans, systematically engage in training to meet the identified needs, and demonstrate mastery of standard. They access resources to provide for release time, funding for continuing education, and substitute support. These practices are judged through the assessment of relevant student outcomes.

Student Outcomes	Evidence-Based Practices
6.1. *Talent Development.* Students develop their talents and gifts as a result of interacting with educators who meet the national teacher preparation standards in gifted education.	6.1.1. Educators systematically participate in ongoing, research-supported professional development that addresses the foundations of gifted education, characteristics of students with gifts and talents, assessment, curriculum planning and instruction, learning environments, and programming.
	6.1.2. The school district provides professional development for teachers that models how to develop environments and instructional activities that encourage students to express diverse characteristics and behaviors that are associated with giftedness.
	6.1.3. Educators participate in ongoing professional development addressing key issues such as anti-intellectualism and trends in gifted education such as equity and access.
	6.1.4. Administrators provide human and material resources needed for professional development in gifted education (e.g., release time, funding for continuing education, substitute support, webinars, or mentors).
	6.1.5. Educators use their awareness of organizations and publications relevant to gifted education to promote learning for students with gifts and talents.

Student Outcomes	Evidence-Based Practices
6.2. *Socio-Emotional Development*. Students with gifts and talents develop socially and emotionally as a result of educators who have participated in professional development aligned with national standards in gifted education and National Staff Development Standards.	6.2.1. Educators participate in ongoing professional development to support the social and emotional needs of students with gifts and talents.
6.3. *Lifelong Learners*. Students develop their gifts and talents as a result of educators who are life-long learners, participating in ongoing professional development and continuing education opportunities.	6.3.1. Educators assess their instructional practices and continue their education in school district staff development, professional organizations, and higher education settings based on these assessments.
	6.3.2. Educators participate in professional development that is sustained over time, that includes regular follow-up, and that seeks evidence of impact on teacher practice and on student learning.
	6.3.3. Educators use multiple modes of professional development delivery including online courses, online and electronic communities, face-to-face workshops, professional learning communities, and book talks.
	6.3.4. Educators identify and address areas for personal growth for teaching students with gifts and talents in their professional development plans.
6.4. *Ethics*. Students develop their gifts and talents as a result of educators who are ethical in their practices.	6.4.1. Educators respond to cultural and personal frames of reference when teaching students with gifts and talents.
	6.4.2. Educators comply with rules, policies, and standards of ethical practice.

Source: National Association for Gifted Children. (2010). *NAGC Pre-K–Grade 12 Gifted Programming Standards: A blueprint for quality gifted education programs.* Washington, DC: Author. Reprinted with permission.

Index

CORWIN HAS ONE MISSION: to enhance education through intentional professional learning.

We build long-term relationships with our authors, educators, clients, and associations who partner with us to develop and continuously improve the best evidence-based practices that establish and support lifelong learning.

The National Association for Gifted Children (NAGC) is an organization of parents, teachers, educators, other professionals, and community leaders who unite to address the unique needs of children and youth with demonstrated gifts and talents as well as those children who may be able to develop their talent potential with appropriate educational experiences.

We support and develop policies and practices that encourage and respond to the diverse expressions of gifts and talents in children and youth from all cultures, racial and ethnic backgrounds, and socioeconomic groups. NAGC supports and engages in research and development, staff development, advocacy, communication, and collaboration with other organizations and agencies who strive to improve the quality of education for all students.

Solutions you want. Experts you trust. Results you need.